THE ESSEN

GOLFERS

IRELAND

GW00370755

CASSIDY PUBLISHING

PUBLISHED BY:
CASSIDY PUBLISHING
UNIT 1,
DERRYKNOCKANE VIEW
BALLYCUMMIN, RAHEEN
LIMERICK

ISBN 0-9545055-0-6

Designed by
AViD Graphic Design
Limerick
Tel. 061 328046
Email. avid@elive.ie

Printed by
Jaycee Printers, Galway

The Essential Golfers Guide Ireland 2003

Welcome to the first edition of The Essential Golfers Guide. This unique publication covers many aspects of the game in Ireland and the people involved in it. It provides extensive, reliable and easily accessible information on the who's who and what's what in Irish golf.

The importance of golf as a significant contributor to the overall economy of Ireland should not be underestimated. However, the huge income that is currently generated by the game is a fairly recent development. Only thirty years ago there was less than half the number of Golf Clubs that exist now; most of them welcomed new members with open arms. Only a generation later, there is in excess of 400 Irish Clubs open for business. Membership is in such demand that many of them do not even accept applications from new aspirants to the game. Furthermore, pre-1980 less than 50,000 overseas visitors came here to play golf. In 2001, we had 217,000 visiting golfers; a parallel explosion to the number of new native golfers and number of new courses for them to play.

The Central Statistics Office returns illustrate clearly the growth of the Irish golf industry. Visiting golfers alone parted with a staggering €144 million in 2001, while at the same time domestic golfers were spending €350 million. For every one million euro spent by tourists, 44 Irish jobs are supported. On their own, golfing visitors support in the region of 6000 Irish jobs. Based on current annual growth rates, 350,000 golfers are likely to visit Ireland annually by the time the 2006 Ryder Cup matches are played in the K-Club, Co. Kildare. The publicity given to this popular event can only further increase awareness of Irish Golf.

The primary reason for Ireland's popularity as a golf destination is our wonderful, natural, golf courses. With in excess of fifty, we possess roughly one third of all of the genuine, seaside links courses in the entire world. They are the jewels in our crown and are recognised by the experts as the best in the world. But neither should we forget all of the wonderful parkland, heathland and even bogland golf courses that are also at our disposal.

I hope you enjoy this publication but most of all...
...ENJOY YOUR GOLF

Edel Cassidy MBA
Publisher

PULLING POWER

Now available in a new 1.4 litre diesel

THE PEUGEOT 307 1.4 HDI FROM €21,095
* Beauty and brawn can make perfect partners. The Peugeot 307 has a sleek, sporty design, and all the ride and handling you'd expect from a Peugeot. But with a 1.4 HDi engine that's much more powerful than you'd expect, a roomy interior and a generous amount of storage space, it can also carry everything a car in its class should. And because the 307 has driver and passenger airbags, ABS, Electronic Braking Assistance, and remote central locking, it offers a compelling level of safety and security. So call into your local Peugeot dealer. We think you'll find the 307 irresistible.

Standard features: • 5 door • Power assisted steering • Remote central locking • Engine immobiliser • ABS • Tinted glass • Driver passenger / side / curtain airbags • Electric front windows • Brake assistance • Remote control radio / CD player • Electronic brake force distribution • Three rear head restraints

* Delivery related charges not included. Minimum Fuel Consumption: 7.9 (litres / 100 Km) mixed. CO_2 Emissions: 188 G / Km. 2 Litre XSi Petrol model

www.peugeot.ie

1850 PEUGEOT
FOR PRODUCT INFORMATION CALL 1850 738 4368

PEUGEOT. THE DRIVE OF YOUR LIFE

307 HDI

PEUGEOT

Message from John O'Donoghue T.D. Minister for Arts, Sport & Tourism

Golfers are an international community who speak a common language that crosses all creeds and boundaries. Golf is one of our most popular sports and it brings immense enjoyment to many people.

There are the thousands of Irish people who play golf in more than 400 clubs around the country, but golf also plays a major part in our vital tourism industry. From 1988 to 2001 golf visitors to Ireland increased in numbers from 52,000 to 217,000, contributing approximately €144 million in 2001 to the Irish economy.

The total investment in golf, over the past decade, has been more than €250 million, helping to establish Ireland as one of the world's premier destinations for the sport.

The Government, through the International Sports Tourism Initiative, has set aside an annual budget of €7.62 million up to 2007 to attract and support major sporting events, with an emphasis on golf. Last year the American Express World Championship Golf tournament was held in Ireland, And we were lucky. For four sun-drenched days we had memorable golf, a win for Tiger Woods and an Irish record of 120,000 enthusiastic fans attended the event.

This year the Sports Tourism Initiative is assisting such golfing events as the Nissan Irish Open and the Smurfit European Open. Meanwhile we are looking ahead to the big one, the Ryder Cup, which will be held in Ireland for the first time in 2006.

So, I wish enjoyment and success to all of you who will read this new Guide and a special welcome to our visitors from overseas.

10
LINKS OF HEAVEN

CONNEMARA GOLF CLUB Ballyconneely

ROYAL PORTRUSH GOLF CLUB Portrush

Ten Links of Heaven. Golfers paradise, call it what you will. Enjoy a vacation which combines the excitement of truly magnificent golf with some of the most beautiful and unspoilt scenery in Europe. Imagine the surf salty on your lips, the turf light and dry beneath your feet and 10 great Atlantic Links courses to enjoy on an unforgettable Irish golf vacation.

CARNE GOLF LINKS Belmullet

PORTSTEWART GOLF CLUB Portstewart

- Connemara Golf Club, **Ballyconneely.**
- Carne Golf Links, **Belmullet.**
- Enniscrone Golf Club, **Enniscrone.**
- Co. Sligo Golf Club, **Rosses Point.**
- Donegal Golf Club, **Murvagh.**
- Rosapenna Golf Links, **Rosapenna.**
- Ballyliffin Golf Club, **Ballyliffin.**
- Castlerock Golf Club, **Castlerock.**
- Portstewart Golf Club, **Portstewart.**
- Royal Portrush Golf Club, **Portrush.**

ENNISCRONE GOLF CLUB Enniscrone

CASTLEROCK GOLF CLUB Castlerock

CO. SLIGO GOLF CLUB Rosses Point

BALLYLIFFIN GOLF CLUB Ballyliffin

DONEGAL GOLF CLUB Murvagh

ROSAPENNA GOLF LINKS Rosapenna

NORTH & WEST COAST LINKS

IRELAND

FOR FURTHER INFORMATION CONTACT:

John McLaughlin, Marketing Manager,
North & West Coast Links,
Galway Golf Centre, Salthill, Co. Galway, Ireland.
Tel: +353 (0) 91 526737. Fax: +353 (0) 91 528200
Email: wclgolf@iol.ie   Web: http://www.westcoastlinks.com

Table of Contents

Photography

Golfing Union of Ireland
L.P.G.A.
P.G.A. (Irish Region)
Ivan Morris Library
Phil Sheldon Golf Picture Library
Doonbeg Golf Club
Old Head Golf Links
Ping
Images of Ireland's West Coast - Volume 172
Shannon Development and Fly Shannon Ireland
Photodisc

Cover Shot: Doonbeg Golf Club

Publisher
Edel Cassidy

Editorial Contributions
'The Professional Golfers
Association' written by
Adrian Feane.
All other editorial written by
Ivan Morris

**Senior Advertising
Executive**
Helen O'Connor

**Advertising Sales
Executives**
Carol O'Regan
Lisa Quigley
Fergus McGrath

Media Consultants
Mary Hayes
Ronan Cassidy

Production Manager
Mark Feane

Production
Adrian Feane
Thomas Kennedy

Editorial Consultant
Ivan Morris

Published by
Cassidy Publishing
Limerick
Ireland

*Inspired by an eminent Junior
Golfer - John*

Ring of Kerry Golf & Country Club

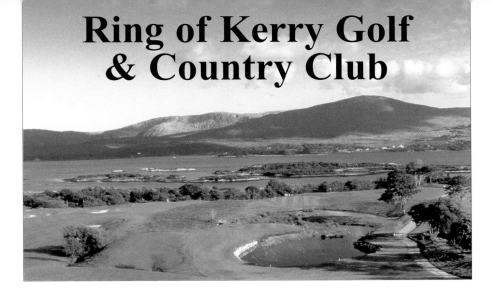

Famed for its spectacular scenery, its VIP playing guest list and the intoxicating hospitality of the Kerry people, the Ring of Kerry Golf and Country Club provides the perfect venue for any discerning golfer visiting Ireland's South West. This par 72, championship course, nestling between two mountain ranges and overlooking Kenmare Bay, has to be seen to be believed.

The Club is situated just 4 miles from the picturesque and vibrant town of Kenmare, home to two of Ireland's top 5* hotels and numerous other hotels, fine restaurants, pubs and bars. A visit to the Ring of Kerry Golf & Country Club, together with a stay in the town of Kenmare, is a memorable experience not to be missed.

Also available:
Corporate Days • Group Rates • Golf Society Packages • Memberships

Templenoe, Kenmare, Co Kerry, Ireland
Tel: 00 353 (0)64 42000
E Mail:reservations@ringofkerrygolf.com
www.ringofkerrygolf.com
Managed and Operated by Universal Golf Consulting Ltd

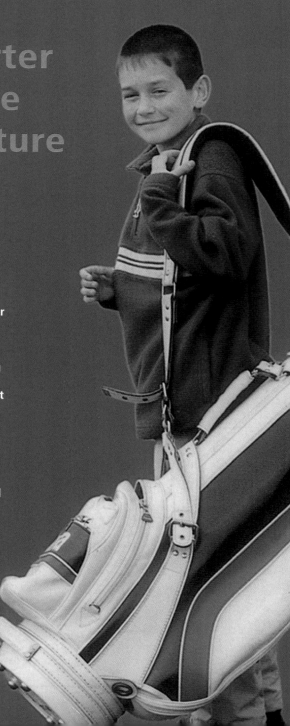

Junior Golf Charter Takes Care of the Future

The GUI takes great pride, and rightly so, in the prize exhibits of their Coaching System – Darren Clarke, Padraig Harrington and Paul McGinley. However, they will also be the first to admit that there is a lot more to their Junior Golf Charter than developing Ryder or Solheim Cup players. Many hundreds of youngsters have benefited from regular coaching at club, provincial and international panel level without ever-achieving fame or fortune. To be honest, most of the coaching that takes place is geared more at increasing the numbers of young people coming into the game and making sure that they know and understand the rules, traditions and etiquette of the game than producing world-beaters. Most of all, junior golf needs to be organised in a controlled manner so that the game will provide a welcoming, safe, enjoyable and challenging environment for everybody, not just the super talented. Any youngster as talented and as motivated as Darren, Padraig and Paul were will succeed no matter what system is in place.

The standard of Irish golf has improved steadily in recent years as more and more youngsters take up the game and are coached by professionals who also have done their bit to educate themselves properly so that they will be in a position to pass on the do's and don'ts in an intelligible manner. In fact, the standard of coaching golf in Ireland has improved at a more rapid rate than we can produce champions. The IPGA training programme for their own recruits is turning out excellent, top class teachers nowadays, many of whom find good jobs overseas, especially in Europe. Could this be a fine career opportunity that is being overlooked perhaps? Most Golf Clubs at home and abroad see the advantage in having a fully qualified resident teaching professional to coach their members and juniors.

Apart from the big three mentioned Ireland's junior golf programmes have also produced Graeme McDowell who is already a tournament winner as a professional. Gary Murphy and Peter Lawrie, both former Irish Close Champions, have recently acquired full European Tour privileges while Denis O'Sullivan is going great guns on the Seniors Tour with five wins to his credit. Des Smyth who is a certainty to achieve great things in seniors' golf in the USA came through the ranks under guidance of Bobby Browne, IPGA professional at Laytown and Bettystown, a man who may have developed more raw talent into fine players than anyone else in Ireland.

Paul McGinley came through the ranks of Junior Golf in Ireland.

3

It is also a matter of some pride in GUI circles that they can also boast of producing the World Open Junior Champion, Cian McNamara from Limerick, who beat competition from all over the World at Musselburgh, Scotland last July. The success rate achieved by Ireland in producing golfers of world standard is proportionately much higher than the English, Scots or Welsh. Perhaps only the Swedes do a better job than us in developing young talent. Why?

Perhaps, the various IPGA trained coaches appointed by the GUI will have had something to do with it. But it is more likely that all the support given to young golfers across the board at grass roots level by parents and ordinary club members who give huge commitment and vast amounts of time to caring for Junior golf at club level, are the true reason why we enjoy so much success.

Junior Golfers from Edmonstown National School perfect their swing under the instruction of teaching professional Brian O'Brien.

The Professional Golfers' Association (Irish Region)

IRISH REGION

J.H. Taylor was a member of the so-called Great Triumvirate of Golf; i.e. Harry Vardon, James Braid and Taylor that won The Open Championship on no less than sixteen occasions between them. Perhaps Taylor's sweetest victory coming in 1894, when he broke the Scottish stranglehold on the claret jug to become the first Englishman to win the Open Championship. But it was as a golfing pioneer that Taylor, a brilliant self-educated man with wide interests, may have made his most lasting contribution to the game because he was the prime mover and first chairman of The Professional Golfers Association that was founded in 1901 and carried on in that capacity for over forty years. He also captained several Ryder Cup teams.

The first professional to be engaged by an Irish Golf Club was Alexander Day from Musselburgh, who was appointed greenkeeper and clubmaker at the Royal Belfast Golf Club in February 1889. In 1907, the Golfing Union of Ireland formed a sub-committee to organize an Irish Professional Championship, the first tournament open to professionals ever held in Ireland and also to run professional golf in Ireland. James Edmundson from Belfast was the first recipient of the winner's cheque for £24.

The first official meeting of the association took place at the North Star Hotel in Dublin. Although the IPGA had been conducting its own affairs more or less independently since 1929, it was 1965 before the IPGA finally broke entirely free of the GUI and formed its own constitution and management structure.

The Irish PGA, now an independent body, agreed to join forces with the British PGA in 1975. In due course, this new entity became the Professional Golfers Association of Great Britain & Ireland. F. Barry Browne became the first secretary in 1965 and served until 1975. Brian Campbell succeeded him and the current serving secretary for the Irish region is Michael McCumiskey. The PGA in Ireland comprises a total of over 400 Professionals who cater for the needs of 300,000 amateur golfers in all parts of the country.

Michael McCumiskey

Kevan Whitson

Brendan McGovern

The current Chairman is Kevan Whitson, the resident professional at Royal County Down Golf Club. One of Kevan's duties will be to sit on the panel of people who will interview the candidates for the highly significant position of National Coach for the Golfing Union of Ireland. Whitson's contribution to Ulster & Irish Golf has been commendable. He has served as the coach to the Ulster branch of the Irish Ladies Golf Union for 6 years. He has also trained many young professionals who have done rather well for themselves. David Kearney of the Galway Golf Centre and the current National Coach for the ILGU is one of many whom Kevin guided by taking them under his wing.

The Irish Professional Golfers Association celebrated one hundred years of unstinting service to Irish golf in appropriate style at the Burlington Hotel, Dublin in 2001 with the mercurial Spanish maestro Seve Ballesteros in attendance. The centenary Captain was Bobby Browne of Laytown and Bettystown, one in Ireland's greatest servants of golf.

The in-coming Captain for 2003 is Brendan McGovern of Headfort Golf Club; a fine, well-respected tournament performer and excellent teacher.

Contact:
Professional Golfers' Association (Irish Region)
Dundalk Golf Club, Blackrock, Co. Louth.
Secretary – Michael McCumiskey
Tel:00353-42-9321193
Fax:00353-429321899

2003 Fixtures
The 2003 list of IPGA fixtures has recently been completed. There will be 50 events comprising a total of 100 days of competition with the impressive figure of €875,000 in total prize money. This figure represents an impressive increase from 1985, Michael McCumiskey's first year in office, when prize money totaled €180,000. As well as established events at Connemara, City of Derry, Monkstown and Cairndhu, there are new additions at East Clare, Headfort, Malahide and Downpatrick to name but a few, this year.

PGA Diploma Programme

Being a qualified golf professional is a career choice of great interest to many young Irish golfers. If you are over 18 years-old and hold a handicap of 4 or better (men) 6 or better (ladies) and meet the minimum academic requirements, the PGA Diploma programme could open up an excellent and rewarding career path. The opportunity to learn a skilled and valued trade under a qualified Golf Professional is tempting. The chance to spend your life immersed in the golf trade is attractive for many and varied reasons.

POPULAR BOB

As I am sure the many golfers in Ireland would testify the local club Professional is often the centre or heart of a Golf Club. The PGA has many great characters and loyal servants among its' ranks, but perhaps none more so than Bob Walker the Professional at Cairndhu Golf Club in Co. Antrim. Bob, who is a youthful 83, is known far and wide in golfing circles. Popular Bob as the members of Cairndhu refer to him has been the Professional at the Club since the 28th July 1947. A staggering and remarkable 56 years of service is quite an achievement. Bob's story is truly amazing. During the Second World War he joined the Royal Air Force, seeing service mostly in the Middle East. It was in Egypt during this period that he met his wife Madge.

On demob in 1947 Bob returned to Donaghadee and was appointed Professional at Larne Town Golf Club. Unfortunately Bob's green keeping duties prevented him from reaching his full golfing potential, but he recalls many happy times, when for instance he took the Legendary Fred Daly to the last hole in the semi – final of the Ulster Championship which Fred went on to win. When the Club moved to Cairndhu, Bob followed and in 1970 he took on the additional duties of Head green keeper, a position he held for over 20 years.

Bob Walker's service to golf was acknowledged when he was awarded the British Empire Medal in the New Years Honours List in 1992. Thus Bob is now Robert Walker PGA Professional MBE! He completes 56 years service to his Club this year and must be one of the longest, if not the longest serving Club Professional in the game.

Always friendly, unless one transgresses on Club etiquette, cheerful and helpful Bob is certainly one of Ulster and Irish golf's remaining characters.

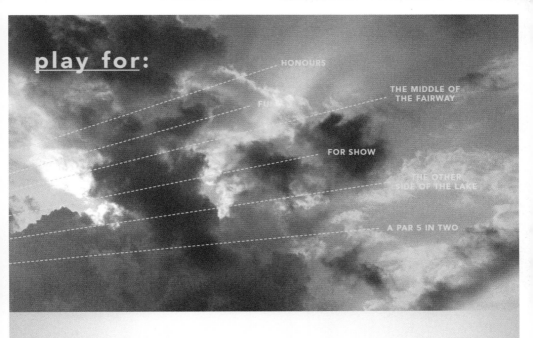

play for:

HONOURS

THE MIDDLE OF
THE FAIRWAY

FOR SHOW

THE OTHER
SIDE OF THE LAKE

A PAR 5 IN TWO

play the: NEW Si3™ DRIVER

*The thin, fully forged face wraps
around the body of the driver for greater
energy transfer and more forgiveness.*

*Hosels colour-coded for face and lie angle
help you hit straighter, more consistent drives.*

play: LONGER, STRAIGHTER DRIVES

The Si3™ Driver – 340ccs of power and performance. Its thin, fully forged face provides the power and forgiveness to play your best. A total weight near 300 grams, the result of a new lightweight shaft and grip, means increased clubhead speed for more distance. And it's custom fit for accuracy. Every spec, including shaft flex and loft, is matched to your needs. So whatever your handicap, we'll custom build a driver just for you. You'll also find a tall, deep face for a confidence-inspiring look at address. To see for yourself, stop by a PING Club Fitting Specialist, or visit pingeurope.com

PING®
play: YOUR BEST™

"Best New International Course 2002" *Golf Digest*

DOONBEG

866 DOONBEG   www.doonbeggolfclub.com

GOLF
PROFESSIONALS

The PGA Professionals listed in this section have fully stocked golf shops with the skills and experience to offer you expert advice. For all your golfing requirements, from equipment to tuition, just remember, that your local PGA Professional is only a phone call away.

THE ESSENTIAL
GOLFERS GUIDE
IRELAND 2003

ANTRIM

GARY MCNEILL
(PGA PRO)

Royal Portrush Golf Club

Dunluce Road, Portrush,
Co. Antrim BT56 8JQ.
T: (028) 7082335
F: (028) 70823139
Fully stocked shop, full tuition including video and indoor lessons. Club repairs & custom fitting also provided.

ANTRIM

MAURICE KELLY
(PGA PRO)

Belvoir Park Golf Club

73/75 Church Road, Newtownbreda,
Belfast BT8 4AN. Co. Antrim.
T: (028) 90491693
E: mauricekelly@belvoirparkgolfclub.com

Golf coaching utilising the V1 swing analysis system.

ARMAGH

PAUL STEVENSON
(PGA PRO)

Portadown Golf Club

192 Gilford Rd, Portadown, Co. Armagh.
T: (028) 38334655
E: paulstevenson@btconnect.com

One of the best stocked shops in the North, Full tuition using the V1 teaching programme.

CARLOW

ANDREW GILBERT
(PGA PRO)

Carlow Golf Club

Deerpark, Carlow, Co. Carlow.
T: (0503) 41745

Personal & group tuition. Video swing analysis. Club repairs a specialty.

CAVAN

BILL NOBLE
(PGA PRO)

County Cavan Golf Club

Arnmore House, Drumelis, Co. Cavan.
T: (049) 4331388

Fully stocked shop, tuition & club repair service available.

CLARE

BOB McCAVERY
(PGA PRO)

Lahinch Golf Club

Lahinch, Co. Clare.
T: (065) 7081408
E: lgc@iol.ie

Custom club maker. Fully stocked shop. Club repair & tuition service.

BRIAN SHAW
(Head Golf Professional)

Doonbeg Golf Club

CLARE

Doonbeg, Co. Clare
T: (065) 9055246

Fully staffed golf academy, club rental, drive cart & trolley hire all available at this world class new addition to Irish golf.

PADDY O'BOYLE
(PGA PRO)

Bandon Golf Club

CORK

Bandon, Co. Cork.
T: (023) 42224
E: paddyoboylegolfpro@eircom.net

Top class golf shop, lessons, and club repair.

LIAM BURNS
(PGA PRO)

Youghal Golf Club

CORK

Knockaverry, Youghal, Co. Cork.
T: (024) 92590

Fully stocked shop. Tuition a specialty using golf psychology with groups, juniors & individuals.

DAVID KEATING
(PGA PRO)

Charleville Golf Club

CORK

Ardmore, Charleville, Co. Cork.
T: (063) 21269
E: keatingda@eircom.net
W: www.charleville.com/davekeating
Digital computerised lessons available. Corporate golf days arranged. Fully stocked pro shop.

PETER HICKEY
(PGA PRO)

Cork Golf Club

CORK

Little Island, Co. Cork.
T: (021) 4353421

Fully stocked shop, tuition, club & trolley hire available. Member of Pro7 buying group.

IAN BLAIR
(PGA PRO)

Castlerock Golf Club

DERRY

65 Circular Road, Castlerock, Co. Derry BT51 4TS.
T: (028) 70849424
E: castlerock18@hotmail.com

Fully stocked golf retail shop. Golf tuition a priority. Electric caddy-car servicing centre.

DONEGAL	**FRANCIS HOWLEY** *(PGA PRO)* **Ballyliffin Golf Club**	Inishowen, Co. Donegal. T: (074) 9376119 E: francis@ballyliffingolfclub.com *Fully stocked shop, lessons & repairs available.*
DONEGAL	**DAVID T. ROBINSON** *(PGA PRO)* **Bundoran Golf Club**	Bundoran, Co. Donegal. T: (072) 41302 *All top brands available. Full tuition service, catering for all standards.*
DOWN	**PAUL MCCRYSTAL** *(PGA PRO)* **Scrabo Golf Club**	233 Scrabo Road, Newtownards, Co. Down. BT23 4SL T: (028) 91817848 *Equipment sales, full tuition & club repair service available.*
DOWN	**KEVAN WHITSON** *(Chairman of the Irish PGA)* **Royal Co.Down Golf Club**	Newcastle, Co. Down. T: (028) 43722419 E: kevanwhitson@aol.com *Fully stocked retail outlet, tuition service, club customisation & repair service.*
DOWN	**ROBERT HUTTON** *(PGA PRO)* **Downpatrick Golf Club**	43 Saul Road, Downpatrick, Co. Down. T: (048) 4461 5947 *All leading brands stocked. Club repair service. Tuition by appointment.*
DUBLIN	**STEPHEN RAYFUS** *(PGA PRO)* **Balcarrick Golf Club**	Corballis, Donabate, Co. Dublin. T: (01) 8434034 E: stephenreyfus2@37.com *All major brands & products. Special discounts for societies. Club repair service & lessons available.*

DOMINIC REILLY
(PGA PRO)

Leopardstown Golf Centre

Foxrock, Dublin 18.
T: (01) 2893511

Fully stocked golf retail outlet. Full tuition & club repair service available. See display advert page 5.

JOEY PURCELL
(PGA PRO)

Portmarnock Golf Club

Portmarnock, Co. Dublin.
T: (01) 8462634

Golf equipment including clubs, bags, shoes and clothing of all top brands. Individual, group & corporate tuition.

JOHN DIGNAM
(PGA PRO)

Slade Valley Golf Club

Lynch Park, Brittas, Co. Dublin.
T: (01) 4582183

All brands stocked. Specialising in club repairs & custom fitting. Tuition available on request.

DAVID O'SULLIVAN
(PGA PRO)

St. Margaret's Golf & Country Club

The Cobra Golf Academy
St. Margaret's, Co. Dublin.
T: (01) 8640400 M: (087)8789659
E: reservations@stmargaretsgolf.com
Professional tuition using computer coaching equipment. Full practice facilities on site. Custom fit centre.

MARK CALLAN
(PGA PRO)

Clontarf Golf Club

Malahide Road, Dublin 3.
T: (01) 8331877
E: markcallan@eircom.net

Golf shop with all top equipment & club repair service. Lessons for members & visitors by appointment.

SUE BAMFORD
(PGA PRO)
(Founder Member of Ladies European Tour)

Blanchardstown Golf Centre

Tyrrelstown House, Mulhuddart, Co. Dublin.
T: (01) 8213206
F: (01) 8217431

Top-class 32 bay driving range, with 18 hole par three course. Individual, corporate & group tuition available.

DAVID KEARNEY
(PGA PRO)

Galway Golf Centre & Driving Range

Salthill, Galway.
T: (091) 526737
E: dkgolf@eircom.net

The Galway Golf Centre is the finest new golfing facility in the West of Ireland, catering for all your golfing needs.

RAYMOND RYAN
(PGA PRO)

Athenry Golf Club

Palmerstown, Oranmore, Co. Galway.
T: (091) 790599
E: rayryan4golf@eircom.net

Fully stocked golf shop, lessons & repairs. Driving range.

RICHARD CLARKE
(Richard Clarke Sports)
(Head Golf Professional)

Portumna Golf Club

Brendan Street, Portumna, Co. Galway.
T/F:(0509) 41049
M: (087) 2359572
Computerised tuition. Junior golf academy. Golfsmith custom club making and repair. Fully stocked shop at golf club & in Portumna.

STEVE FAHY
(Director Of Golf)

Ceann Sibéal Golf Club

Ballyferriter, Tralee, Co. Kerry.
T: (066) 9156255
E: dinglegc@iol.ie

Fully stocked golf shop.

BRIAN O'CALLAGHAN
(PGA PRO)

Ballybunion Golf Club

Ballybunion, Co. Kerry.
T: (068) 27842
F: (068) 27387
E: bbgcproshop@iol.ie
First-class pro shop. Tuition, club repairs, club hire, trolley hire all available.

LIAM HIGGINS
BRIAN HIGGINS
DAVID HIGGINS
(3 PGA PRO'S)
Waterville Golf Club

Waterville, Co. Kerry.
T: (066) 9474102
M: (087) 2337609

Fully stocked pro shop. Individual, group & corporate tuition available. Brian also teaches at The Kerries Driving Range, Tralee.

KILDARE

JOHN MCHENRY
(PGA PRO)
PETER O'HAGAN
(PGA PRO)

The K Club

Straffan, Co. Kildare.
T: (01) 6017321
E: john.mchenry@kclub.ie

Fully stocked pro shop. First class tuition packages for individuals, groups and corporate occasions.

KILDARE

GERRY EGAN
(PGA PRO)

Castlewarden Golf & Country Club

Straffan, Co. Kildare.
T: (01) 4588219
E: info@castlewardengolfclub.com

Fully stocked shop with all major brands at excellent prices, full tuition service provided.

KILDARE

GERRY BURKE
(PGA PRO)

The Curragh Golf Club

The Curragh, Co. Kildare.
T: (045) 441896
F: (045) 442476

Wide range of stock. "We will match the best prices in Ireland". Tuition is a speciality. Instant repair service.

KILKENNY

SEAN COTTER
(PGA PRO)

Mount Juliet Golf Academy

Thomastown, Co.Kilkenny
T: (056) 73071
E: s.cotter@mountjuliet.ie
World-class golf academy with driving range & full size 3 hole course. Individual & group tuition service for all standards.

KILKENNY

JOHN O'DWYER
(Head Golf Professional)

Callan Golf Club

Callan, Co. Kilkenny.
T: (086) 8172464
E: jodprom@oceanfree.net

Golf retail sales, full tuition, club fitting & repair service.

LIMERICK

KEVIN BENNIS
(Golf Shop)

Castletroy Golf Club

Castletroy, Co. Limerick.
T: (061) 330450

Fully stocked golf shop with all major brands.

LIMERICK

DONAL MCSWEENEY
(PGA PRO)

Limerick County Golf and Country Club

Ballyneety, Co. Limerick.
T: (061) 352905
E: mcsweeneygolf@msn.com

Four PGA Pros providing all year round tuition using the V1 coaching system. Fully stocked shop offering club fitting services.

LIMERICK

BARBARA HACKETT
(Ladies European Tour PRO)

Limerick Driving Range

Coonagh, Co. Limerick.
T: (061) 455584
M: (086) 8116255
E: barbarahackett@eircom.net
Floodlit driving range facilities. Full tuition service for golfers of all levels, including beginners & juniors.

LONGFORD

DAVID KEENAGHAN
(PGA PRO)

Providing Golf Professional services to Golfers in Longford.

T: (086) 8722924
E: cardav@eircom.net

Corporate, group & individual tuition. Available to travel for tuition. Club repair service.

LOUTH

DAVID CARROLL
(PGA PRO)

Seapoint Golf Club

Termonfeckin, Co. Louth.
T: (041) 9881066

Tuition for beginners and advanced players, including on-course lessons. Fully stocked shop. Repairs also available.

LOUTH

JOE FRAWLEY
(PGA PRO)

Joe & Anne Frawley Golf & Leisure

Long Walk Shopping Centre, Dundalk, Co. Louth.
T: (042) 9352999
E: anne027@gofree.indigo.ie
Full tuition service available at Carnbeg Golf Club & Iniskeen Driving Range.
See display advert page 5.

MEATH

ROBIN MACHIN
(PGA PRO)

County Meath Golf Club

Newtownmoynagh, Trim, Co. Meath.
T: (046) 31463
E: mrobin@gofree.indigo.ie

All leading brands stocked: Callaway, Titliest, Footjoy, Ping and Macgregor. Tuition for individuals & groups. Video lessons.

MEATH

EMMANUEL RIBLET
(PGA PRO)

Navan Golf Club

Proudstown, Navan, Co. Meath.
T: (046) 72888

Fully stocked golf shop. Individual, group & corporate tuition service.

MEATH

BOBBY BROWNE
(PGA PRO)

Laytown & Bettystown Golf Club

Bettystown, Co. Meath.
T: (041) 9828739
E: bettystowngolfclub@utvinternet

Golf retail sales, full tuition, club fitting & repair service.

MONAGHAN

MAURICE CASSIDY
(PGA PRO)

Nuremore Golf Club

Carrickmacross, Co. Monaghan.
T: (042) 9664016
E: mmcassidy@eircom.net

Director of Golf, providing full pro shop services and tuition.

OFFALY

DONAGH MCARDLE
(PGA PRO)

Tullamore Golf Club

Tullamore, Co. Offaly.
T: (0506) 51757
E: donmacpro2001@yahoo.com

Fully stocked golf shop, repairs & tuition available.

ROSCOMMON

MARTIN QUINN
(PGA PRO)

Athlone Golf Club

Hodson Bay, Athlone, Co. Roscommon
T: (0902) 92073/92868

Fully stocked golf shop, repair, service & tuition available.

SLIGO

JIM ROBINSON
(PGA PRO)

County Sligo Golf Club

Robbo Golf, Rosses Point, Co. Sligo
T: (071) 77171
E: robbogolf@eircom.net

Fully stocked golf shop, full club repair & tuition service available.

TIPPERARY

GER JONES
(PGA PRO)

Tipperary Golf Club

Rathanny, Tipperary.
T: (062) 51119

Fully stocked pro shop with all leading brands. Computerised golf tuition 'The Neat System' for group and individual lessons.

TIPPERARY

ROBERT KELLY
(PGA PRO)

Nenagh Golf Club

Beechwood, Nenagh, Co. Tipperary.
T: (067) 33242

Well-stocked shop. Repair of golf equipment. Tuition for individuals & groups.

TIPPERARY

JOHN O'DWYER
(Golf Professional)

The Golf Store

Unit 4/5, Clonmel Business Park,
Co. Tipperary
T: (086) 8172464
E: jodprom@oceanfree.net

Golf retail sales, full tuition, club fitting & repair service.

TYRONE

GARY CHAMBERS
(PGA PRO)

Killymoon Golf Club

200 Killymoon Rd, Cookstown
Co.Tyrone, BT80 8TW
T: (028) 86763460
E: chambers.golf@btopenworld.com

Fully stocked golf shop, full club repair & tuition service available to all.

WATERFORD

JAMES KANE-NASH
(Head Golf Professional)

Dunmore East Golf Club

Dunmore, Co. Waterford.
T: (051) 383151
M: (086) 8731045
E: kane-nashgolf@eircom.net

Individual, group & corporate tuition available. Video swing analysis.

WATERFORD

DERRY KIELY
(PGA PRO)

Faithlegg Golf Club

Faithlegg, Co. Waterford.
T: (051) 382241
M: (087) 2398856

Golf tuition available to all standards of golfers. On-course lessons on request.

WESTMEATH	**JOHN BURNS** *(PGA PRO)* **Mullingar Golf Club**	Mullingar, Co. Westmeath. T: (044) 40085 *Fully stocked shop. Tuition & overnight club repair service. Advice on course construction.*
WESTMEATH	**DAVID KEENAGHAN** *(PGA PRO)* **Mount Temple Golf Club**	Moate, Co. Westmeath. T: (086) 8722924 E: cardav@eircom.net *Corporate, group & individual tuition. Available to travel for tuition. Club repair service.*
WEXFORD	**JOHN COONE** *(PGA PRO)* **Courtown Golf Club**	Kiltennel, Gorey, Co. Wexford. T: (055) 25166 *All top brands of equipment, clothing and shoes. Tuition by appointment. Trolley, buggy and club hire.*
WEXFORD	**JOHNNY YOUNG** *(PGA PRO)* **Rosslare Golf Club**	Rosslare Strand, Co. Wexford. T: (053) 32032 F: (053) 32203 M: (087) 2251330 W: www.johnnyyoung.ie *Large stock of golfing goods at very competitive prices. Custom fit, repair service. Tuition for all standards.*
WICKLOW	**PETER DUIGNAN** *(PGA PRO)* **Charlesland Golf & Country Club**	Greystones, Co. Wicklow. T: (01) 2874350 E: peteduignan@yahoo.co.uk *The new V1 digital golf-coaching system available. Fully stocked shop.*
WICKLOW	**PETER JONES** *(PGA PRO)* **Coollattin Golf Club**	Shillelagh, Co. Wicklow. T: (055) 29125 M: (087)5800193 *Golf lessons provided. (Video optional) All top brands at competitive prices. Plus many special offers.*

Newcomers to the Irish Golf Scene

THE HERITAGE GOLF & COUNTRY CLUB
Co. Laois.

Tom Keane had a dream. He told his friends, "I want my hero Seve Ballesteros to help me make it come true." Nobody who knows this far-seeing Portlaoise property developer and hotelier would dare to question his powers of persuasion. The Heritage Golf and Country Club, situated near the charming village of Killenard in County Laois, just off the motorway that is the main Dublin-Cork road, about forty miles south-west of Dublin, is due to open for play in July 2003 and Keane's brave vision will become a reality.

By all accounts, it did not need a lot of coaxing to bring Ballesteros on board. The great Spaniard was quick to reiterate his affinity for Irish golf and was delighted to link up with the well-known Irish-based course builder and golf architect, Jeff Howes. The Midlands of Ireland is not exactly over-flowing with golf courses of championship quality but The Heritage will take care of that situation presently. What was once fertile farmland has been transformed by an imaginative parkland design. The most striking feature is the introduction of five artificial lakes, the largest of these covers no less than five acres and it will come into play at both the ninth and eighteenth holes.

The course is built on beautiful, easily drained, limestone countryside that includes all the necessary features of water and trees, changes in elevation and rolling undulations that will be both a joy and a challenge to play. At 7345 yards, off the back tees, The Heritage will have enough length and variety to test anybody and it is hoped that Ballesteros will bring the top professionals of Great Britain and Ireland to play against the best pros from Continental Europe for his own Seve Trophy to this rich and fertile part of Ireland as soon as the course and all of its facilities are in full swing. The clubhouse, with accompanying bars, restaurants and spa will be superbly luxurious and every conceivable comfort will be available to any member or visitor intent on spoiling themselves. Side by side with the golf course is the possibility of living in these tranquil surroundings. Luxury homes and lodges are being developed in tandem with the golf course.

The Club is now actively seeking members and the contact person is former Irish Team Captain, Eddie Dunne. For information telephone him at 0502 61700 or Email: info@theheritagegolf.com

CARTON HOUSE GOLF CLUB, Co. Kildare

Dating from 1176 to 1920, the Carton Desmense, near Maynooth, was the ancestral home of successive Lord FitzGeralds, the Earls of Kildare, one of the most prominent ruling families in Irish history. Just a thirty-mile drive from the city centre of Dublin and the Dublin International Airport, one of Ireland's greatest and most historic Estates contains a superbly preserved 18th century mansion house, surrounded by 1100 acres of rolling countryside. The Carton Estate has been turned into two totally contrasting golf courses, one designed by Colin Montgomerie, the other by Mark O'Meara. Standing side by side, both courses are ready to challenge the most adventurous golfers.

In order to play 21st century golf at its best, you enter walled grounds that bring you into surroundings of a rich heritage stretching back over 800 years. The Mark O'Meara course is a modern tree-lined parkland layout, with a river running through the property and has been gaining rave reviews in the world's golf media. While the Colin Montgomerie links, naturally enough, resembles a great Scottish seaside links with large undulating greens, pot bunkers and penal rough with a distinct shortage of trees.

Carton House has already established itself as a hugely worthwhile experience. The exemplary quality of the two golf courses plus the unique atmosphere in the clubhouse will ensure that every aspect of a day out will be memorably enjoyable.

For more information on membership or green fees visit www.carton.ie or telephone: 01 628 6271

CASTLEISLAND GOLF CLUB, Co. Kerry

On a trip from Limerick to Killarney a couple of years ago I noticed what appeared to be a golf course under construction on the side of a "mountain" just off the N21 motorway as it snakes its way down into the busy town of Castleisland. "That is an extraordinary place to put a golf course," I said to my wife. "Players will need ski-lifts to get around". Kerry people are noted for their ingenuity so I should not have been too surprised to find out later when I was invited to play the golf course with its designer, Dr. Arthur Spring, that I was completely wrong. As I imagined, it was no easy task constructing a golf course on such a landscape but Arthur and his team succeeded beyond their wildest expectations. This is a hidden jewel of a golf course in a county that is already festooned in golfing lore.

Although there is a considerable change in elevation from the top of the course to its lowest point, there is little sensation or effort in the climbing and descending. The clever routing takes one diagonally and sideways along terraced fairways. It may also appear inhospitable, albeit attractive, bog land in places but the fairways and greens are superbly dry underfoot all year round. All thanks to the way that Dr. Spring did his work. Rather than wait for seeding to take place, herringbone surface drains were inserted at an early stage of construction. Not only was this to prove a cheaper way of drainage, it was also less disruptive and helped to bring the finished article to conclusion ahead of schedule. This latest addition to Kerry's magnificent golfing kingdom is a splendid test. There isn't a weak hole in sight. The views from several of the tees are breath taking. While the course is eminently playable by all grades of golfers there are still plenty of hazardous wetlands teeming with vegetation and wildlife along the edges of the fairways ready to gobble up loose and errant golf balls.

The clubhouse is unique and simple, being a converted rifle shooting gallery but it is more than adequate comfort-wise and perfectly utilitarian. Castleisland GC is certainly well worth a visit at any time for a casual game or a golf society outing.

For bookings contact the
Club Manager, Michael Coote
Telephone: 066 714 1709 or
Email: managercastleislandgolfclub@eircom.net

ROGANSTOWN Golf & Country Club, Swords, Co. Dublin

Christy O'Connor Junior, the Irish touring professional star for so many years, is the proud designer of twenty-four courses in Ireland. Roganstown Golf and Country Club, 2 miles east of the N1 motorway at Swords, Co. Dublin is his latest venture. Christy can be very proud of what he has helped to achieve.

Natural water from the Broadmeadow River that runs through the property provided the opportunity for plentiful water hazards to be exploited to the full on a site that also features gentle rolling terrain. Christy Junior and his course builder, Tom Bryan, must have had as much fun and satisfaction creating this fine addition to Ireland's growing number of top class facilities as the golfers will now have playing it. The €40 million development will not only have its own classic golf course but also a 52-room luxury hotel, a conference venue, a state of the art leisure club with all facilities, some holiday homes and townhouses (for short term rental) as well as twenty-five exclusive detached residences.

**Telephone: 01 843 3118 for more information or
Email: info@roganstown.com or look up
www.roganstown.com**

SEAFIELD GOLF & COUNTRY CLUB
Gorey, Co. Wexford

It's rare indeed that one comes across a golf course that combines the normally incompatible characteristics of woodland, heath land and seaside golf all on one location. Such is the case at Seafield near Gorey. About one hour's drive from Dublin and only twenty minutes south of The European Club at Brittas Bay, Seafield Golf and Country Club has developed remarkably well since it opened with rare flair in mid-2002 with a televised shoot-out exhibition match between Padraig Harrington, Retief Goosen and Barry Lane.

Seafield is an extremely attractive proposition for golfers from the Dublin area wanting to get away for day trips or even an overnight stay. No expense was spared getting the top class quality of this project perfectly right. An hour's drive from Dublin will be nothing compared to the reward of being here. At 6447 yards, Seafield is a short course by modern standards but course designer, Peter McEvoy, the former champion golfer and Walker Cup captain, has ensured that every club in the bag will be tested as well as the strength and power of one's concentration because of the spectacular terrain and views overlooking Ballymoney Strand and the Irish Sea. There are also plans for a hotel and some discreet housing in a village style setting on the 170-acre site to give it a true resort feel.

**Contact the on-site
Director of Golf, Dara O'Neill at 055 24777 or
Email: info@seafield.com or
www.seafield.com for further information.**

DOONBEG GOLF CLUB, County Clare

"The sensitivity of this piece of property required a totally hands-on approach. You do not get many opportunities to work on a piece of land like this. It is unique. I am going to make sure the end result is 100%. I know I am not going to please everybody but I will give it my best effort. This is a course that I want to be identified with. One that I will be able to say with pride, I did this one. I may be the luckiest designer in the world because of the uniqueness of this site. It's Ireland, it's Irish golf, it's links golf; sand hills like you'll never see again". The enthusiasm of Greg Norman for what he was about to achieve at Doonbeg is only matched by the feeling of satisfaction now that the links has opened for play and has been in receipt of a string of accolades that would be difficult to surpass in the history of new course openings anywhere.

Doonbeg Golf Club in County Clare opened for play after a particularly troublesome gestation in July 2002. This great new links is located on a narrow crescent of cone shaped sand dunes at the edge of the Atlantic Ocean named Donoughmore Bay, six miles north of Kilkee, twenty miles south of Lahinch and about forty miles from Shannon Airport. Greg Norman, the world-renowned Australian golfer, visited the site twenty-two times during the construction process taking a laudable, highly active, hands-on approach at all stages of the project. Clearly, he and his team have done a remarkable job. The construction process was impeded and virtually handcuffed at various stages of its development by objections from misguided environmentalists who claimed that they wished to protect a tiny indigenous snail named Vertigo Angustior. Somehow the objectors had inexplicably failed to acknowledge that ancestors of the same snail family had managed to survive the activities of the golfing fraternity at nearby Lahinch for well over a century. Doonbeg is one of the last courses of its type that will ever be built anywhere. The land needed to create a genuine links like this one is almost extinct. Indeed, Norman is quick to say how grateful he is that he had such a rare opportunity and is sanguine about ever having the chance to work with land of similar quality ever again.

To stand on the high altar-like first tee at Doonbeg with driver at the ready is an inspiration all by itself. Looking down the first fairway with the ocean on one's left and the straight-out route to the ninth green stretching as much as two and one half miles into the distance is enough to help anybody put their best game face on and perform above themselves, for one day at least. A small pot bunker in the middle of the fairway about 110 yards short of the first green dominates the hole with a seemingly magnetic force. The half circle of enormous dunes surrounding the green site is stunning to look at but hardly come into play. Although the 7th hole is only a par three of 184 yards, more dirt was moved here than at any other place on the course. The hole is totally artificial but you never think so from looking at the finished article. The entire golf course looks as if it has been waiting for the mere act of putting grass mowers on it and cutting the holes and putting in flagsticks. That is the highest compliment you can pay any golf architect and course builder.

Unlike so many new golf courses these days Doonbeg is not overly long but there is fantastic variety to be savoured. Some of the most unusual green sites ever created will cause many a puzzle to those who find themselves on the "wrong" side of any of the greens. There are several Scottish type eccentricities such as deep, cavernous bunkers that face the "wrong way", a sand trap in the centre of the 12th green and several crossover shots. All will guarantee that a game at Doonbeg will be anything but dull. This is a course that everybody should play at least once whether they are Irish or from Paraparamaumau.

For full information on memberships or tee-times
Telephone: 065 9055246 or
Email: info@doonbeggolfclub.com

GOLF CLUBS

The golf industry in Ireland is changing to meet new demands and challenges. The golf clubs and resorts in this section are now well equipped to service every standard of golfer. This commitment ensures that the game of golf is enjoyed by members and visitors alike.

THE ESSENTIAL
GOLFERS GUIDE
IRELAND 2003

ABBEYFEALE GOLF CLUB
No. of holes: 9

Dromtrasna, Collins
Abbeyfeale, Co. Limerick.
T: (068) 32033
E: abbeyfealegolf@hotmail.com

Contact Name: Maurice O'Riordan
Secretary\Manager
Captain 2003: John Haugh
Green Fees: Weekdays: €10
Weekends: €10
G/C: N   **P/C :** N   **G/S :** N
Course Distance C'ship: 4,072m

ABBELYLEIX GOLF CLUB
No. of holes: 18

Rathmoyle, Abbeyleix, Portlaois, Co. Laois.
T: (0502) 31450

Contact Name: Michael Martin
Hon\Secretary
Captain 2003: Brian Gee
Green Fees: Weekdays: €15
Weekends: €25
G/C: N   **P/C :** Y   **G/S :** N
Course Distance C'ship: 5,583m
Ladies: 4,572m

ACHILL ISLAND GOLF CLUB
No. of holes: 9

Keel, Achill, Co. Mayo.
T: (098) 43456
F: (098) 43265

Contact Name: Sean Connelly
Hon. Secretary
Captain 2003: Leo Smith
Green Fees: Weekdays: €15
Weekends: €20
G/C: N   **P/C :** Y   **G/S :** N
Course Distance C'ship: 5,416m
Ladies: 4,640m

ADARE GOLF CLUB
No. of holes: 18

Adare Manor, Adare, Co. Limerick.
T: (061) 395044
F: (061) 396987
E: golf@adaremanor.com
W: www.adaremanor.com

Contact Name: Will Hickey
Pro Shop Manager
Green Fees: Weekdays: €115
Weekends: €115
G/C: Y   **P/C :** Y   **G/S :** Y
Course Distance C'ship: 5,583m
Ladies: 4,927m

ADARE MANOR GOLF CLUB
No. of holes: 18

Adare, Co. Limerick
T: (061) 396204
F: (061) 396800
E: info@adaremanorgolfclub.com
W: www.adaremanorgolfclub.com
Contact Name: Pat O'Brien
Hon\Secretary
Captain 2003: Charlie Daly
Green Fees: Weekdays: €35
Weekends: €35
G/C: N   **P/C :** Y   **G/S :** Y
Course Distance C'ship: 6,303m
Ladies: 4,637m

ANTRIM GOLF CLUB
No. of holes: 18

45 Castle Road, Antrim BT41 4NA
T: (028) 94429001
E: antrimgolfclub@aol.com

Contact Name: Marie Agnew
Secretary\Manager
Captain 2003: Allan Jardine
Green Fees: Weekdays: Stg £15.50
Weekends: Stg £17.50
G/C: N   **P/C :** Y   **G/S :** Y
Course Distance C'ship: 6,015m
Ladies: 5,021m

Golf Carts = G/C   Pull Carts = P/C   Golf shop = G/S

ARDACONG GOLF CLUB
No. of holes: 18

Milltown Road, Tuam, Co. Galway
T: (093) 25525/24343
E: ardaconggc@eircom.net

Contact Name: Paul Kelly
Captain 2003: John Byrne
Green Fees: Weekdays: €15
Weekends: €18
G/C: N **P/C :** Y **G/S :** N
Course Distance C'ship: 5,486m
Ladies: 4,599m

ARDEE GOLF CLUB
No. of holes: 18

Townspark, Ardee, Co. Louth
T: (041) 6853227
F: (041) 6856137
E: ardeegolfclub@eircom.net
W: www.ardeegolfclub.com
Contact Name: M.P. Conoluty
Secretary\Manager
Captain 2003: Noel Malone
Green Fees Weekdays: €35
Weekends: €50
G/C: Y **P/C :** Y **G/S :** Y
Course Distance C'ship: 6,030m
Ladies: 4,947m

ARDFERT GOLF CLUB
No. of holes: 18

Sackville, Ardfert, Co. Kerry.
T: (066) 7134744
F: (066) 7134744

Contact Name: Tom Lawlor
Secretary\Manager
Captain 2003: P.J. O'Riordan
Green Fees: Weekdays: €22
Weekends: €22
G/C: N **P/C :** Y **G/S :** N
Course Distance C'ship: 5,214m
Ladies: 4,680m

ARDGLASS GOLF CLUB
No. of holes: 18

Castle Place, Ardglass, Co. Down.
T: (028) 44841219
F: (028) 44841841
E: info@ardglassgolfclub.com
W: www.ardglassgolfclub.com
Contact Name: Debbie Polly
Secretary\Manager
Captain 2003: Harry Dougherty
Green Fees: Weekdays: Stg £28
Weekends: Stg £40
G/C: N **P/C :** Y **G/S :** Y
Course Distance C'ship: 6,065m
Ladies: 5,293m

ARDMINNAN GOLF CLUB
No. of holes: 9

15a Ardminnan Road, Portaferry,
Co. Down BT22 1QJ.
T: (028) 42771321
F: (028) 42771321
E: info@ardminnan.com
Contact Name: Eamonn McGrattan
Secretary\Manager
Captain 2003: Ted McCartney
Green Fees Weekdays: Stg £10
Weekends: Stg £15
G/C: N **P/C :** Y **G/S :** Y
Course Distance C'ship: 5,532m
Ladies: 5,116m

ARKLOW GOLF CLUB
No. of holes: 18

Abbeylands, Arklow, Co. Wicklow.
T: (0402) 32492
F: (0402) 91604
E: arklowgolflinks@eircom.net
W: www.arklowgolflinks.com
Contact Name: Brendan Timons
Hon\Secretary
Captain 2003: Tony Hewitt
Green Fees Weekdays: €40
Weekends: €40
G/C: N **P/C :** Y **G/S :** N
Course Distance C'ship: 5,665m
Ladies: 4,836m

Golf Carts = G/C   Pull Carts = P/C   Golf shop = G/S

Golf Clubs

ASHBOURNE GOLF CLUB
No. of holes: 18

Archerstown, Ashbourne, Co. Meath.
T: (01) 8352005/8352562
F: (01) 8359261
E: ashgc@iol.ie
W: www.ashbournegolfclub.ie
Contact Name: Des O'Hare
 Secretary\Manager
Captain 2003: Martin Power
Green Fees Weekdays: €40
 Weekends: €50
G/C: Y P/C : Y G/S : Y
Course Distance C'ship: 5,884m
Ladies: 5,081m

ASHFIELD GOLF CLUB
No. of holes: 18

Freeduff, Cullyhanna, Newry,
Co. Down BT35 0JJ.
T: (028) 30868180
F: (028) 30868611
E: ashfield.golfing@virgin.net
W: www.freespace.virgin.net/ashfield.golfing
Contact Name: John Murphy Hon\Secretary
Captain 2003: Christy O'Brien
Green Fees Weekdays: Stg £12
 Weekends: Stg £15
G/C: Y P/C : Y G/S : N
Course Distance C'ship: 5,110m
Ladies: 4,780m

ATHENRY GOLF CLUB
No. of holes: 18

Palmerstown, Oranmore, Co. Galway.
T: (091) 794466
F: (091) 794971
E: athenrygc@eircom.net
W: www.ebookireland.com/athenrygolf.htm
Contact Name: Padraig Flaherty
 Secretary/Manager
Captain 2003: John Reidy
Green Fees Weekdays: €30
 Weekends: €35
G/C: N P/C : Y G/S : Y
Course Distance C'ship: 5,687m
Ladies: 4,966m

ATHLONE GOLF CLUB
No. of holes: 18

Hodson Bay, Athlone, Co. Roscommon.
T: 0902-92073
F: 0902-94080
Contact Name: Ita Dockery
 Secretary\Manager
Captain 2003: Larry Fagan
Green Fees Weekdays: €25
 Weekends: €30
G/C: Y P/C : Y G/S : Y
Course Distance C'ship: 5,973m
Ladies: 5,045m

ATHY GOLF CLUB
No. of holes: 18

Geraldine, Athy, Kildare.
T: 0507-31729
F: 0507-34710
E: info@athygolfclub.com
W: www.athygolfclub.com
Contact Name: Pat Fleming
 Hon\Secretary
Captain 2003: Paddy Brereton
Green Fees Weekdays: €20
 Weekends: €30
G/C: Y P/C : Y G/S : Y
Course Distance C'ship: 5,599m
Ladies: 5,000m

AUGHNACLOY GOLF CLUB
No. of holes: 9

99 Tullyvar Road, Aughnacloy
Co. Tyrone BT69 6BL.
T: 028-85557050

Contact Name: Everet Clarke
 Secretary\Manager
Captain 2003: Thomas Strain
Green Fees Weekdays: Stg £10
 Weekends: Stg £12
G/C: N P/C : Y G/S : N
Course Distance C'ship: 5,017m

36

Golf Carts = G/C   **Pull Carts = P/C**   **Golf shop = G/S**

BALBRIGGAN GOLF CLUB
No. of holes: 18

Blackhall, Balbriggan, Co. Dublin.
T: 01-8412229
F: 01-8413927
E: balbriggangolfclub@eircom.net
W: www.balbirggangolfclub.com
Contact Name: Michael O'Halloran
Secretary\Manager
Captain 2003: Ian Fraher
Green Fees Weekdays: €34
Weekends: €37
G/C: N   P/C : Y   G/S : N
Course Distance C'ship: 5,922m
Ladies: 5,172m

BALCARRICK GOLF CLUB
No. of holes: 18

Corballis, Donabate, Co. Dublin.
T: 01-8436957
F: 01-8436228
E: balcarr@iol.ie
W: www.balcarrickgolfclub.com
Contact Name: Patricia Fennelly
Secretary\Manager
Captain 2003: Ron Nolan
Green Fees Weekdays: €32
Weekends: €40
G/C: Y   P/C : Y   G/S : Y
Course Distance C'ship: 6,191m
Ladies: 5,093m

BALLAGHADEREEN GOLF CLUB
No. of holes: 9

Aughalustia, Ballaghadereen,
Co. Roscommon.
T\F: 0907-60295
W: www.ballaghadereen.com/golf.html

Contact Name: John Corcoran
Hon\Secretary
Captain 2003: Basil Clancy
Green Fees Weekdays: €15
Weekends: €15
G/C: N   P/C : Y   G/S : N
Course Distance C'ship: 5,339m
Ladies: 4,602m

BALLINA GOLF CLUB
No. of holes: 18

Mossgrove, Shanaghy, Ballina, Co. Mayo.
T: 096-21050
F: 096-21718
E: ballinagc@eircom.net
W: www.ballinagc.net
Contact Name: Padraig Connolly
Hon\Secretary
Captain 2003: Eamonn Ruddy
Green Fees Weekdays: €28
Weekends: €35
G/C: Y   P/C : Y   G/S : N
Course Distance C'ship: 5,580m
Ladies: 4,872m

BALLINAMORE GOLF CLUB
No. of holes: 9

Ballinamore, Co. Leitrim
T: 078-44346
F: 078-45951
W: www.ballinamore.com

Contact Name: P Reynolds
Hon\Secretary
Captain 2003: Vincent McMorrow
Green Fees Weekdays: €15
Weekends: €15
G/C: N   P/C : Y   G/S : N
Course Distance C'ship: 5,514m
Ladies: 4,526m

BALLINASLOE GOLF CLUB
No. of holes: 18

Portumna Road, Ballinasloe, Co. Galway.
T: 0909-642126
F: 0909-642538
E: ballinasloegolfclub@eircom.net
W: www.ballinasloegolfclub.com
Contact Name: Conor Carr
Hon\Secretary
Captain 2003: Liam Farrell
Green Fees Weekdays: €22
Weekends: €28
G/C: Y   P/C : Y   G/S : N
Course Distance C'ship: 5,865m
Ladies: 5,023m

Golf Carts = G/C   Pull Carts = P/C   Golf shop = G/S

BALLINLOUGH CASTLE GOLF CLUB
No. of holes: 18

Clonmellon, Co. Westmeath.
T\F: 044-64544
E: tonyinballinlough@eircom.net
W: www.ballinloughcastle.com

Contact Name: Tony Brady
Secretary\Manager
Captain 2003: Oliver O'Sullivan
Green Fees Weekdays: €25
Weekends: €25
G/C: N   P/C : Y   G/S: N
Course Distance C'ship: 6,144 m

BALLINASCORNEY GOLF CLUB
No. of holes: 9

Kilmashogue Lane, Rathfarnham, Dublin 16.
T: 01-4937475
E: info@ballinascorneygolfclub.com
W: www.ballinascorneygolfclub.com

Contact Name: Vincent P. Byrne
Hon\Secretary
Captain 2003: Liam Redmond
Green Fees Weekdays: €15
Weekends: €20
G/C: N   P/C : Y   G/S: N
Course Distance C'ship: 4,507m
Ladies: 4,074m

BALLINROBE GOLF CLUB
No. of holes: 18

Cloonacastle, Ballinrobe, Co. Mayo.
T: 094-9541118
F: 094-9541889
E: bgcgolf@iol.ie

Contact Name: Tom Moran
Secretary\Manager
Captain 2003: Seamus McHugh
Green Fees Weekdays: €30
Weekends: €35
G/C: Y   P/C : Y   G/S: N
Course Distance C'ship: 6,234m
Ladies: 5,136m

BALLYBOFEY & STRANORLAR GOLF CLUB
No. of holes: 18

The Glebe, Stranorlar, Co. Donegal.
T: 074-31093
F: 074-31058

Contact Name: John McCaughan
Hon\Secretary
Captain 2003: Joe Blee
Green Fees Weekdays: €20
Weekends: €25
G/C: N   P/C : Y   G/S : Y
Course Distance C'ship: 5,371m
Ladies: 4,791m

BALLYBUNION GOLF CLUB
No. of holes: 36

Sandhill Road, Ballybunion, Co. Kerry.
T: 068-27146   **F:** 068-27387
E: bbgolfc@iol.ie
W: www.ballybuniongolfclub.ie
Contact Name: Jim McKenna
Secretary\Manager
Captain 2003: Gerard Walsh
Green Fees
Weekdays: €110(Old)   €75(Cashen)
Weekends: €110(Old)   €75(Cashen)
G/C: N   P/C : Y   G/S: Y
Course Distance C'ship: 5,994m
Ladies: 4,795m

BALLYCASTLE GOLF CLUB
No. of holes: 18

2 Cushendall Road, Ballycastle, Co. Antrim
BT54 6QP.
T: 028-20762536
F: 028-20769909
E: info@ballycastlegolfclub.com
W: www.ballycastlegolfclub.com
Contact Name: B.J. Dillon – Hon\Secretary
Captain 2003: Colm Henry
Green Fees Weekdays: Stg £20
Weekends: Stg £30
G/C: N   P/C : Y   G/S: Y
Course Distance C'ship: 5,406m
Ladies: 4,829m

Golf Carts = G/C   Pull Carts = P/C   Golf shop = G/S

BALLYCLARE GOLF CLUB
No. of holes: 18

25 Springvale Road, Ballyclare BT39 9JW.
T: 028-93322696
F: 028-93324542
E: ballyclaregolfclub@supanet.com
W: www.ballyclaregolfclub.supanet.com
Contact Name: Harry McConnell
Secretary\Manager
Captain 2003: Sam Maxwell
Green Fees Weekdays: Stg £20
Weekends: Stg £24
G/C: Y P/C : Y G/S : Y
Course Distance C'ship: 5,745m
Ladies: 4,893m

BALLYHAUNIS GOLF CLUB
No. of holes: 9

Coolnaha, Ballyhaunis, Co. Mayo.
T: 0907-30014

Contact Name: John Mooney
Hon\Secretary
Captain 2003: Ger Henry
Green Fees Weekdays: €20
Weekends: €20
G/C: N P/C : N G/S : N
Course Distance C'ship: 5,413m

BALLYHEIGUE CASTLE GOLF CLUB
No. of holes: 9

Ballyheigue, Co. Kerry.
T: 066-7133555
F: 066-7133934

Contact Name: John Casey
Secretary\Manager
Captain 2003: Richard O'Reilly
Green Fees Weekdays: €23
Weekends: €23
G/C: N P/C : Y G/S : Y
Course Distance C'ship: 6,292m
Ladies: 4,719m

BALLYKISTEEN GOLF CLUB
No. of holes: 18

Ballykisteen, Limerick Junction,
Co. Tipperary.
T: 062-33333
F: 062-33711

Contact Name: Josephine Ryan
Secretary\Manager
Captain 2003: Michael Greensmith
Green Fees Weekdays: €35
Weekends: €40
G/C: Y P/C : Y G/S : Y
Course Distance C'ship: 6,765m
Ladies: 5,559m

BALLYLIFFIN GOLF CLUB
No. of holes: 39

Ballyliffin, Inishowen, Co. Donegal.
T: 077-76119
F: 077-76672
E: info@ballyliffingolfclub.com
W: www.ballyliffingolfclub.com
Contact Name: Cecil Doherty
Secretary\Manager
Captain 2003: Barney Mullan
Green Fees Weekdays: €60
Weekends: €70
G/C: Y P/C : Y G/S : Y
Course Distance C'ship: 7,230m
Ladies: 5,861m

BALLYMENA GOLF CLUB
No. of holes: 18

128 Raceview Road, Ballymena,
Co. Antrim.
T: 028-25861487
F: 028-25861487

Contact Name: Seamus Crummey
Hon\Secretary
Captain 2003: James McCloy
Green Fees Weekdays: Stg £17
Weekends: Stg £22
G/C: N P/C : Y G/S : Y
Course Distance C'ship: 5,299m
Ladies: 4,848m

40

Golf Carts = G/C   Pull Carts = P/C   Golf shop = G/S

BALLYMOTE GOLF CLUB
No. of holes: 9

Ballynascarrow, Ballymote, Co. Sligo.
T: 071-83504
W: www.ballymotegolfclub.com

Contact Name: Damien Mullaney
Hon\Secretary
Captain 2003: Sean Henry
Green Fees Weekdays: €15
Weekends: €15
G/C: N   P/C : N   G/S : N
Course Distance C'ship: 5281m

BALMORAL GOLF CLUB
No. of holes: 18

518 Lisburn Road, Belfast BT9 6QX.
T: 028-90381514
F: 028-90666759
E: admin@balmoralgolf.com

Contact Name: Terry Graham
Secretary\Manager
Captain 2003: Pat Mullaney
Green Fees Weekdays: Stg £20
Weekends: Stg £30
G/C: N   P/C : Y   G/S : Y
Course Distance C'ship: 5,705m
Ladies: 5,147m

BALTINGLASS GOLF CLUB
No. of holes: 9

Baltinglass, Co. Wicklow.
T: 0508-81350
F: 0508-82842
E: baltinglass@eircom.net
W: wwwbaltinglassgc.com
Contact Name: Owen Cooney
Hon\Secretary
Captain 2003: Eamon Sweeney
Green Fees Weekdays: €20
Weekends: €30
G/C: Y   P/C : Y   G/S : Y
Course Distance C'ship: 5,912m
Ladies: 4,744m

BANBRIDGE GOLF CLUB
No. of holes: 18

116 Huntly Road, Banbridge, Co. Down BT32 3UR.
T: 028-40662211
F: 028-40669400
E: info@banbridgegolf.freeserve.co.uk
W: www.banbridge-golf.freeserve.co.uk
Contact Name: Jacqueline Anketell
Secretary\Manager
Captain 2003: Jack Bickerstaff
Green Fees Weekdays: Stg £17
Weekends: Stg £22
G/C: Y   P/C : Y   G/S : Y
Course Distance C'ship: 5,590m
Ladies: 4,416m

BANDON GOLF CLUB
No. of holes: 18

Castlebernard, Bandon, Co. Cork.
T: 023-41111
F: 023-44690
E: bandongolfclub@eircom.net

Contact Name: Paula Reardon
Secretary\Manager
Captain 2003: Finbar McCarthy
Green Fees Weekdays: €35
Weekends: €40
G/C: Y   P/C : Y   G/S : Y
Course Distance C'ship: 5,377m
Ladies: 4,739m

BANGOR GOLF CLUB
No. of holes: 18

Broadway, Bangor, Co. Down BT20 4RH.
T: 028-91270922
F: 028-91453394
E: bgcsecretary@aol.com
W: www.golfclubworldinfo.com
Contact Name: David Ryan
Secretary\Manager
Captain 2003: John Whittle
Green Fees Weekdays: Stg £25
Weekends: Stg £30
G/C: N   P/C : Y   G/S : Y
Course Distance C'ship: 5,913m
Ladies: 5,154m

Golf Carts = G/C   Pull Carts = P/C   Golf shop = G/S

BANTRY BAY GOLF CLUB
No. of holes: 18

Donemark, Bantry, West Cork.
T: 027-50579
F: 027-53790
E: info@bantrygolf.com
W: www.bantrygolf.com
Contact Name: John O'Sullivan
                  Secretary\Manager
Captain 2003: Cathal McCarthy
Green Fees Weekdays: €35
              Weekends: €40
G/C: Y   P/C : Y   G/S : Y
Course Distance C'ship: 5,910m
Ladies: 4,770m

BEARNA GOLF CLUB
No. of holes: 18

Corboley, Baran, Co. Galway.
T: 091-592677
F: 091-592674
E: info@bearnagolfclub.com
W: www.bearnagolfclub.com
Contact Name: Michael Meade
                  Secretary\Manager
Captain 2003: Pat Ward/Mary Wyer
Green Fees Weekdays: €35
              Weekends: €45
G/C: Y   P/C : Y   G/S : N
Course Distance C'ship: 6,174m
Ladies: 4,684m

BEAUFORT GOLF CLUB
No. of holes: 18

Churchtown, Beaufort, Killarney, Co. Kerry.
T: 064-44440
F: 064-44752
E: beaufortgc@tinet.ie
W: www.globalgolf.com
Contact Name: Colm Kelly
                  Secretary\Manager
Captain 2003: Pat O'Sullivan
Green Fees Weekdays: €45
              Weekends: €55
G/C: Y   P/C : Y   G/S : Y
Course Distance C'ship: 6,023m
Ladies: 4,855m

BEAVERSTOWN GOLF CLUB
No. of holes: 18

Donabate, Co. Dublin.
T: 01-8436439
F: 01-8435059
E: manager@beaverstown.com
W: www.beaverstown.com
Contact Name: Declan Monaghan
                  Secretary\Manager
Captain 2003: Aidan O'Kennedy
Green Fees Weekdays: €52
              Weekends: €68
G/C: Y   P/C : Y   G/S : N
Course Distance C'ship: 5,972m
Ladies: 5,095m

BEECH PARK GOLF CLUB
No. of holes: 18

Johnstown, Rathcoole, Co. Dublin.
T: 01-4580522   **F:** 01-4588365
E: info@beechpark.ie
W: www.beeckpark.ie
Contact Name: Paul Muldowney
                  Secretary\Manager
Captain 2003: Gerry Diggins
                  Adrienne Kelly
Green Fees Weekdays: €38
              Weekends: N\A
G/C: N   P/C : Y   G/S : N
Course Distance C'ship: 5,735m
Ladies: 4,878m

BELMULLET GOLF CLUB
No. of holes: 18

Carne Golf Links, Carne, Belmullet,
Co. Mayo.
T: 097-82292   **F:** 097-81477
E: carnegolf@aol.com
W: www.belmulletgolfclub.ie
Contact Name: Evelynn Keane
                  Secretary\Manager
Captain 2003: Kevin Donnelly/Sheila Talbot
Green Fees Weekdays: €45
              Weekends: €50
G/C: N   P/C : Y   G/S : N
Course Distance C'ship: 6,119m
Ladies: 4,704m

Golf Carts = G/C   Pull Carts = P/C   Golf shop = G/S

BELTURBET GOLF CLUB
No. of holes: 9

Erne Hill, Belturbet, Co. Cavan.
T: 049-9522287
F: 049-9524044

Contact Name: Liam Crotty
                 Secretary\Manager
Captain 2003: Tony Garby
Green Fees   Weekdays: €15
                 Weekends: €15
G/C: Y   P/C : Y   G/S : N
Course Distance C'ship: 5,347m
Ladies: 4,768m

BELVOIR PARK GOLF CLUB
No. of holes: 18

73 Church Road, Newtownbreda, Belfast
BT8 7AN.
T: 028-90491693
F: 028-90646113

Contact Name: Ann Vaughan
                 Secretary\Manager
Captain 2003: Larry Andrews
Green Fees   Weekdays: Stg £38
                   Weekends: Stg £45
G/C: Y   P/C : Y   G/S : Y
Course Distance C'ship: 5,956m
Ladies: 5,589m

BENBURB VALLEY GOLF CLUB
No. of holes: 9

Maydown Road, Benburb
Co. Tyrone BT71 7LJ.
T: 028-37549868
F: 028-37548236
W: www.benburbvalley.co.uk

Contact Name: Robert Irwin - Owner
Captain 2003: Adrian Murphy
Green Fees   Weekdays: Stg £11
                   Weekends: Stg £14
G/C: Y   P/C : Y   G/S : Y
Course Distance C'ship: 5,923m
Ladies: 4,784m

BEREHAVEN GOLF CLUB
No. of holes: 9

Millcove, Castletownbere, Co. Cork.
T\F: 027-70700
E: bearagolfclub@eircom.net
W: www.bearagolf.com

Contact Name: Karan Crowley
                 Secretary\Manager
Captain 2003: David Kelly
Green Fees   Weekdays: €20
                   Weekends: €25
G/C: N   P/C : Y   G/S : N
Course Distance C'ship: 5,174m
Ladies: 3,982m

BIRR GOLF CLUB
No. of holes: 18

The Glenn's, Birr, Co. Offaly.
T: 0509-20082
F: 0509-22155
E: birrgolfclub@eircom.net
W: www.globalgolf.com
Contact Name: Joan Grimes
                 Secretary\Manager
Captain 2003: George Boyd
Green Fees   Weekdays: €25
                   Weekends: €35
G/C: Y   P/C : Y   G/S : N
Course Distance C'ship: 5,824m
Ladies: 4,860m

BLACKBUSH GOLF CLUB
No. of holes: 27

Thomastown, Dunshaughlin, Co. Meath.
T: 01-8250021
F: 01-8250400
E: golf@blackbush.iol.ie

Contact Name: Kate O'Rourke
                 Administrator
Captain 2003: Tom Foran
Green Fees   Weekdays: €30
                   Weekends: €35
G/C: Y   P/C : Y   G/S : Y
Course Distance C'ship: 6,260m
Ladies: 5,148m

43

Golf Carts = G/C   Pull Carts = P/C   Golf shop = G/S

BLACKLION GOLF CLUB
No. of holes: 9

Toam, Blacklion, Co. Cavan.
T: 072-53024

Contact Name: Pat Gallery
Hon\Secretary
Captain 2003: Aidan Malanaphy
Green Fees Weekdays: €15
Weekends: €20
G/C: N P/C: Y G/S : N
Course Distance C'ship: 5,634m

BLACKWOOD GOLF CLUB
No. of holes: 18

150 Crawfordsburn Road, Clandeboyle,
Bangor, Co. Down BT19 1GB.
T: 028-91852706
F: 028-91853785

Contact Name: James Kennedy
Secretary\Manager
Captain 2003: Owen McMullen
Green Fees Weekdays: Stg £20
Weekends: Stg £25
G/C: N P/C : Y G/S : Y
Course Distance C'ship: 5,844m
Ladies: 4,867m

BLAINROE GOLF CLUB
No. of holes: 18

Blainroe, Co. Wicklow.
T: 0404-68168
F: 0404-69369
E: blainroegolfclub@eircom.net
W: www.blainroe.com

Contact Name: Phil Noble - Administrator
Captain 2003: Harry Whittaker
Green Fees Weekdays: €45
Weekends: €60
G/C: N P/C : Y G/S : Y
Course Distance C'ship: 6,175m
Ladies: 5,450m

BODENSTOWN GOLF CLUB
No. of holes: 36

Sallins, Co. Kildare.
T: 045-897096

Contact Name: Rita Mather
Secretary\Manager
Captain 2003: Art O'Molloy
Green Fees Weekdays: €18
Weekends: €18
G/C: Y P/C : Y G/S : Y
Course Distance C'ship: 6,132m
Ladies: 5,095m

BORRIS GOLF CLUB
No. of holes: 9

Deerpark, Borris, Co. Carlow.
T: 0503-73310
F: 0503-73750

Contact Name: Nollaig Lucas
Secretary\Manager
Captain 2003: Pat O'Neill
Green Fees Weekdays: €20
Weekends: €20
G/C: Y P/C : Y G/S : N
Course Distance C'ship: 5,596m
Ladies: 5,009m

BOYLE GOLF CLUB
No. of holes: 9

Knockadoo, Brusna, Boyle,
Co. Roscommon.
T: 079 62594

Contact Name: Don Conlon
Hon\Secretary
Captain 2003: Willie Tiernan
Green Fees Weekdays: €15
Weekends: €15
G/C: N P/C : N G/S : N
Course Distance C'ship: 4,914m
Ladies: 4,700m

Golf Carts = G/C   Pull Carts = P/C   Golf shop = G/S

BOYSTOWN GOLF CLUB
No. of holes: 9

Baltyboys, Blessington, Co. Wicklow.
T: 045-867146

Contact Name: Donal McAvoy
Secretary\Manager
Captain 2003: Tony McGinley
Green Fees Weekdays: €22
Weekends: €22
G/C: N P/C : Y G/S : N
Course Distance C'ship: 6,352m
Ladies: 4,954m

BRAY GOLF CLUB
No. of holes: 18

Ravenswell Road, Bray, Co. Wicklow.
T\F: 01-2862484
E: braygolfclub@eircom.net
W: www.braygolfclub.com

Contact Name: Gerry Montgomery
Secretary\Manager
Captain 2003: Denis Walsh
Green Fees Weekdays: €60
Weekends: €70
G/C: Y P/C : Y G/S : Y
Course Distance C'ship: 5,893m
Ladies: 5,091m

BRIGHT CASTLE GOLF CLUB
No. of holes: 18

14 Coniamstown Road, Bright,
Downpatrick, Co. Down BT30 8LU.
T\F: 048-44841319

Contact Name: Arnold Ennis - Owner
Captain 2003: Mel Carney
Green Fees Weekdays: Stg £12
Weekends: Stg £14
G/C: Y P/C : Y G/S : Y
Course Distance C'ship: 6,407m
Ladies: 5,484m

BROWN TROUT GOLF CLUB
No. of holes: 9

209 Agivey Road, Aghadowey,
Co. Londonderry BT51 4AD.
T: 028-70868209
E: bill@browntroutinn.com
W: www.browntroutinn.com
Contact Name: Bill O'Hara
Secretary\Manager
Captain 2003: Mr. Cashley
Green Fees Weekdays: Stg £10
Weekends: Stg £15
G/C: N P/C : Y G/S : Y
Course Distance C'ship: 5,488m
Ladies: 4,734m

BUNCRANA GOLF CLUB
No. of holes: 9

Ballymacarry, Buncrana, Co. Donegal.
T: 077-62279

Contact Name: Francis McGrory
Secretary\Manager
Captain 2003: Dennis Doherty
Green Fees Weekdays: €13
Weekends: €13
G/C: N P/C : Y G/S : Y
Course Distance C'ship: 4,250m
Ladies: 4,150m

BUNDORAN GOLF CLUB
No. of holes: 18

Bundoran, Co. Donegal.
T: 072-41302
F: 072-42014
E: bundorangolfclub@eircom.net
W: www.bundorangolfclub.com
Contact Name: John McGagh
Secretary\Manager
Captain 2003: Padraic McGowan
Green Fees Weekdays: €35
Weekends: €45
G/C: Y P/C : Y G/S : Y
Course Distance C'ship: 5,688m
Ladies: 5,116m

Golf Carts = G/C   Pull Carts = P/C   Golf shop = G/S

BURNFIELD HOUSE GOLF CLUB
No. of holes: 9

Newtownabbey, Co. Antrim BT36 5BN.
T: 028-90838737
F: 028-93838448

Contact Name: M Jackson
Hon\Secretary
Captain 2003: D Cahill
Green Fees Weekdays: Stg £10
Weekends: Stg £12
G/C: Y   P/C : Y   G/S : N
Course Distance C'ship: 5,490m

BUSHFOOT GOLF CLUB
No. of holes: 9

50 Bushfoot Road, Portballintree BT57 8RR,
Co. Antrim.
T: 028-20731317
F: 028-20731852

Contact Name: J. Knox Thompson
Secretart\Manager
Captain 2003: B. Rodgers
Green Fees Weekdays: Stg £15
Weekends: Stg £19
G/C: N   P/C : Y   G/S : N
Course Distance C'ship: 5,323m
Ladies: 4,700m

CABRA CASTLE GOLF CLUB
No. of holes: 9

Kingscourt, Co. Cavan.
T: 042-9667030

Contact Name: Tom Lynch
Hon\Secretary
Captain 2003: Paul Heavey
Green Fees Weekdays: €15
Weekends: €15
G/C: N   P/C : Y   G/S : N
Course Distance C'ship: 5,261m

CAHIR PARK GOLF CLUB
No. of holes: 18

Kilcommon, Cahir, Co. Tipperary.
T: 052-41474
F: 052-42727

Contact Name: Michael Costello
Club Secretary
Captain 2003: Phillip Shealy
Green Fees Weekdays: €25
Weekends: €30
G/C: Y   P/C : Y   G/S : Y
Course Distance C'ship: 5,802m
Ladies: 4,934m

CAIRNDHU GOLF CLUB
No. of holes: 18

192 Coast Road, Ballygally, Larne BT40 2QG.
T\F: 028-28583324
E: cairndhugc@utvinternet.com

Contact Name: Michael Corsar
General Manager
Captain 2003: Hugh Logue
Green Fees Weekdays: Stg £20
Weekends: Stg £25
G/C: Y   P/C : Y   G/S : Y
Course Distance C'ship: 5,611m
Ladies: 4,861m

CALLAN GOLF CLUB
No. of holes: 18

Geraldine, Callan, Co. Kilkenny.
T: 056-55875
F: 056-55155
E: info@callangolfclub.com
W: www.callangolfclub.com
Contact Name: Liam Duggan
Secretary\Manager
Captain 2003: John Grace
Green Fees Weekdays: €25
Weekends: €30
G/C: Y   P/C : Y   G/S : Y
Course Distance C'ship: 5,872m
Ladies: 4,984m

Golf Carts = G/C   Pull Carts = P/C   Golf shop = G/S

CARLOW GOLF CLUB
No. of holes: 18

Deerpark, Carlow.
T: 0503-31695
F: 0503-40065
E: carlowgolfclub@eircom.net
W: www.carlowgolfclub.com
Contact Name: Donard McSweeney
Secretary\Manager
Captain 2003: Tom McDonald
Green Fees Weekdays: €45
Weekends: €60
G/C: Y   P/C : Y   G/S : Y
Course Distance C'ship: 5,974m
Ladies: 5,303m

CARNALEA GOLF CLUB
No. of holes: 18

Station Road, Bangor, Co. Down BT19 1EZ.
T: 028-91270368
F: 028-91273989

Contact Name: Gary Steele
Secretary\Manager
Captain 2003: D. Loughran
Green Fees Weekdays: Stg £16.50
Weekends: Stg £21.50
G/C: N   P/C : Y   G/S : Y
Course Distance C'ship: 5,647m
Ladies: 5,192m

CARNBEG GOLF CLUB
No. of holes: 18

Carnbeg, Dundalk, Co. Louth.
T/F: 042-9332518
E: carnbeggolfcourse@eircom.net
W: www.carnbeggolfcourse.ie

Contact Name: Patrick McCaffrey
Secretary\Manager
Captain 2003: Kevin Morgan
Green Fees Weekdays: €20
Weekends: €28
G/C: Y   P/C : Y   G/S : Y
Course Distance C'ship: 5,645m
Ladies: 4,656m

CARRICKFERGUS GOLF CLUB
No. of holes: 18

35 North Road, Carrickfergus, Co. Antrim BT38 8LP.
T: 028-93363713
F: 028-93363023
E: carrickfergusgc@talk21.com
Contact Name: Ian McLean
Secretary\Manager
Captain 2003: Stephen Nash
Green Fees Weekdays: Stg £19.50
Weekends: Stg £26.50
G/C: N   P/C : Y   G/S : Y
Course Distance C'ship: 5,768m
Ladies: 5,257m

CARRICKMINES GOLF CLUB
No. of holes: 9

Golf Road, Carrickmines, Dublin 18.
T: 01-2955972

Contact Name: Tim Webb
Hon\Secretary
Captain 2003: Chris Henderson
Green Fees Weekdays: €33
Weekends: €38
G/C: N   P/C : N   G/S : N
Course Distance C'ship: 5,542m
Ladies: 4,545m

CARRICK-ON-SHANNON GOLF CLUB
No. of holes: 9

Woodbrook, Carrick-on-Shannon, Co. Roscommon.
T\F: 071-9667015
E: ckgc3@eircom.net

Contact Name: Liz McCarthy - Treasurer
Captain 2003: Michael Daly
Green Fees Weekdays: €20
Weekends: €20
G/C: N   P/C : Y   G/S : N
Course Distance C'ship: 5,571m
Ladies: 5,214m

Golf Carts = G/C   Pull Carts = P/C   Golf shop = G/S

CARRICK-ON-SUIR GOLF CLUB
No. of holes: 18

Garravoone, Carrick-on-Suir, Co. Waterford.
T: 051-640047
F: 051-640558
E: cosgc@eircom.net
Contact Name: Aidan Murphy
Secretary\Manager
Captain 2003: Louis Dowley
Green Fees Weekdays: €25
Weekends: €30
G/C: Y   P/C : Y   G/S : Y
Course Distance C'ship: 6,061m
Ladies: 4,933m

CARTON HOUSE GOLF CLUB
No. of holes: 36

Maynooth, Co. Kildare.
T: 01-6286271
F: 01-6286555
E: golf@carton.ie
W: www.carton.ie
Contact Name: David Fleming
Secretary\Manager
Captain 2003: Willie Coonan
Green Fees Weekdays: €110
Weekends: €110
G/C: Y   P/C : Y   G/S : Y
Course Distance C'ship: 6,369m
Ladies: 5,645m

CASTLE GOLF CLUB
No. of holes: 18

Woodside Drive, Rathfarnham, Dublin 14.
T: 01-4904207
F: 01-4920264
E: info@castlegc.ie
Contact Name: John McCormack
Secretary\Manager
Captain 2003: Ken O'Neill
Niamh Leonard
Green Fees Weekdays: €60
Weekends: €80
G/C: N   P/C : Y   G/S : Y
Course Distance C'ship: 5,733m
Ladies: 5,104m

CASTLE BARNA GOLF CLUB
No. of holes: 18

Castlebarnagh, Daingean, Co. Offaly.
T: 0506-53384
F: 0506-53077
E: info@castlebarna.ie
W: www.castlebarna.ie
Contact Name: Kieran Mangan
Secretary\Manager
Captain 2003: J.J. Mulligan
Green Fees Weekdays: €17
Weekends: €22
G/C: Y   P/C : Y   G/S : N
Course Distance C'ship: 5,708m
Ladies: 4,755m

CASTLE HUME GOLF CLUB
No. of holes: 18

Ballyhose, Castle Hume, Enniskillen, Co. Fermanagh BT93 7ED.
T: 028-66327077
F: 028-66327076

Contact Name: Wilma Connor
Office/Admin.
Captain 2003: Billy Mulligan
Green Fees Weekdays: Stg £20
Weekends: Stg £25
G/C: Y   P/C : Y   G/S : Y
Course Distance C'ship: 5,932m
Ladies: 4,941m

CASTLEBAR GOLF CLUB
No. of holes: 18

Hawthorn Avenue, Rocklands, Castlebar, Co. Mayo.
T: 094-9021649   **F:** 094-9026088
E: castlebargolf@eircom.ie
W: www.castlebar.net
Contact Name: James McGovern
Hon\Secretary
Captain 2003: Gerry Needham
Green Fees Weekdays: €25
Weekends: €32
G/C: Y   P/C : Y   G/S : Y
Course Distance C'ship: 5,901m
Ladies: 4,840m

Golf Carts = G/C   Pull Carts = P/C   Golf shop = G/S

CASTLEBLAYNEY GOLF CLUB
No. of holes: 9

Onomy, Castleblayney, Co. Monaghan.
T: 042-9740451
E: castleblayneygolfclub@eircom.net
W: www.castleblayneygolfclub.com

Contact Name: Raymond Kernan
Hon\Secretary
Captain 2003: Raymond McHugh
Green Fees Weekdays: €12
Weekends: €14
G/C: N   P/C : N   G/S : N
Course Distance C'ship: 4,921m
Ladies: 4,571m

CASTLECOMER GOLF CLUB
No. of holes: 18

Drumgoole, Castlecomer, Co. Kilkenny.
T\F: 056-41139
E: castlecomergolf@eircom.net
W: www.castlecomergolf.com

Contact Name: Matt Dooley
Hon\Secretary
Captain 2003: Tom Rothwell
Green Fees Weekdays: €50
Weekends: €50
G/C: Y   P/C : Y   G/S : N
Course Distance C'ship: 5,923m
Ladies: 4,836m

CASTLEGREGORY GOLF CLUB
No. of holes: 9

Stradbally, Castlegregory, Co. Kerry.
T: 066-7139444

Contact Name: Martin Lynch
Secretary\Manager
Captain 2003: Pat Moynihan
Green Fees Weekdays: €25
Weekends: €25
G/C: N   P/C : Y   G/S : Y
Course Distance C'ship: 5,386m
Ladies: 4,114m

CASTLEISLAND GOLF CLUB
No. of holes: 18

Castleisland, Co. Kerry.
T: 066-7141709
F: 066-7142090
E: managercastleislandgolfclub@eircom.net
W: www.castleislandgolfclub.com

Contact Name: Michael Coote - Manager
Captain 2003: Martin O'Donoghue
Green Fees Weekdays: €35
Weekends: €40
G/C: Y   P/C : Y   G/S : Y
Course Distance C'ship: 6,041m
Ladies: 4,922m

CASTLEREA GOLF CLUB
No. of holes: 9

Clonalis, Castlerea, Co. Roscommon.
T: 0907-20068
E: castlereagolf@oceanfree.net

Contact Name: E. McNiff
Secretary\Manager
Captain 2003: Ignatius Hayden
Green Fees Weekdays: €15
Weekends: N\A
G/C: N   P/C : Y   G/S : Y
Course Distance C'ship: 5,154m
Ladies: 4,096m

CASTLEROCK GOLF CLUB
No. of holes: 27

65 Circular Road, Castlerock, Co. Derry.
T: 028-70848314   **F:** 028-70849440
E: info@castlerockgc.co.uk
W: www.castlerockgc.co.uk

Contact Name: Mark Steen
Secretary\Manager
Captain 2003: Raymond Eakin
Green Fees Weekdays: Stg £35
Weekends: Stg £60
G/C: N   P/C : Y   G/S : Y
Course Distance C'ship: 6,112m
Ladies: 5,382m

Golf Carts = G/C   Pull Carts = P/C   Golf shop = G/S

CASTLEROSSE GOLF CLUB
No. of holes: 9

Killarney, Co. Kerry.
T: 064-31144
F: 064-31031
E: castler@iol.ie
W: www.castlerosse-killarney.com

Contact Name: Danny Bowe
Secretary\Manager
Captain 2003: Matt O'Neill
Green Fees Weekdays: €28
Weekends: €28
G/C: N P/C : Y G/S : N
Course Distance C'ship: 6,146m

CASTLETROY GOLF CLUB
No. of holes: 18

Castletroy, Co. Limerick.
T: 061-335753
F: 061-335373
E: cgc@iol.ie

Contact Name: Paddy Keane
Secretary\Manager
Captain 2003: Sean G. Meaney
Green Fees Weekdays: €40
Weekends: €50
G/C: Y P/C : Y G/S : Y
Course Distance C'ship: 5,802m
Ladies: 5,241m

CASTLEWARDEN GOLF CLUB
No. of holes: 18

Castlewarden, Straffan, Co. Kildare.
T: 01-4589254
F: 01-4588972
E: info@castlewardengolfclub.com
W: www.castlewardengolfclub.com
Contact Name: J. McGowan
Hon\Secretary
Captain 2003: E.Gavin
Green Fees Weekdays: €38
Weekends: €38
G/C: Y P/C : Y G/S : Y
Course Distance C'ship: 6,025m
Ladies: 5,309m

CEANN SIBÉAL GOLF CLUB
No. of holes: 18

Ballyoughtra, Ballyferiter, Co. Kerry.
T: 066-9156255
F: 066-9156409
E: dinglegc@iol.ie
W: www.dingelinks.com
Contact Name: Steve Fahy
Secretary\Manager
Captain 2003: Tom Curran
Green Fees Weekdays: €55
Weekends: €65
G/C: Y P/C : Y G/S : Y
Course Distance C'ship: 6,081m
Ladies: 4,735m

CELBRIDGE ELM HALL GOLF CLUB
No. of holes: 9

Co. Kildare.
T: 01-6288208

Contact Name: Seamus Lawless - Owner
Captain 2003: Austin McCartney
Green Fees Weekdays: €22
Weekends: €27
G/C: N P/C : Y G/S : N
Course Distance C'ship: 5,210m
Ladies: 4,848m

CHARLESLAND GOLF CLUB
No. of holes: 18

Greystones, Co. Wicklow.
T: 01-2874350
F: 01-2874360
E: teetime@charlesland.com
W: www.charlesland.com
Contact Name: Patrick Bradshaw
Secretary\Manager
Captain 2003: Tom King
Green Fees Weekdays: €45
Weekends: €60
G/C: Y P/C : Y G/S : Y
Course Distance C'ship: 6,169m
Ladies: 5,046m

Golf Carts = G/C   Pull Carts = P/C   Golf shop = G/S

CHARLEVILLE GOLF CLUB
No. of holes: 18

Ardmore, Charleville, Co. Cork.
T: 063-81257
F: 063-81274
E: charlevillegolf@eircom.net
W: www.charlevillegolf.com
Contact Name: Pat Nagle
Secretary\Manager
Captain 2003: Michael Fitzgerald
Green Fees Weekdays: €30
Weekends: €35
G/C: Y   P/C : Y   G/S : Y
Course Distance C'ship: 5,970m
Ladies: 4,663m

CHRISTY O'CONNOR GOLF CLUB
No. of holes: 18

Silloge Park Golf Club, Ballymun Road,
Swords, Co. Dublin.
T: 01-8620464   **F:** 01-8441250
E: christyo@indigo.ie
W: www.christyoconnor.com
Contact Name: Denis D'Arcy
Secretary\Manager
Captain 2003: Ben Finlay
Green Fees Weekdays: €16
Weekends: €24
G/C: Y   P/C : Y   G/S : Y
Course Distance C'ship: 5,924m
Ladies: 4,899m

CILL DARA GOLF CLUB
No. of holes: 9

Little Curragh, Kildare, Co. Kildare.
T: 045-521295
F: 045-522945
E: cilldaragc@eircom.net

Contact Name: Dan Doody
Secretary\Manager
Captain 2003: John Rooney
Green Fees Weekdays: €20
Weekends: €25
G/C: N   P/C : Y   G/S : Y
Course Distance C'ship: 5,852m
Ladies: 4,966m

CITYWEST GOLF CLUB
No. of holes: 18

Saggart, Co. Dublin.
T: 01-4010878
F: 01-4010945
E: mlloyd@citywesthotel.com
W: www.citywesthotel.com
Contact Name: Margaret Lloyd
Secretary\Manager
Captain 2003: Barry Phelan
Green Fees Weekdays: €35
Weekends: €40
G/C: Y   P/C : Y   G/S : Y
Course Distance C'ship: 5,154m
Ladies: 4,419m

CITY OF DERRY GOLF CLUB
No. of holes: 27

49 Victoria Road, Derry BT47 2PU.
T: 028-71346369
F: 028-71310008
E: cityofderry@aol.com

Contact Name: Noreen Allen
Secretary\Manager
Captain 2003: Eddie Leonard
Green Fees Weekdays: Stg £17
Weekends: Stg £21
G/C: N   P/C : Y   G/S : Y
Course Distance C'ship: 5,877m
Ladies: 5,338m

CLANDEBOYE GOLF CLUB
No. of holes: 36

51 Tower Road, Conlig, Newtownards, Co.
Down BT23 3PN.
T: 028-91271767   **F:** 028-91473711
E: contact@cgc-ni.com
W: www.cgc-ni.com

Contact Name: Rhonda Eddis Administrator
Captain 2003: Ted Spence
Green Fees Weekdays: Stg £27.50
Weekends: Stg £33
G/C: Y   P/C : Y   G/S : Y
Course Distance C'ship: 6,559m
Ladies: 5,770m

Golf Carts = G/C   Pull Carts = P/C   Golf shop = G/S

CLAREMORRIS GOLF CLUB
No. of holes: 18

Castlemacgarrett, Claremorris, Co. Mayo.
T: 094-71527
F: 094-72919
E: claremorrisgc@ebookireland.com
W: www.ebookireland.com
Contact Name: Chris Rush
Secretary\Manager
Captain 2003: Eamon Blake
Green Fees Weekdays: €25
Weekends: €30
G/C: N   P/C : Y   G/S : Y
Course Distance C'ship: 6,143m
Ladies: 4,882m

CLIFTONVILLE GOLF CLUB
No. of holes: 9

44 Westland Road, Belfast BT14 6NH.
T: 028-90746595
F: 028-90744158

Contact Name: E. Lusty – Hon\Secretary
Captain 2003: H. McLean
Green Fees Weekdays: Stg £18
Weekends: Stg £20
G/C: Y   P/C : Y   G/S : Y
Course Distance C'ship: 5,665m
Ladies: 5,298m

CLONES GOLF CLUB
No. of holes: 9

Hilton Park, Clones, Co. Monaghan.
T: 047-56913
F: 047-56913
E: clonesgolfclub@eircom.net
W: www.clonesgolf.com
Contact Name: Martin Taylor
Secretary\Manager
Captain 2003: Gerry Douglas
Green Fees Weekdays: €25
Weekends: €25
G/C: N   P/C : Y   G/S : N
Course Distance C'ship: 5,549m
Ladies: 4,624m

CLONLARA GOLF CLUB
No. of holes: 12

Clonara, Co. Clare.
T: 061-349807
F: 061-342288
E: markmorris@oceanfree.net

Contact Name: Mark Morris
Secretary\Manager
Captain 2003: Tony McMahon
Green Fees Weekdays: €12
Weekends: €15
G/C: N   P/C : Y   G/S : N
Course Distance C'ship: 4,854m
Ladies: 3,875m

CLONMEL GOLF CLUB
No. of holes: 18

Lyreanearla, Clonmel, Co. Tipperary.
T: 052-24050
F: 052-83349
E: cgc@indigo.ie
W: www.clonmelgolfclub.com
Contact Name: Aine Myles-Keating
Secretary\Manager
Captain 2003: Liam White
Green Fees Weekdays: €30
Weekends: €35
G/C: Y   P/C : Y   G/S : Y
Course Distance C'ship: 5,845m
Ladies: 5,579m

CLONTARF GOLF CLUB
No. of holes: 18

Donnycarney House, Malahide Road,
Dublin 3.
T: 01-8331892   **F:** 01-8331933
E: info.cgc@indigo.ie
W: www.clontarfgolfclub.ie
Contact Name: Arthur Cahill
Secretary\Manager
Captain 2003: Hal Kellett
Green Fees Weekdays: €50
Weekends: €60
G/C: N   P/C : Y   G/S : Y
Course Distance C'ship: 5,317m
Ladies: 4,949m

Golf Carts = G/C   Pull Carts = P/C   Golf shop = G/S

CLOUGHANEELY GOLF CLUB
No. of holes: 9

Cloughabeely, Falcarragh, Co. Donegal.
T: 074-65416
F: 074-65416

Contact Name: Michael Murray
Secretary\Manager
Captain 2003: Alan Crawley
Green Fees Weekdays: €13
Weekends: €15
G/C: N   P/C : Y   G/S : Y
Course Distance C'ship: 6,088m
Ladies: 5,274m

CLOVERHILL GOLF CLUB
No. of holes: 18

Lough Road, Mullaghbawn, Co. Armagh
BT35 9XP.
T/F: 028-30889374
E: info@cloverhillgc.com
W: www.cloverhillgc.com

Contact Name: Margaret Smyth - Owner
Captain 2003: Seamus McCoy
Green Fees Weekdays: Stg £12
Weekends: Stg £15
G/C: N   P/C : Y   G/S : Y
Course Distance C'ship: 5,536m
Ladies: 4,913m

COUNTY ARMAGH GOLF CLUB
No. of holes: 18

The Demesne, 7 Newry Road, Armagh
BT60 1EN.
T: 028-37525861   **F:** 028-37525861
E: ruth@golfarmagh.co.uk
W: www.golfarmagh.co.uk
Contact Name: June McParland
Secretary\Manager
Captain 2003: S. Swift
Green Fees Weekdays: Stg £15
Weekends: Stg £20
G/C: Y   P/C : Y   G/S : Y
Course Distance C'ship: 5,678m
Ladies: 4,427m

COUNTY CAVAN GOLF CLUB
No. of holes: 18

Arnmore House, Drumelis, Cavan.
T/F: 049-4331541
E: info@cavangolf.ie
W: www.cavangolf.ie

Contact Name: Brian Fitzsimons
Hon\Secretary
Captain 2003: Seamus McConnon
Green Fees Weekdays: €25
Weekends: €30
G/C: Y   P/C : Y   G/S : Y
Course Distance C'ship: 5,634m
Ladies: 4,815m

COUNTY LONGFORD GOLF CLUB
No. of holes: 18

Glack, Dublin Road, Longford.
T: 043-46310
F: 043-47082
E: colonggolf@eircom.net

Contact Name: Dan Rooney
Hon\Secretary
Captain 2003: Denis Hughes
Green Fees Weekdays: On Request
Weekends: On Request
G/C: Y   P/C : Y   G/S : Y
Course Distance C'ship: 5,527m
Ladies: 4,844m

COUNTY LOUTH GOLF CLUB
No. of holes: 18

Baltray, Drogheda, Co. Louth
T: 041-9881530
F: 041-9881531
E: info@countylouthgolfclub.com
W: www.countylouthgolfclub.com
Contact Name: Michael Delany
Secretary\Manager
Captain 2003: Thomas Collier
Green Fees Weekdays: €90
Weekends: €110
G/C: N   P/C : Y   G/S : Y
Course Distance C'ship: 6,200m
Ladies: 5,368m

Golf Carts = G/C   Pull Carts = P/C   Golf shop = G/S

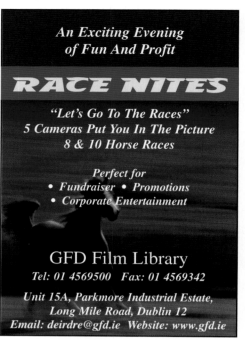

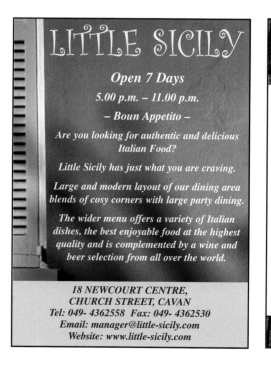

COUNTY MEATH GOLF CLUB
No. of holes: 18

Newtownmoynagh, Trim, Co. Meath.
T: 046-31463
F: 046-67554
E: sec@trimgolf.com
W: www.trimgolf.net
Contact Name: Deirdre Cullen
Secretary\Manager
Green Fees Weekdays: €30
Weekends: €35
G/C: Y   P/C : Y   G/S : Y
Course Distance C'ship: 6,135m
Ladies: 5,067m

COUNTY SLIGO GOLF CLUB
No. of holes: 27

Rosses Point, Co. Sligo.
T: 071-9177134
F: 071-9177460
E: cosligo@iol.ie
W: www.countysligogolfclub.ie
Contact Name: Jim Ironside - Manager
Captain 2003: Padraig McMunn
Green Fees Weekdays: €60
Weekends: €75
G/C: Y   P/C : Y   G/S : Y
Course Distance C'ship: 6,043m
Ladies: 5,280m

COUNTY TIPPERARY GOLF CLUB
No. of holes: 18

Dundrum, Co. Tipperary.
T: 062-71717
F: 062-71718
E: dundrumh@iol.ie
W: www.dundrumhousehotel.com
Contact Name: William Crowe
Director of Golf
Captain 2003: John Ryan
Green Fees Weekdays: €40
Weekends: €50
G/C: Y   P/C : Y   G/S : Y
Course Distance C'ship: 6,415m
Ladies: 4,794m

COBH GOLF CLUB
No. of holes: 9

Ballywilliam, Cobh, Co. Cork.
T: 021-4812399
F: 021-4812615

Contact Name: H. Cunnighham
Secretary\Manager
Captain 2003: Joe O'Brien
Green Fees Weekdays: €16
Weekends: N\A
G/C: N   P/C : N   G/S : N
Course Distance C'ship: 5,006m
Ladies: 4,156m

COLDWINTERS GOLF CLUB
No. of holes: 27

Newtown House, St. Margaret's, Co. Dublin.
T: 01-8640324
F: 01-8341400

Contact Name: Graham Beattie
Secretary\Manager
Captain 2003: Eamonn Dagger
Green Fees Weekdays: €17
Weekends: €25
G/C: Y   P/C : Y   G/S : Y
Course Distance C'ship: 5,973m
Ladies: 5,117m

COLIN VALLEY GOLF CLUB
No. of holes: 9

115 Blacks Road, Dunmurry, Belfast BT10 0NF.
T: 028-90601133
F: 028-90601694
E: colinvalley@btconnect.com

Contact Name: Joe McCaffrey
Secretary\Manager
Captain 2003: P. Dixon
Green Fees Weekdays: Stg £6
Weekends: Stg £8
G/C: N   P/C : Y   G/S : N
Course Distance C'ship: 4,746m

Golf Carts = G/C   Pull Carts = P/C   Golf shop = G/S

CONNEMARA GOLF CLUB
No. of holes: 27

Ballyconneely, Clifden, Co. Galway.
T: 095-23502
F: 095-23662
E: links@iol.ie
W: www.westcoastlinks.com
Contact Name: Richard Flaherty
Secretary\Manager
Captain 2003: Lorcan Geoghegan
Green Fees Weekdays: €50
Weekends: €55
G/C: Y   P/C : Y   G/S : Y
Course Distance C'ship: 6,666m
Ladies: 4,927m

CONNEMARA ISLES GOLF CLUB
No. of holes: 9

Annaghvane, Lettermore, Co. Galway
T: 091-572498
F: 091-572214
E: connemaraisles@eircom.net

Contact Name: Tony Lynch
Secretary\Manager
Captain 2003: Michael Carter
Green Fees Weekdays: €15
Weekends: €20
G/C: N   P/C : Y   G/S : N
Course Distance C'ship: 4,855m
Ladies: 4,032m

COOLLATTIN GOLF CLUB
No. of holes: 18

Shillelagh, Co. Wicklow.
T/F: 055-29125

Contact Name: Dennis Byrne - Secretary
Captain 2003: Perry Kelly
Green Fees Weekdays: €35
Weekends: €45
G/C: Y   P/C : Y   G/S : Y
Course Distance C'ship: 5,622m
Ladies: 4,766m

COOSHEEN GOLF CLUB
No. of holes: 9

Coosheen, Schull, Co. Cork.
T: 028-28182

Contact Name: Donal Morgan
Secretary\Manager
Captain 2003: Paddy Barry-Murphy
Green Fees Weekdays: €20
Weekends: €20
G/C: N   P/C : Y   G/S : N
Course Distance C'ship: 4,046m
Ladies: 3,670m

CORK GOLF CLUB
No. of holes: 18

Little Island, Co. Cork.
T: 021-4353451
F: 021- 4353410
E: corkgolfclub@eircom.net
W: www.corkgolf.ie
Contact Name: Matt Sands
Secretary\Manager
Captain 2003: Dermot Duggan
Green Fees Weekdays: €75
Weekends: €85
G/C: N   P/C : Y   G/S : Y
Course Distance C'ship: 6,119m
Ladies: 5,185m

CORRSTOWN GOLF CLUB
No. of holes: 27

Corrstown, Kilsallaghan, Co. Dublin.
T: 01-8640533
F: 01-8640537
E: info@corrstowngolfclub.com
W: www.corrstowngolfclub.com
Contact Name: Jason Kelly
Secretary\Manager
Captain 2003: Tommy Doyle
Green Fees Weekdays: €40
Weekends: €50
G/C: Y   P/C : Y   G/S : Y
Course Distance C'ship: 6,298m
Ladies: 5,232m

Golf Carts = G/C   Pull Carts = P/C   Golf shop = G/S

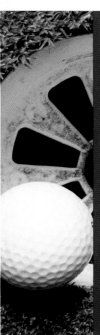

COURTOWN GOLF CLUB
No. of holes: 18

Kiltennel, Gorey, Co. Wexford.
T: 055-25166
F: 055-25553
E: courtown@iol.ie
W: www.courtowngolfclub.com
Contact Name: Sharon O'Hara
Secretary\Manager
Captain 2003: Enda Murphy
Green Fees Weekdays: €36
Weekends: €42
G/C: Y   P/C : Y   G/S : Y
Course Distance C'ship: 5,344m
Ladies: 4,539m

CRADDOCKSTOWN GOLF CLUB
No. of holes: 18

Blessington Road, Naas, Co. Kildare.
T: 045-897610
E: 045-896968
E: gaynolan@craddockstown.com

Contact Name: Gay Nolan
Secretary\Manager
Captain 2003: Pat Corrigan
Green Fees Weekdays: €30
Weekends: €40
G/C: Y   P/C : Y   G/S : N
Course Distance C'ship: 6,125m
Ladies: 4,949m

CROSSGAR GOLF CLUB
No. of holes: 9

231 Derryboy Road, Crossgar,
Downpatrick, Co. Down BT30 9DL.
T: 028-44831523

Contact Name: Dennis Keenan
Hon\Secretary
Captain 2003: Geoffrey Casement
Green Fees Weekdays: Stg £10
Weekends: Stg £11
G/C: N   P/C : Y   G/S : Y
Course Distance C'ship: 4,139m
Ladies: 3,600m

CRUIT ISLAND GOLF CLUB
No. of holes: 9

Cruit Island, Kincasslagh, Co. Donegal.
T: 075-43296
F: 075-48028

Contact Name: Dermot Devenney
Secretary\Manager
Captain 2003: Terence Gallagher
Green Fees Weekdays: €20
Weekends: €20
G/C: N   P/C : Y   G/S : Y
Course Distance C'ship: 5,141m
Ladies: 4,780m

CURRA WEST GOLF CLUB
No. of holes: 18

Currawest, Kylebrack, Loughrea, Co.
Galway.
T: 0509-45121
F: 0509-45121

Contact Name: Justin O'Byrne - Secretary
Captain 2003: Roderick Rohan
Green Fees Weekdays: €15
Weekends: €17
G/C: Y   P/C : Y   G/S : N
Course Distance C'ship: 4,546m
Ladies: 3,960m

CURRAGH GOLF CLUB
No. of holes: 18

Curragh, Co. Kildare.
T: 045-441714
F: 045-442476
E: curraghgolf@eircom.net
W: www.curraghgolfclub.com
Contact Name: Ann Culleton
Secretary\Manager
Captain 2003: John Cremin
Green Fees Weekdays:€32
Weekends: €37
G/C: N   P/C : N   G/S : Y
Course Distance C'ship: 6,035m
Ladies: 4,928m

Golf Carts = G/C   Pull Carts = P/C   Golf shop = G/S

CUSHENDALL GOLF CLUB
No. of holes: 9

21 Shore Road, Cushendall, Co. Antrim
BT44 0NG.
T/F: 028-21771318
W: www.antrim-glens.demon.co.uk

Contact Name: Shaun McLaughlin
　　　　　　　　Hon\Secretary
Captain 2003: Geordie Wheeler
Green Fees Weekdays: Stg £13
　　　　　　　Weekends: Stg £18
G/C: N　　P/C : Y　　G/S : N
Course Distance C'ship: 4,384m
Ladies: 3,996m

DEER PARK GOLF CLUB
No. of holes: 36

Deer Park Hotel, Howth, Co. Dublin
T: 01-8322624
F: 01-8326039

Contact Name: Damien Daly
　　　　　　　　Hon\Secretary
Captain 2003: Colin Tracy
Green Fees Weekdays: N\A
　　　　　　　Weekends: €23
G/C: N　　P/C : Y　　G/S : Y
Course Distance C'ship: 6,245m
Ladies: 4,797m

DELGANY GOLF CLUB
No. of holes: 18

Delgany, Co. Wicklow.
T: 01-2874536
F: 01-2873977
E: delganygolf@eircom.net

Contact Name: Peter M. Ribeiro
　　　　　　　　General Manager
Captain 2003: Dermot Harrington
Green Fees Weekdays: €40
　　　　　　　Weekends: €50
G/C: Y　　P/C : Y　　G/S :Y
Course Distance C'ship: 5,480m
Ladies: 4,860m

DELVIN CASTLE GOLF CLUB
No. of holes: 18

Clonyn, Delvin, Co. Westmeath.
T: 044-64315
F: 044-64315

Contact Name: Fiona Dillon
　　　　　　　　Owner\Manager
Captain 2003: Nicky Dunne
Green Fees Weekdays: €25
　　　　　　　Weekends: €30
G/C: N　　P/C : Y　　G/S :Y
Course Distance C'ship: 5,500m
Ladies: 4,780m

DJOUSE GOLF CLUB
No. of holes: 9

Roundwood, Co. Wicklow
T: 01-2818585
F: 01-2012904
E: djousegc@ireland.com
W: www.ecoast-midlandstravel.ie
Contact Name: Donal McGillycuddy
　　　　　　　　Manager\Proprietor
Captain 2003: Eamonn McGee
Green Fees Weekdays: €15
　　　　　　　Weekends: €20
G/C: N　　P/C : Y　　G/S :N
Course Distance C'ship: 5,724m
Ladies: 5,153m

DONABATE GOLF CLUB
27 holes

Balcarrick, Donabate, Co. Dublin.
T: 01-8436346
F: 01-8435012
E: golfclub@indigo.ie

Contact Name: Betty O'Connor
　　　　　　　　Secretary\Manager
Captain 2003: Leslie Brooks
Green Fees Weekdays: €45
　　　　　　　Weekends: €55
G/C: Y　　P/C : Y　　G/S :Y
Course Distance C'ship: 5,960m
Ladies: 5,146m

Golf Carts = G/C　　　　**Pull Carts = P/C**　　　　**Golf shop = G/S**

DONAGHADEE GOLF CLUB
No. of holes: 18

84 Warren Road, Donaghadee BT21 0PQ, Co. Down.
T: 028-91883624
F: 028-91888891
E: deegolf@freenet.co.uk
Contact Name: Ron Thomas
Secretary\Manager
Captain 2003: Freddie Green
Green Fees Weekdays: Stg £22
Weekends: Stg £25
G/C: Y   P/C : Y   G/S : Y
Course Distance C'ship: 5,570m
Ladies: 5,132m

DONEGAL GOLF CLUB
No. of holes: 18

Murvagh, Laghey, Co. Donegal.
T: 073-34054
F: 073-34377
E: info@donegalgolfclub.ie
W: www.donegalgolfclub.ie
Contact Name: Patrick Nugent
General Manager
Captain 2003: Brian Boyle
Green Fees Weekdays: €50
Weekends: €65
G/C: Y   P/C : Y   G/S : Y
Course Distance C'ship: 6,332m
Ladies: 5,398m

DONERAILE GOLF CLUB
No. of holes: 9

Doneraile, Co. Cork.
T: 022-24137

Contact Name: Jim O'Leary
Hon\Secretary
Captain 2003: Richard Moloney
Green Fees Weekdays: €20
Weekends: €20
G/C: Y   P/C : Y   G/S : N
Course Distance C'ship: 5,455m
Ladies: 5,145m

DOOKS GOLF CLUB
No. of holes: 18

Glenbeigh, Co. Kerry
T: 066-9768205
F: 066-9768476
E: office@dooks.com
W: www.dooks.com
Contact Name: Declan Mangan
Secretary\Manager
Captain 2003: Eric Black
Green Fees Weekdays: €40
Weekends: €40
G/C: N   P/C : Y   G/S : Y
Course Distance C'ship: 5,519m
Ladies: 5,225m

DOONBEG GOLF CLUB
No. of holes: 18

Doonbeg, Co. Clare.
T: 065-9055246
F: 065-9055247
E: links@doonbeggolfclub.com
W: www.doonbeggolfclub.com

Contact Name: Brian Shaw
Director of Golf
Green Fees Weekdays: €185
Weekends: €185
G/C: Y   P/C : Y   G/S : Y
Course Distance C'ship: 6,885m
Ladies: 4808m

DOUGLAS GOLF CLUB
No. of holes: 18

Douglas, Co. Cork.
T/F: 021-4895297
E: admin@douglasgolfclub.ie
W: www.douglasgolfclub.ie

Contact Name: Brian Kiely
Secretary\Manager
Captain 2003: Bob Casey
Green Fees Weekdays: €40
Weekends: €50
G/C: Y   P/C : Y   G/S : Y
Course Distance C'ship: 5,972m
Ladies: 4,952m

Golf Carts = G/C   Pull Carts = P/C   Golf shop = G/S

DOWN ROYAL GOLF CLUB
No. of holes: 27

Dunygarton Road, Maze, Lisburn,
Co. Antrim BT27 5RT
T/F: 028-92621339

Contact Name: Cameron Allen
Secretary\Manager
Captain 2003: -
Green Fees Weekdays: Stg £17
Weekends: Stg £20
G/C: N   P/C : Y   G/S : Y
Course Distance C'ship: 6,237m
Ladies: 4,940m

DOWNPATRICK GOLF CLUB
No. of holes: 18

43 Saul Road, Downpatrick, Co. Down, BT30 6PA.
T: 028-44615947
F: 028-44617502
E: info@downpatrickgolfclub.com
W: www.downpatrickgolfclub.org
Contact Name: Barbara Ann Hitchens
Manager
Captain 2003: J.J. Kelly
Green Fees Weekdays: Stg £20
Weekends: Stg £25
G/C: Y   P/C : Y   G/S : Y
Course Distance C'ship: 5,564m
Ladies: 4,931m

DROMOLAND GOLF CLUB
No. of holes: 18

Newmarket-on-Fergus, Co. Clare.
T: 061-368444
F: 061-368498
E: dromolandgc@eircom.net
W: www.dromoland.ie
Contact Name: John O'Halloran
Secretary\Manager
Captain 2003: John O'Brien
Green Fees: Weekdays: €50
Weekends: €60
G/C: Y   P/C : Y   G/S : Y
Course Distance C'ship: 5,565m
Ladies: 4,441m

DRUIDS GLEN GOLF CLUB
No. of holes: 18

Newtownmountkennedy, Co. Wicklow.
T: 01-2873600
F: 01-2873699
E: info@druidsglen.ie
W: www.druidsglen.ie
Contact Name: Donal Finn
Secretary\Manager
Captain 2003: Tim O'Connor
Green Fees Weekdays: €140
Weekends: €140
G/C: Y   P/C : Y   G/S : Y
Course Distance C'ship: 5,714m
Ladies: 5,066m

DUBLIN CITY GOLF CLUB
No. of holes: 18

Ballinascorney, Dublin 24.
T: 01-4516430
F: 01-4598445
E: info@dublincitygolf.com
W: www.dublincitygolf.com
Contact Name: Francis Bagnall
Secretary\Manager
Captain 2003: Tom McGrath
Green Fees Weekdays: €25
Weekends: €35
G/C: Y   P/C : Y   G/S : Y
Course Distance C'ship: 5,568m
Ladies: 5,297m

DUBLIN MOUNTAIN GOLF CLUB
No. of holes: 18

Gortlum, Brittas, Co. Dublin.
T: 01-4582622
F: 01-4582048

Contact Name: Deborah Carolan
Course Manager
Captain 2003: Joe Maher
Green Fees Weekdays: €14
Weekends: €18
G/C: N   P/C : Y   G/S : Y
Course Distance C'ship: 5,635m
Ladies: 5,169m

Golf Carts = G/C   **Pull Carts = P/C**   **Golf shop = G/S**

DUN LAOIGHAIRE GOLF CLUB
No. of holes: 18

Eglington Park, Tivoli Road,
Dun Laoighaire, Co. Dublin.
T: 01-2803916
F: 01-2804868
W: www.dunlaoighairegolfclub.ie
Contact Name: Dennis Peacock
General Manager
Captain 2003: Edward Dempsey
Green Fees Weekdays: €55
Weekends: €55
G/C: N P/C : Y G/S : Y
Course Distance C'ship: 5,313m
Ladies: 4,980m

DUNDALK GOLF CLUB
No. of holes: 18

Blackrock, Dundalk, Co. Louth.
T: 042-9321731
F: 042-9322022
E: dkgc@iol.ie
W: www.eiresoft.com/dundalkgc
Contact Name: Terry Sloane
Secretary\Manager
Captain 2003: Gerry O'Keeffe
Green Fees Weekdays: €55
Weekends: €55
G/C: Y P/C : Y G/S : Y
Course Distance C'ship: 6,160m
Ladies: 5,134m

DUNFANAGHY GOLF CLUB
No. of holes: 18

Kill, Dunfanaghy via Letterkenny, Co. Donegal.
T: 074-9136335
F: 074-9136684
E: dunfanaghygolf@eircom.net
W: www.golfdunfanaghy.com
Contact Name: Sandra McGinley
Club Secretary
Captain 2003: Patrick Hunter
Green Fees Weekdays: €25
Weekends: €30
G/C: Y P/C : Y G/S : Y
Course Distance C'ship: 5,247m
Ladies: 4,544m

DUNGANNON GOLF CLUB
No. of holes: 18

34 Springfield Lane, Dungannon, Co. Tyrone
BT70 1QX.
T: 028-87722098 **F:** 028-87727338
E: info@dungannongolfclub.com
W: www.dungannongolfclub.com
Contact Name: Brenda McKenna
Secretary\Manager
Captain 2003: Dr. Joseph Hackett
Green Fees Weekdays: £18
Weekends: £22
G/C: Y P/C : Y G/S : Y
Course Distance C'ship: 6,061m
Ladies: 5,419m

DUNGARVAN GOLF CLUB
No. of holes: 18

Knocknagranagh, Dungarvan, Co. Waterford.
T: 058-43310
F: 058-44113
E: dungarvangc@eircom.net
W: www.dungarvangolfclub.com
Contact Name: Irene Howell
Secretary\Manager
Captain 2003: Eugene Slater
Green Fees Weekdays: €30
Weekends: €40
G/C: Y P/C : Y G/S : Y
Course Distance C'ship: 6,017m
Ladies: 4,992m

DUNLOE GOLF CLUB
No. of holes: 9

Dunloe, Beaufort, Killarney, Co. Kerry.
T: 064-44578
F: 064-44733
E: enquiries@dunloegc.com
W: www.dunloegc.com
Contact Name: Kieran Crehan
Secretary\Manager
Captain 2003: Kevin Clarke
Green Fees Weekdays: €23
Weekends: €23
G/C: N P/C : Y G/S : Y
Course Distance C'ship: 4,706m
Ladies: 4,024m

Golf Carts = G/C **Pull Carts = P/C** **Golf shop = G/S**

DUNMORE GOLF CLUB
No. of holes: 9

Muckross, Clonakilty, Co. Cork.
T: 023-34644

Contact Name: Laurence O'Donovan -
Secretary
Captain 2003: Richard Barrett
Green Fees Weekdays: €20
Weekends: N\A
G/C: N   P/C : Y   G/S : N
Course Distance C'ship: 4,500m
Ladies: 4,364m

DUNMORE DEMESNE GOLF CLUB
No. of holes: 9

Tuam Road, Dunmore, Co. Galway.
T: 093-38709
E: ddgc@eircom.net

Contact Name: Carmel Howley
Hon\Secretary
Captain 2003: Niall Cloonan
Green Fees Weekdays: €13
Weekends: €13
G/C: N   P/C : N   G/S : N
Course Distance C'ship: 5,278m
 Ladies: 4,763m

DUNMORE EAST GOLF CLUB
No. of holes: 18

Dunmore East, Co. Waterford.
T: 051-383151
W: www.dunmoreeastgolfclub.ie

Contact Name: Mary Skehan
Secretary\Manager
Captain 2003: Hugh McAllister
Green Fees Weekdays: €25
Weekends: €30
G/C: Y   P/C : Y   G/S : Y
Course Distance C'ship: 6,070m
Ladies: 5,011m

DUNMURRY GOLF CLUB
No. of holes: 18

91 Dunmurr Lane, Dunmurry, Belfast BT17 9JS.
T: 028-90610834
F: 028-90602540
E: dunmurrygc@hotmail.com
W: www.dunmurrygolfclub.co.uk

Contact Name: Tony Cassidy – Golf Manager
Captain 2003: J.A.L. Campbell
Green Fees Weekdays: Stg £27
Weekends: Stg £37
G/C: N   P/C : Y   G/S : Y
Course Distance C'ship: 5,574m
Ladies: 5,002m

EAST CLARE GOLF CLUB
No. of holes: 18

Bodyke, Co. Clare.
T: 061-921322
F: 061-921717
E: eastclaregolfclub@eircom.net

Contact Name: Mildred O'Hanlon
Secretary\Manager
Captain 2003: Paul Nesbitt
Green Fees Weekdays: €25
Weekends: €30
G/C: Y   P/C : Y   G/S : Y
Course Distance C'ship: 5,922m
Ladies: 4,860m

EAST CORK GOLF CLUB
No. of holes: 18

Gortacrue, Midleton, Co. Cork.
T: 021-4631687
F: 021-4631273

Contact Name: Maurice Moloney
Secretary\Manager
Captain 2003: Killian McGrath
Green Fees Weekdays: €25
Weekends: €30
G/C: N   P/C : Y   G/S : Y
Course Distance C'ship: 5,012m
Ladies: 4,788m

Golf Carts = G/C   **Pull Carts = P/C**   **Golf shop = G/S**

EDENDERRY GOLF CLUB
No. of holes: 18

Kishawanny, Edenderry, Co. Offaly.
T: 0405-9731072
F: 0405-9733911
E: enquiries@edenderrygolfclub.com
W: www.edenderrygolfclub.com
Contact Name: Paula Mooney
Secretary\Manager
Captain 2003: Declan Conlon
Green Fees Weekdays: €30
Weekends: €35
G/C: N   P/C: Y   G/S: Y
Course Distance C'ship: 6029m
Ladies: 4879m

EDENMORE GOLF CLUB
No. of holes: 18

Edenmore House, 70 Drumnabreeze Road,
Magherlin, Craigavon, Co. Down BT67 0RH.
T: 028-92619241   **F:** 028-92613310
E: info@edenmore.com
W: www.edenmore.com
Contact Name: Robert McDowell
Hon\Secretary
Captain 2003: Chris Laird
Green Fees Weekdays: Stg £15
Weekends: Stg £20
G/C: Y   P/C: Y   G/S: Y
Course Distance C'ship: 5,591m
Ladies: 4,811m

EDMONDSTOWN GOLF CLUB
No. of holes: 18

Edmonstown Road, Rathfarnham, Dublin 16.
T: 01-4931082
F: 01-4933152
E: info@edmonstowngolfclub.ie
W: www.edmondstowngolfclub.ie
Contact Name: Selwyn Davies
Secretary\Manager
Captain 2003: Donal Casey
Green Fees Weekdays: €55
Weekends: €65
G/C: Y   P/C: Y   G/S: Y
Course Distance C'ship: 6,011m
Ladies: 4,875m

ELM GREEN GOLF CLUB
No. of holes: 18

Castleknock, Dublin 15.
T: 01-8200797
F: 01-8226668
E: elmgreen@golfdublin.com
W: www.golfdublin.com
Contact Name: Gerry Carr
General Manager
Captain 2003: Fred Brereton
Green Fees Weekdays: €22
Weekends: €30
G/C: Y   P/C: Y   G/S: Y
Course Distance C'ship: 5,307m
Ladies: 4,496m

ELM PARK GOLF CLUB
No. of holes: 18

Nutley House, Nutley Lane, Donnybrook,
Dublin 4.
T: 01-2693438
F: 01-2694505
E: office@elmparkgolfclub.ie
Contact Name: Adrian McCormack
Secretary\Manager
Captain 2003: Denis Bergin
Green Fees Weekdays: €70
Weekends: €80
G/C: N   P/C: Y   G/S: Y
Course Distance C'ship: 5,355m
Ladies: 4,974m

ENNIS GOLF CLUB
No. of holes: 18

Drumbiggle, Ennis, Co. Clare.
T: 065-6824074
F: 065-6841848
E: egc@eircom.net
W: www.golfclub.ennis.ie
Contact Name: Niall O'Donnell
Manager
Captain 2003: Tom Saunders
Green Fees Weekdays: €30
Weekends: €35
G/C: Y   P/C: Y   G/S: Y
Course Distance C'ship: 5,592m
Ladies: 4,998m

Golf Carts = G/C   Pull Carts = P/C   Golf shop = G/S

ENNISCORTHY GOLF CLUB
No. of holes: 18

Knockmarshall, Enniscorthy, Co. Wexford.
T: 054-33191
F: 054-37637
E: engc@eircom.net
Contact Name: Sean O'Leary
Hon/Secretary
Captain 2003: Paul Leacy
Green Fees Weekdays: €25
Weekends: €35
G/C: Y P/C : Y G/S : Y
Course Distance C'ship: 6,385m
Ladies: 5,189m

ENNISCRONE GOLF CLUB
No. of holes: 27

Enniscrone, Co. Sligo.
T: 096-36297
F: 096-36657
E: enniscronegolf@eircom.net
W: www.enniscronegolf.com
Contact Name: Michael Staunton
Secretary\Manager
Captain 2003: Bernard Flynn
Green Fees Weekdays: €48
Weekends: €60
G/C: Y P/C : Y G/S : Y
Course Distance C'ship: 6,195m
Ladies: 5,121m

ENNISKILLEN GOLF CLUB
No. of holes: 18

Castlecoole, Enniskillen, Co. Fermanagh
BT74 6HZ.
T/F: 028-66325250
E: enquiries@enniskillengolfclub.com
W: www.enniskillengolfclub.com
Contact Name: Darryl Robinson
Bar Steward
Captain 2003: William McBrian
Green Fees Weekdays: Stg £18
Weekends: Stg £22
G/C: Y P/C : Y G/S : N
Course Distance C'ship: 5,664m
Ladies: 4,944m

ESKER HILLS GOLF CLUB
No. of holes: 18

Tullamore, Co. Offaly.
T: 0506-55999
F: 0506-55021
E: info@eskerhillsgolf.com
W: www.eskerhillsgolf.com
Contact Name: Caroline Guinan
Secretary\Manager
Captain 2003: John O'Shea
Green Fees Weekdays: €30
Weekends: €40
G/C: Y P/C : Y G/S : Y
Course Distance C'ship: 6,016m
Ladies: 4,585m

FAITHLEGG GOLF CLUB
No. of holes: 18

Faithlegg, Co. Waterford.
T: 051-382241
F: 051-382664
E: golf@faithlegg.com
W: www.faithlegg.com
Contact Name: Dick Brennan
Director of Golf
Captain 2003: Paul Townely
Green Fees Weekdays: €40
Weekends: €55
G/C: Y P/C : Y G/S : Y
Course Distance C'ship: 6,629m
Ladies: 5,501m

FAUGHAN VALLEY GOLF CLUB
No. of holes: 18

Carmoney Road, Campsie, Derry BT47 3JH.
T: 048-71860707

Contact Name: John Cleghorn
Secretary\Manager
Captain 2003: Ronnie Ross
Green Fees Weekdays: Stg £8
Weekends: Stg £10
G/C: N P/C : Y G/S : Y
Course Distance C'ship: 5,232m

Golf Carts = G/C   **Pull Carts = P/C**   **Golf shop = G/S**

Golf Clubs

65

FERMOY GOLF CLUB
No. of holes: 18

Corrin, Fermoy, Co. Cork.
T: 025-32694
F: 025-33072
E: fermoygolfclub@eircom.net

Contact Name: Kathleen Murphy
Secretary\Manager
Captain 2003: John O'Grady
Green Fees Weekdays: €20
Weekends: €30
G/C: N   P/C : Y   G/S : Y
Course Distance C'ship: 5,846m
Ladies: 4,722m

FERNHILL GOLF CLUB
No. of holes: 18

Carrigaline, Co. Cork.
T: 021-4372226
F: 021-4371011
E: fernhill@iol.ie
W: www.fernhillgolfhotel.com
Contact Name: Claire McCarthy
Admininstrator\Secretary
Captain 2003: Dermot O'Sullivan
Green Fees Weekdays: €20
Weekends: €28
G/C:Y   P/C : Y   G/S : Y
Course Distance C'ship: 5,755m
Ladies: 5,205m

FINTONA GOLF CLUB
No. of holes: 18

7 Klin Street, Fintona, Co. Tyrone BT78 2BJ.
T: 028-82840777
F: 028-82841480
E: fintonagolfclub@freenet.uk.com

Contact Name: Vincent McCarney
Hon\Secretary
Captain 2003: David Abraham
Green Fees Weekdays: Stg £10
Weekends: Stg £15
G/C: N   P/C : N   G/S : Y
Course Distance C'ship: 5,765m
Ladies: 5,507m

FORREST LITTLE GOLF CLUB
No. of holes: 18

Cloghran, Co. Dublin.
T: 01-8401763
E: info@forrestlittle.com
W: www.forrestlittlegolfclub.com

Contact Name: Kevin McIntyre
Secretary\Manager
Captain 2003: Harry Reilly
Green Fees Weekdays: €45
Weekends: N\A
G/C: Y   P/C : Y   G/S : Y
Course Distance C'ship: 5,902m
Ladies: 5,075m

FORTWILLIAM GOLF CLUB
No. of holes: 18

Downview Avenue, Belfast BT15 4EZ.
T: 028-90370770
F: 028-90781891

Contact Name: Michael Purdy
Hon\Secretary
Captain 2003: Ivan McMichael
Green Fees Weekdays: Stg £22
Weekends: Stg £29
G/C: Y   P/C : Y   G/S : Y
Course Distance C'ship: 5,430m
Ladies: 4,915m

FOTA ISLAND GOLF CLUB
No. of holes: 18

Fota Island, Carrigtwohill, Co. Cork.
T: 021-4883700
F: 021-4883713
E: kmaccann@fotaisland.ie
W: www.fotaisland.com
Contact Name: Kate MacCann
Managing Director
Captain 2003: Joe O'Connor
Green Fees Weekdays: €83
Weekends: €98
G/C: Y   P/C : Y   G/S : Y
Course Distance C'ship: 6,297m
Ladies: 5018m

Golf Carts = G/C   Pull Carts = P/C   Golf shop = G/S

FOXROCK GOLF CLUB
No. of holes: 9

Torquay Road, Foxrock, Dublin 18.
T: 01-2893992
F: 01-2894943
E: fgc@indigo.ie
W: www.foxrockgolfclub.com
Contact Name: Frank Hayes
Secretary\Manager
Captain 2003: Anthony P. Walshe
Green Fees Weekdays: €50
Weekends: €50
G/C: Y   P/C : Y   G/S : Y
Course Distance C'ship: 5,667m
Ladies: 5,113m

FOYLE GOLF CLUB
No. of holes: 18

12 Alder Road, Derry BT48 8DB.
T: 028-71352222
F: 028-71353967
E: mail@foylegolfclub24.co.uk
W: www.foylegolfcentre.com
Contact Name: Margaret Lapsley
Secretary\Manager
Captain 2003: Alan Harkens
Green Fees Weekdays: £12
Weekends: £15
G/C: N   P/C : Y   G/S : Y
Course Distance C'ship: 6,678m
Ladies: 5,507m

FRANKFIELD GOLF CLUB
No. of holes: 9

Frankfield, Grange, Cork.
T: 021-4363124
F: 021-4366205
E: frankgolf@eircom.net
Contact Name: Eamonn O'Donovan
Secretary\Manager
Captain 2003: Fred Lotty
Green Fees Weekdays: €10
Weekends: €10
G/C: N   P/C : Y   G/S : Y
Course Distance C'ship: 4,732m
Ladies: 4,437m

GALGORM CASTLE GOLF CLUB
No. of holes: 18

200 Galgorm Road, Ballymena, Co. Antrim
BT42 1HL.
T: 028-25646161   **F:** 028-25651151
E: golf@galgormcastle.com
W: www.galgormcastle.com
Contact Name: Barbara McGeown
Manager
Captain 2003: Sean Donnelly
Green Fees Weekdays: Stg £25
Weekends: Stg £30
G/C: Y   P/C : Y   G/S : Y
Course Distance C'ship: 6,124m
Ladies: 4,961m

GALWAY GOLF CLUB
No. of holes: 18

Blackrock, Salthill, Galway.
T: 091-522033
F: 091-529783
E: galwaygolf@eircom.net
Contact Name: Padraic Fahy
Secretary\Manager
Captain 2003: Diarmuid Caulfield
Green Fees Weekdays: €40
Weekends: €50
G/C: Y   P/C : Y   G/S : Y
Course Distance C'ship: 5,916m
Ladies: 4,958m

GALWAY BAY GOLF & COUNTRY CLUB
No. of holes: 18

Rinville, Oranmore, Co. Galway.
T: 091-790503
F: 091-792510
E: gbay@iol.ie
W: www.gbaygolf.com
Contact Name: Eugene O'Connor
Head Professional
Captain 2003: Tom Sands
Green Fees Weekdays: €55
Weekends: €70
G/C: Y   P/C : Y   G/S : Y
Course Distance C'ship: 6,355m
Ladies: 5,136m

Golf Carts = G/C   Pull Carts = P/C   Golf shop = G/S

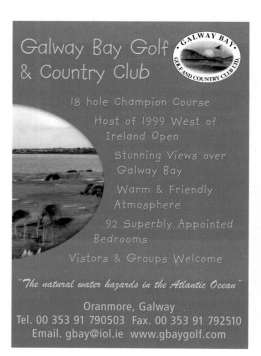

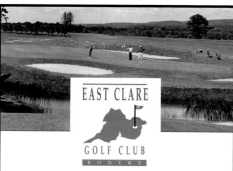

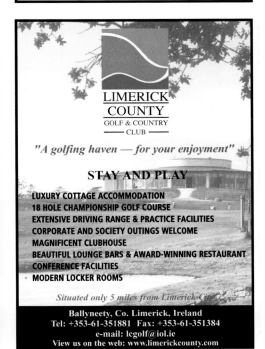

GILNAHIRK GOLF CLUB
No. of holes: 9

Manns Corner, Upper Braniel Road,
Gilnahirk, Belfast BT5 7TX.
T: 028-90448477

Contact Name: Andrew Carson
Secretary\Manager
Captain 2003: Alan Tipping
Green Fees Weekdays: Stg £10
Weekends: Stg £12
G/C: N   P/C: Y   G/S: Y
Course Distance C'ship: 5,398m
Ladies: 4,522m

GLASSON GOLF CLUB
No. of holes: 18

Glasson, Athlone, Co. Westmeath.
T: 0902-85120
F: 0902-85444
E: info@glassongolf.ie
W: www.glassongolf.ie
Contact Name: Fidelma Reid
Secretary\Manager
Captain 2003: Joe Kenny
Green Fees Weekdays: €55
Weekends: €65
G/C: Y   P/C: Y   G/S: Y
Course Distance C'ship: 6,472m
Ladies: 5,078m

GLEN OF THE DOWNS GOLF CLUB
No. of holes: 18

Coolnaskeagh, Delgany, Co. Wicklow.
T: 01-2876240
F: 01-2870063
E: info@glenofthedowns.com
W: www.glenofthedowns.com
Contact Name: Gavin Hunt
General Manager
Captain 2003: Colm O'Hagan
Green Fees Weekdays: €65
Weekends: €80
G/C: Y   P/C: Y   G/S: Y
Course Distance C'ship: 5,857m
Ladies: 4,800m

GLENCULLEN GOLF CLUB
No. of holes: 9

Glencullen, Co. Dublin.
T: 01-2940898
F: 01-2952895
E: admin@glencullengolfclub.ie
W: www.glencullengolfclub.ie
Contact Name: Georgina Davy
Secretary\Manager
Captain 2003: Neal Johnston
Green Fees Weekdays: €17
Weekends: €22
G/C: N   P/C: Y   G/S: N
Course Distance C'ship: 4,786m
Ladies: 4,247m

GLENGARRIFF GOLF CLUB
No. of holes: 9

Glengarriff, Co. Cork.
T: 027-63150

Contact Name: Noreen Deasy
Secretary\Manager
Captain 2003: Tony McElhinney
Green Fees Weekdays: €20
Weekends: €25
G/C: N   P/C: Y   G/S: N
Course Distance C'ship: 4,514m
Ladies: 4,202m

GLENLO ABBEY GOLF CLUB
No. of holes: 18

Glenlo Abbey Hotel, Bushy Park, Galway.
T: 091-519698
F: 091-519699
E: glenlo@iol.ie
W: www.glenlo.com

Contact Name: Bill Daly - Manager
Captain 2003: Brian Bourke
Green Fees Weekdays: €15
Weekends: €20
G/C: N   P/C: Y   G/S: Y
Course Distance C'ship: 6,437m
Ladies: 4,998m

Golf Carts = G/C   Pull Carts = P/C   Golf shop = G/S

GLENMALURE GOLF CLUB
No. of holes: 18

Ballintombay, Rathdrum, Co. Wicklow.
T: 0404-46679
F: 0404-46783

Contact Name: Patrick Daye
Secretary\Manager
Captain 2003: Jack Goucher
Green Fees   Weekdays: €25
Weekends: €35
G/C: Y   P/C : Y   G/S : N
Course Distance C'ship: 4,820m
Ladies: 4,740m

GOLDCOAST GOLF CLUB
No. of holes: 18

Ballinacourty, Dungarvan, Co. Waterford.
T/F: 058-44055
E: golfcoastgolf@eircom.net

Contact Name: Tom Considine
Secretary\Manager
Captain 2003: Tom White
Green Fees   Weekdays: €35
Weekends: €45
G/C: Y   P/C : Y   G/S : Y
Course Distance C'ship: 6,171m
Ladies: 5,028m

GORT GOLF CLUB
No. of holes: 18

Castlequarter, Gort, Co. Galway.
T: 091-632244
F: 091-632387
E: info@gortgolf.com
W: www.gortgolf.com
Contact Name: Andrew Crawford
Administrator\Secretary
Captain 2003: Joe Byrne
Green Fees   Weekdays: €25
Weekends: €30
G/C: Y   P/C : Y   G/S : Y
Course Distance C'ship: 5,974m
Ladies: 4,889m

GOWRAN GOLF CLUB
No. of holes: 18

Gowran Park, Co. Kilkenny.
T: 056-26699
F: 056-26173
E: gowranpk@eircom.net
Contact Name: Michael O'Sullivan
Secretary\Manager
Captain 2003: James Walsh
Green Fees   Weekdays: €35
Weekends: €45
G/C: Y   P/C : Y   G/S : Y
Course Distance C'ship: 6,110m
Ladies: 5,456m

GRACEHILL GOLF CLUB
No. of holes: 18

143 Ballinlea Road, Stamocum,
Ballymoney, Co. Antrim BT53 8PX.
T: 028-20751209   **F:** 028-20751074
E: golf@gracehillgolfclub.co.uk
W: www.gracehillgolfclub.co.uk
Contact Name: Margaret McClure
Secretary\Manager
Captain 2003: Rory McCartney
Green Fees   Weekdays: Stg £18
Weekends: Stg £22
G/C: N   P/C : Y   G/S : Y
Course Distance C'ship: 6,000m
Ladies: 5,500m

GRANGE GOLF CLUB
No. of holes: 18

Whitechurch Road, Rathfarnham, Dublin 16.
T: 01-4932889
F: 01-4939490
E: grangegc@eircom.net
W: www.grangegc.com
Contact Name: J.A. O'Donoghue
Secretary\Manager
Captain 2003: Tom Shaw
Green Fees   Weekdays: €65
Weekends: N\A
G/C: N   P/C : Y   G/S : Y
Course Distance C'ship: 5,839m
Ladies: 5,063m

Golf Carts = G/C   Pull Carts = P/C   Golf shop = G/S

GRANGE CASTLE GOLF CLUB
No. of holes: 18

Nangor Road, Clondalkin, Dublin 22.
T: 01-4641043
F: 01-4641039
E: grangecastle@golfdublin.com
W: www.golfdublin.com

Contact Name: Gary Duncan
Secretary\Manager
Captain 2003: Colm Tyndell
Green Fees Weekdays: €19
Weekends: €27
G/C: Y   P/C : Y   G/S : Y
Course Distance C'ship: 5,966m

GREENACRES GOLF CLUB
No. of holes: 18

153 Ballyrobert Road, Ballyclare,
Co. Antrim BT39 9RT.
T: 028-93354111
F: 028-93354166
W: www.greenacresgolfclub.co.uk
Contact Name: Peter Watson
Secretary\Manager
Captain 2003: J Montgomery
Green Fees Weekdays: Stg £14
Weekends: Stg £20
G/C: Y   P/C : Y   G/S : Y
Course Distance C'ship: 5,839m
Ladies: 5,063m

GREENCASTLE GOLF CLUB
No. of holes: 18

Greencastle, Co. Donegal.
T/F:074-9381015
E: b-mc-caul@yahoo.com
W: www.greencastlegolfclub.com

Contact Name: Billy McCaul
Hon\Secretary
Captain 2003: Brian Doherty
Green Fees Weekdays: €20
Weekends: €35
G/C: N   P/C : Y   G/S : Y
Course Distance C'ship: 5,145m
Ladies: 4,983m

GREENISLAND GOLF CLUB
No. of holes: 9

156 Upper Road, Greenisland,
Carrickfergus, Co. Antrim BT38 8LP.
T: 028-90862236

Contact Name: Jim McLaughlin
Hon\Secretary
Captain 2003: Mr. I Riddle
Green Fees Weekdays: Stg £12
Weekends: Stg £18
G/C: N   P/C : N   G/S : N
Course Distance C'ship: 5,624m
Ladies: 4,827m

GREENORE GOLF CLUB
No. of holes: 18

Greenore, Co. Louth.
T: 042-9373212
F: 042-9383898
E: greenoregolfclub@eircom.net
W: www.greenoregolf.com
Contact Name: Connie O'Connor
Secretary\Manager
Captain 2003: Brian Rafferty
Green Fees Weekdays: €32
Weekends: €45
G/C: Y   P/C : Y   G/S : Y
Course Distance C'ship: 6,043m
Ladies: 5,210m

GREYSTONES GOLF CLUB
No. of holes: 18

Whitshed Road, Greystones, Co. Wicklow.
T: 01-2874136
F: 01-2873749
E: secretary@greystonesgc.com
W: www.greystonesgc.com
Contact Name: Jim Melody
Secretary\Manager
Captain 2003: Tommy Hayden
Green Fees Weekdays: €45
Weekends: €50
G/C: Y   P/C : Y   G/S : Y
Course Distance C'ship: 5,322m
Ladies: 4,879m

Golf Carts = G/C   **Pull Carts = P/C**   **Golf shop = G/S**

GWEEDORE GOLF CLUB
No. of holes: 9

Magheragallan, Derrybeg PO, Co. Donegal.
T: 075-31140

Contact Name: Seamus McGowan
Hon\Secretary
Captain 2003: Jack White
Green Fees Weekdays: €13
Weekends: €15
G/C: N   P/C : Y   G/S : N
Course Distance C'ship: 5,600m
Ladies: 4,912m

HARBOUR POINT GOLF CLUB
No. of holes: 18

Clash Road, Little Island, Cork.
T: 021-4353094
F: 021-4354408
E: hpoint@iol.com

Contact Name: Aylmer Barrett
General Manager
Captain 2003: Jimmy Lennon
Green Fees Weekdays: €33
Weekends: €38
G/C: Y   P/C : Y   G/S : Y
Course Distance C'ship: 6,163m
Ladies: 5,915m

HAZEL GROVE GOLF CLUB
No. of holes: 9

Mount Seskin Road, Jobstown, Dublin 24.
T: 01-4520911
W: www.hazelgrovegolfclub.com

Contact Name: Pat Foley
Secretary\Manager
Captain 2003: Seamus Gaffney
Green Fees Weekdays: €18
Weekends: €20
G/C: N   P/C : Y   G/S : N
Course Distance C'ship: 5,077m
Ladies: 4,900m

HEADFORT GOLF CLUB
No. of holes: 36

Kells, Co. Meath.
T: 046-40146
F: 046-49282
E: hgcadmin@eircom.net
Contact Name: Nora Murphy
Adminstrator\Secretary
Captain 2003: Niall Clerkin
Green Fees
Weekdays: €55 (New) / €40 (Old)
Weekends: €60 (New) / €45 (Old)
G/C: Y   P/C : Y   G/S : Y
Course Distance C'ship: 6,524\6,164m
Ladies: 5,010m

HELENS BAY GOLF CLUB
No. of holes: 9

Golf Road, Helen's Bay, Bangor, Co. Down
BT19 1TL.
T: 028-91852815
F: 028-91852660
E: mail@helensbaygc.com
Contact Name: Peter B. Clarke
Hon\Secretary
Captain 2003: John Coote
Green Fees Weekdays: Stg £17
Weekends: Stg £20
G/C: Y   P/C : Y   G/S : N
Course Distance C'ship: 5,161m
Ladies: 4,873m

HERMITAGE GOLF CLUB
No. of holes: 18

Lucan, Co. Dublin.
T: 01-6264891
F: 01-6238881
E: hermitagegolf@eircom.net
W: www.hermitagegolf.ie
Contact Name: Pat Maguire
General Manager
Captain 2003: Paul. A. Harney
Green Fees Weekdays: €75
Weekends: €80
G/C: Y   P/C : Y   G/S : Y
Course Distance C'ship: 6,010m
Ladies: 5,261m

Golf Carts = G/C   Pull Carts = P/C   Golf shop = G/S

HIBERNIAN GOLF CLUB
No. of holes: 18

c\o Citywest Hotel, Saggart, Co. Dublin.
T: 01-8510565
F: 01-8315779
E: hiberniangolf@eircom.net
W: www.hiberniangolf.com
Contact Name: Brendan Cooling
General Secretary
Captain 2003: Eamon Cox
Green Fees Weekdays: €40
Weekends: €50
G/C: Y P/C : Y G/S : Y
Course Distance C'ship: 5,843m
Ladies: 4,745m

HIGHFIELD GOLF CLUB
No. of holes: 18

Carbury, Co. Kildare.
T/F: 0405-31021
E: hgc@indigo.ie
W: www.highfield-golf.ie
Contact Name: Margaret Duggan
Secretary\Manager
Captain 2003: Aiden O'Sullivan
Green Fees Weekdays: €25
Weekends: €35
G/C: Y P/C : Y G/S : Y
Course Distance C'ship: 5,782m
Ladies: 4,675m

HILTON TEMPLEPATRICK GOLF CLUB
No. of holes: 18

Castle Upton Estate, Templepatrick
BT39 0DD, Co. Down.
T: 028-94435510
F: 028-94435511
E: bill_donald@hilton.ie
Contact Name: Bill Donald
Secretary\Manager
Captain 2003: Peter McFarland
Green Fees Weekdays: Stg £40
Weekends: Stg £45
G/C: Y P/C : Y G/S : Y
Course Distance C'ship: 6,311m
Ladies: 5,009m

HOLLYSTOWN GOLF CLUB
No. of holes: 27

Hollystown, Co. Dublin.
T: 01-8207444
F: 01-8207447
E: info@hollystown.com
W: www.hollystown.com
Contact Name: Ciaran Barry
Secretary\Manager
Captain 2003: John Lennon
Green Fees Weekdays: €25
Weekends: €35
G/C: Y P/C : Y G/S : N
Course Distance C'ship: 5,818m
Ladies: 4,818m

HOLLYWOOD LAKES GOLF CLUB
No. of holes: 18

Ballyboughal, Co. Dublin.
T: 01-8433407
F: 01-8433002
E: hollywoodlakesgc@eircom.net
W: www.hollywoodlakesgolfclub.com
Contact Name: Sid Baldwin
Secretary\Manager
Captain 2003: Niall Hickey
Green Fees Weekdays: €35
Weekends: €45
G/C: Y P/C : Y G/S : Y
Course Distance C'ship: 6,088m
Ladies: 5,763m

HOLYWOOD GOLF CLUB
No. of holes: 18

Nuns Walk, Demesne Road, Holywood,
Co. Down BT18 9LE.
T: 028-90425503 **F:** 028-90425040
E: mail@holywoodgolfclub.co.uk
W: www.holywoodgolfclub.co.uk
Contact Name: Gerry Fyfe
Secretary\Manager
Captain 2003: John Paterson
Green Fees Weekdays: Stg £17
Weekends: Stg £26
G/C: N P/C : Y G/S : Y
Course Distance C'ship: 5,480m
Ladies: 4,835m

Golf Carts = G/C   Pull Carts = P/C   Golf shop = G/S

HOWTH GOLF CLUB
No. of holes: 18

Carrickbrack Road, Sutton, Dublin 13.
T: 01-8323055
F: 01-8321793
E: secretary@howthgolfclub.ie
W: www.howthgolfclub.ie
Contact Name: Ann MacNeice
    Secretary\Manager
Captain 2003: Don Mahony
Green Fees Weekdays: €50
    Weekends: €50
G/C: Y   P/C : Y   G/S : Y
Course Distance C'ship: 5,643m
Ladies: 4,952m

KANTURK GOLF CLUB
No. of holes: 18

Fairyhill, Kanturk, Co. Cork.
T: 029-50534
F: 029-20951

Contact Name: Tony McAuliffe
    Hon\Secretary
Captain 2003: Gerald Crotty
Green Fees Weekdays: €20
    Weekends: €25
G/C: N   P/C : Y   G/S : N
Course Distance C'ship: 5,297m
Ladies: 4,333m

KENMARE GOLF CLUB
No. of holes: 18

Kenmare, Co. Kerry.
T: 064-41291
F: 064-42061
E: info@kenmaregolfclub.com
W: www.kenmaregolfclub.com
Contact Name: Simon Duffield
    Secretary\Manager
Captain 2003: Jackie Tuohy
Green Fees Weekdays: €15
    Weekends: €15
G/C: N   P/C : Y   G/S : Y
Course Distance C'ship: 5,173m
Ladies: 4,502m

THE KERRIES GOLF CLUB
No. of holes: 9

Tralee, Co. Kerry.
T: 066-7122112
F: 066-7120085
E: thekerriesgolfcourse@eircom.net

Contact Name: Maurice Barrett
    Secretary\Manager
Captain 2003: David Doyle
Green Fees Weekdays: €15
    Weekends: €15
G/C: N   P/C : Y   G/S : Y
Course Distance C'ship: 5,832m
Ladies: 4,365m

KILCOCK GOLF CLUB
No. of holes: 18

Gallow, Kilcock, Co. Meath.
T: 01-6287592
F: 01-6287283
E: kilcockgolfclub@eircom.net
W: www.kilcockgolfclub.com
Contact Name: Seamus Kelly
    Secretary\Manager
Captain 2003: Ken Lawless
Green Fees Weekdays: €25
    Weekends: €30
G/C: Y   P/C : Y   G/S : Y
Course Distance C'ship: 5,812m
Ladies: 5,107m

KILCOOLE GOLF CLUB
No. of holes: 9

Newcastle Road, Kilcoole, Co. Wicklow.
T: 01-2872066
F: 01-2010497
E: adminkg@eircom.net
W: www.kilcoolegolfclub.com
Contact Name: Eddie Lonergan
    Secretary\Manager
Captain 2003: Con Thomas
Green Fees Weekdays: €30
    Weekends: €35
G/C: N   P/C : Y   G/S : Y
Course Distance C'ship: 5,514m
Ladies: 5,082m

Golf Carts = G/C   Pull Carts = P/C   Golf shop = G/S

KILKEA CASTLE GOLF CLUB
No. of holes: 18

Kilkea, Castledermot, Co. Kildare.
T: 0503-45555
F: 0503-45505
E: kilkeacastlegolfclub@eircom.net
W: www.kilkeacastlehotelgolf.com
Contact Name: John Kissane
General Manager
Captain 2003: Jimmy Barry
Green Fees Weekdays: €38
Weekends: €45
G/C: N P/C : Y G/S : Y
Course Distance C'ship: 6,097m
Ladies: 5,076m

KILKEE GOLF CLUB
No. of holes: 18

East End, Kilkee, Co. Clare.
T: 065-9056048
F: 065-9056977
E: kilkeegolfclub@eircom.net
W: www.kilkeegolfclub.ie
Contact Name: Michael Culligan
Secretary\Manager
Captain 2003: Gerry O'Halloran
Green Fees Weekdays: €25
Weekends: €30
G/C: Y P/C : Y G/S : Y
Course Distance C'ship: 5,421m
Ladies: 4,104m

KILKEEL GOLF CLUB
No. of holes: 18

Mourne Park, Ballyardle, Kilkeel BT34 4LB, Down.
T: 028-41765095
F: 028-41765579
E: srooney@mail.com
Contact Name: Seamus Rooney
General Manager
Captain 2003: Jim Boyd
Green Fees Weekdays: Stg £20
Weekends: Stg £25
G/C: Y P/C : Y G/S : Y
Course Distance C'ship: 6,015m
Ladies: 5,399m

KILKENNY GOLF CLUB
No. of holes: 18

Glendine, Kilkenny.
T: 056-65400
F: 056-23593
E: enquiries@kilkennygolfclub.com
W: www.kilkennygolfclub.com
Contact Name: Anne O'Neill
Secretary\Manager
Captain 2003: Morgan Doyle
Green Fees Weekdays: €35
Weekends: €40
G/C: Y P/C : Y G/S : Y
Course Distance C'ship: 5,682m
Ladies: 5,138m

KILLARNEY GOLF & FISHING CLUB
No. of holes: 3 x 18

Mahony's Point, Killarney, Co. Kerry.
T: 064-31034
F: 064-33065
E: reservations@killarney_golf.com
W: www.killarney_golf.com
Contact Name: Tom Prendergast
Secretary\Manager
Captain 2003: Tommy Cooper
Green Fees Weekdays: €75
Weekends: €75
G/C: Y P/C : Y G/S : Y
Course Distance C'ship: 6,474m
Ladies: 4,938m

KILLEEN GOLF CLUB
No. of holes: 18

Kill, Co. Kildare.
T: 045-866003
F: 045-875881
E: admin@kileengc.ie
W: www.killeengolf.ie
Contact Name: Maurice Kelly
Secretary\Manager
Captain 2003: Liam Burke
Green Fees Weekdays: €35
Weekends: €50
G/C: N P/C : Y G/S : Y
Course Distance C'ship: 6,155m
Ladies: 4,914m

KILLERIG CASTLE GOLF CLUB
No. of holes: 18

Killerig, Co. Carlow.
T: 0503-63000
F: 0503-63005
E: info@killerig-golf.ie
W: www.killerig-golf.ie
Contact Name: Fiona Dillon
  Secretary\Manager
Captain 2003: Jimmy O'Neill
Green Fees Weekdays: €35
  Weekends: €45
G/C: Y P/C : Y G/S : Y
Course Distance C'ship: 6,165m
Ladies: 5,329m

KILLINBEG GOLF CLUB
No. of holes: 18

Killin Park, Dundalk, Co. Louth.
T: 042-9339303

Contact Name: Pat Reynolds
  Secretary\Manager
Captain 2003: Eamon Doherty
Green Fees Weekdays: €20
  Weekends: €25
G/C: Y P/C : Y G/S : Y
Course Distance C'ship: 5,338m
Ladies: 4,783m

KILLINEY GOLF CLUB
No. of holes: 9

Ballinclea, Road Killiney, Co. Dublin.
T: 01-2852823
F: 01-2852861
E: killineygolfclub@eircom.net

Contact Name: Michael Walsh
  Secretary\Manager
Captain 2003: John Morgan
Green Fees Weekdays: €50
  Weekends: €50
G/C: Y P/C : Y G/S : Y
Course Distance C'ship: 5,655m
Ladies: 5,158

KILLORGLIN GOLF CLUB
No. of holes: 18

Stealroe, Killorglin, Co. Kerry.
T: 066-9761979
F: 066-9761437
E: kilgolf@iol.ie

Contact Name: Billy Dodd- Owner
Captain 2003: Brian Spillane
Green Fees Weekdays: €25
  Weekends: €30
G/C: Y P/C : Y G/S : Y
Course Distance C'ship: 5,913m
Ladies: 4,752m

KILLYMOON GOLF CLUB
No. of holes: 18

200 Killymoon Road, Cookstown,
Co. Tyrone BT80 8TW.
T: 028-86763762
F: 028-86763762
E: kgcl@btopenworld.com
W: www.killymoongolf.com
Contact Name: V. Wilson – Manager
Captain 2003: Brendan Conway
Green Fees Weekdays: Stg £20
  Weekends: Stg £25
G/C: Y P/C : Y G/S : Y
Course Distance C'ship: 5,496m
Ladies: 4,939m

KILREA GOLF CLUB
No. of holes: 9

Lasnagrot Road, Kilrea, Co. Derry.
T: 028-2954004

Contact Name: Kevin McWilliams
  Hon\Secretary
Captain 2003: Seamus Quinn
Green Fees Weekdays: Stg £10
  Weekends: Stg £15
G/C: N P/C : Y G/S : N
Course Distance C'ship: 4,104m
Ladies: 3,465m

Golf Carts = G/C   Pull Carts = P/C   Golf shop = G/S

KILRUSH GOLF CLUIB
No. of holes: 18

Parkamoney, Kilrush, Co. Clare.
T: 065-9051138
F: 065-9052633
E: info@kilrushgolfclub.com
W: www.kilrushgolfclub.com
Contact Name: Denis Nagle
Secretary\Manager
Captain 2003: Jimmy McSwiggan
Green Fees Weekdays: €25
Weekends: €30
G/C: Y   P/C : Y   G/S : Y
Course Distance C'ship: 5,215m
Ladies: 4,477m

KILTERNAN GOLF CLUB
No. of holes: 18

Kilternan, Co. Dublin.
T: 01-2955559
F: 01-2955670
E: kgc@kilternan-hotel.ie

Contact Name: Jimmy Kinsella
Secretary\Manager
Captain 2003: Tony Mulligan
Green Fees Weekdays: €27
Weekends: €34
G/C: Y   P/C : Y   G/S : Y
Course Distance C'ship: 5,021m
Ladies: 4,400m

KINSALE GOLF CLUB
No. of holes: 18

Farrangalway, Kinsale, Co. Cork.
T: 021-4774722
F: 021-4773114
E: office@kinsalegolf.com
W: www.kinsale.com
Contact Name: Michael Power
Secretary\Manager
Captain 2003: George Cantwell
Green Fees Weekdays: €35
Weekends: €50
G/C: Y   P/C : Y   G/S : Y
Course Distance C'ship: 6,008m
Ladies: 5,077m

KIRKISTOWN CASTLE GOLF CLUB
No. of holes: 18

142 Main Road, Cloughey, Newtownards,
Co. Down BT22 1JA.
T: 028-42771233   **F:** 028-42771699
E: kirkstown@supanet.com
W: www.kcgc.org
Contact Name: Rosemary Coulter
Secretary\Manager
Captain 2003: David Peacock
Green Fees Weekdays: Stg £20.75
Weekends: Stg £27.75
G/C: Y   P/C : Y   G/S : Y
Course Distance C'ship: 5,596m
Ladies: 5,220m

KNOCK GOLF CLUB
No. of holes: 18

Summerfield, Dundonald, Belfast BT16 2QX.
T: 028-90483251
F: 028-90487277

Contact Name: Anne Armstrong
General Manager
Captain 2003: Harry Flanigan
Green Fees Stg Weekdays: Stg £25
Stg Weekends: Stg £40
G/C: Y   P/C : Y   G/S : Y
Course Distance C'ship: 5,820m
Ladies: 5,270m

KNOCKANALLY GOLF CLUB
No. of holes: 18

Donadea, North Kildare.
T/F: 045-869322

Contact Name: Noel Lyons
Secretary\Manager
Captain 2003: Joe O'Toole
Green Fees Weekdays: €30
Weekends: €50
G/C: Y   P/C : Y   G/S : Y
Course Distance C'ship: 5,874m
Ladies: 4,939m

Golf Carts = G/C   Pull Carts = P/C   Golf shop = G/S

LAHINCH GOLF CLUB
No. of holes: 36

Lahinch, Co. Clare.
T: 065-7081003
F: 065-7081592
E: info@lahinchgolf.com
W: www.lahinchgolf.com
Contact Name: Alan Reardon
Secretary\Manager
Captain 2003: Donal Curtin
Green Fees Weekdays: €110
Weekends: €110
G/C: N P/C : Y G/S : Y
Course Distance C'ship: 6,292m
Ladies: 4,989m

LAMBEG GOLF CLUB
No. of holes: 18

Bells Lane, Lambeg, Lisburn,
Co. Antrim BT27 4RH.
T: 028-92662738 **F:** 028-92693432
E: mmsports@btopenworld.com

Contact Name: Alan Mason
Secretary\Manager
Captain 2003: Stanley Grayham
Green Fees Weekdays: Stg £11
Weekends: Stg £13.20
G/C: Y P/C : Y G/S : Y
Course Distance C'ship: 4,139m
Ladies: 3,660m

LARNE GOLF CLUB
No. of holes: 9

54 Ferris Bay Road, Islandmagee,
Co. Antrim BT40 3RT.
T: 028-93382228 **F:** 028-93382088
E: internet@larnegolfclub.co.uk
W: www.larnegolfclub.co.uk
Contact Name: Sharon Norris
Secretary\Manager
Captain 2003: George R. McLean
Green Fees Weekdays: Stg £10
Weekends: Stg £18
G/C: N P/C : N G/S : N
Course Distance C'ship: 5,745m
Ladies: 5,476m

LAYTOWN & BETTSTOWN GOLF CLUB
No. of holes: 18

Golf Links Road, Bettystown, Co. Meath.
T: 041-9827170
F: 041-9828506
E: bettystowngolfclub@utvinternet.com
W: www.bettystownclub.utvinternet.com
Contact Name: Helen Finnegan
Secretary\Manager
Captain 2003: Joe Costello
Green Fees Weekdays: €45
Weekends: €55
G/C: N P/C : Y G/S : Y
Course Distance C'ship: 5,862m
Ladies: 5,082m

LEE VALLEY GOLF CLUB
No. of holes: 18

Clashanure, Ovens, Co. Cork.
T: 021-7331721
F: 021-7331695
E: leevalleygolfclub@eircom.net
W: www.leevalleygc.ie
Contact Name: Caroline Nyhan
Secretary\Manager
Captain 2003: Redmond Tobin
Green Fees Weekdays: €30
Weekends: €35
G/C: Y P/C : Y G/S : Y
Course Distance C'ship: 6,114m
Ladies: 4,955m

LETTERKENNY GOLF CLUB
No. of holes: 18

Barnhill, Lettekenny, Co. Donegal.
T: 074-21150
F: 074-21175
E: letterkennygc@eircom.net

Contact Name: P.J. Sweeney
Secretary\Manager
Captain 2003: P.J. Keating
Green Fees Weekdays: €20
Weekends: €25
G/C: Y P/C : Y G/S : Y
Course Distance C'ship: 5,672m
Ladies: 4,868m

Golf Carts = G/C   Pull Carts = P/C   Golf shop = G/S

LIMERICK GOLF CLUB
No. of holes: 18

Ballyclough, Co. Limerick.
T: 061-415146
F: 061-319219
E: lgc@eircom.net
W: www.limerickgc.com
Contact Name: Pat Murray
General Manager
Captain 2003: Billy Rice
Green Fees Weekdays: €50
Weekends: €60
G/C: Y P/C : Y G/S : Y
Course Distance C'ship: 5,932m
Ladies: 5,114m

LIMERICK COUNTY GOLF CLUB
No. of holes: 18

Ballyneety, Co. Limerick.
T: 061-351881
F: 061-351384
E: lcgolf@iol.ie
W: www.limerickcounty.com
Contact Name: Sinead O'Donnell
Administrator
Captain 2003: Michael O'Brien
Green Fees Weekdays: €37
Weekends: €50
G/C: Y P/C : Y G/S : Y
Course Distance C'ship: 6,116m
Ladies: 5,049m

LISBURN GOLF CLUB
No. of holes: 18

68 Eglantine Road, Lisburn BT27 5RQ,
Antrim.
T: 028-92677216
F: 028-92603608
E: lisburngolfclub@aol.com
Contact Name: George McVeigh
Secretary\Manager
Captain 2003: Alan McCarthy
Green Fees Weekdays: Stg£30
Weekends: Stg£35
G/C: Y P/C : Y G/S : Y
Course Distance C'ship: 6,078m
Ladies: 5,642m

LISMORE GOLF CLUB
No. of holes: 9

Ballyin, Lismore, Co. Waterford.
T: 058-54026
F: 058-53338
E: lismoregolfclub@eircom.net
W: Under Construction

Contact Name: Bernard Dooley
Hon\Secretary
Captain 2003: Paddy O'Leary
Green Fees Weekdays: €20
Weekends: €20
G/C: N P/C : Y G/S : N
Course Distance C'ship: 5,289m

LISNARICK GOLF CLUB
No. of holes: 9

Drumarkey, Lisnarick BT94 1PN
Co. Fermanagh.
T: 028-68628091
F: 028-68628648

Contact Name: Hilary Sansom
Hon\Secretary
Captain 2003: Packie Robinson
Green Fees Weekdays: Stg £10
Weekends: Stg £10
G/C: N P/C : Y G/S : N
Course Distance C'ship: 3,945m

LISTOWEL GOLF CLUB
No. of holes: 9

Feale View, Listowel, Co. Kerry.
T: 068-21592
F: 068-23387

Contact Name: John Looney
Hon\Secretary
Captain 2003: P.M. O'Sullivan
Green Fees Weekdays: €15
Weekends: €20
G/C: N P/C : Y G/S : N
Course Distance C'ship: 5,208m
Ladies: 4,508m

Golf Carts = G/C   Pull Carts = P/C   Golf shop = G/S

LOUGHGALL GOLF CLUB
No. of holes: 18

11-14 Main Street, Loughgall, Co. Armagh.
T: 028-38892900
F: 028-38892902

Contact Name: Greg Ferson
Secretary\Manager
Captain 2003: David Neill
Green Fees Weekdays: Stg £14
Weekends: Stg £16
G/C: Y   P/C : Y   G/S : N
Course Distance C'ship: 5,663m
Ladies: 5,344m

LOUGHREA GOLF CLUB
No. of holes: 18

Graigue, Loughrea, Co. Galway.
T: 091-841049
F: 091-847472
E: loughreagolfclub@eircom.net

Contact Name: Maura Hawkins
Secretary\Manager
Captain 2003: Joe Barrett
Green Fees Weekdays: €20
Weekends: €20
G/C: Y   P/C : Y   G/S : N
Course Distance C'ship: 5,841m
Ladies: 4,930m

LUCAN GOLF CLUB
No. of holes: 18

Celbridge Road, Lucan, Co. Dublin.
T: 01-6282106
F: 01-6282929
E: lucangolf@eircom.net
Contact Name: Tom O'Donnell
Secretary\Manager
Captain 2003: Willie Doyle
Green Fees Weekdays: €45
Weekends: €45
G/C: Y   P/C : Y   G/S : N
Course Distance C'ship: 5,994m
Ladies: 5,167m

LURGAN GOLF CLUB
No. of holes: 18

Demesne, Lurgan, Co. Armagh BT67 9BN.
T: 028-38322087
F: 028-38316166
E: lurgan@btclick.com
Contact Name: Muriel Sharpe
Secretary\Manager
Captain 2003: Kieran Walsh
Green Fees Weekdays: Stg £15
Weekends: Stg £20
G/C: N   P/C : Y   G/S : Y
Course Distance C'ship: 5,701m
Ladies: 4,907m

LUTTRELLSTOWN CASTLE GOLF CLUB
No. of holes: 18

Castleknock, Dublin 15.
T: 01-8089988
F: 01-8089989
E: golf@luttrellstown.ie
W: www.luttrellstown.ie
Contact Name: Edward Doyle - Professional
Captain 2003: Martin Crawford
Green Fees Weekdays: €85
Weekends: €95
G/C: Y   P/C : Y   G/S : Y
Course Distance C'ship: 6,383m
Ladies: 5,168m

MACROOM GOLF CLUB
No. of holes: 18

Lackadur, Macroom, Co. Cork.
T: 026-41072
F: 026-41391
E: macroomgc@iol.ie

Contact Name: Cathal O'Sullivan
Manager
Captain 2003: Jim Curtin
Green Fees Weekdays: €25
Weekends: €30
G/C: N   P/C : Y   G/S : Y
Course Distance C'ship: 5,586m
Ladies: 4,599m

Golf Carts = G/C   Pull Carts = P/C   Golf shop = G/S

MAHEE ISLAND GOLF CLUB
No. of holes: 9

Mahee Island, Comber, Newtownards
BT23 6EP, Down.
T: 028-97541234

Contact Name: Mervin Marshall
Secretary\Manager
Captain 2003: Trevor Haslett
Green Fees Weekdays: Stg £10
Weekends: Stg £15
G/C: N   P/C : Y   G/S : Y
Course Distance C'ship: 2,908m
Ladies: 2,782m

MAHON GOLF CLUB
No. of holes: 18

Cloverhill, Blackrock, Cork.
T: 021-4294280
E: mahon@golfnet.ie

Contact Name: Tim O'Connor
Secretary\Manager
Captain 2003: Jim Keelan
Green Fees Weekdays: €20
Weekends: €22
G/C: N   P/C : Y   G/S : Y
Course Distance C'ship: 5,192m
Ladies: 4,862m

MALAHIDE GOLF CLUB
No. of holes: 18

Beechwood, The Grange, Malahide
Co. Dublin.
T: 01-8461611
F: 01-8461270
W: www.malahidegolfclub.com
Contact Name: P.J. Smyth
General Manager
Captain 2003: Donal Hughes
Green Fees Weekdays: €50
Weekends: €85
G/C: Y   P/C : Y   G/S : Y
Course Distance C'ship: 6,066m
Ladies: 5,146m

MALLOW GOLF CLUB
No. of holes: 18

Ballyellis, Mallow, Co. Cork.
T: 022-21145
F: 022-42501
E: golmall@gofree.indigo.ie

Contact Name: David Curtin
Secretary\Manager
Captain 2003: Barry White
Green Fees Weekdays: €35
Weekends: €40
G/C: Y   P/C : Y   G/S : Y
Course Distance C'ship: 5,960m
Ladies: 4,897m

MALLUSK GOLF CLUB
No. of holes: 9

Antrim Road, Glengormley,
Newtownabbey, Co. Antrim BT36 4RF.
T: 028-908473799

Contact Name: John Patterson
Hon\Secretary
Captain 2003: Tom Easton
Green Fees Weekdays: Stg £7.20
Weekends: Stg £10
G/C: N   P/C : N   G/S : N
Course Distance C'ship: 4,444m

MALONE GOLF CLUB
No. of holes: 27

240 Upper Malone Road, Dunmurry,
Belfast BT17 9LB.
T: 028-90612758   **F:** 028-90431394
E: manager@malonegolfclub.co.uk
W: www.malonegolfclub.co.uk
Contact Name: Nick Agate
Club Manager
Captain 2003: Dr. Brian Darby
Green Fees Weekdays: Stg £40
Weekends: Stg £45
G/C: N   P/C : Y   G/S : Y
Course Distance C'ship: 6,034m
Ladies: 5,228m

Golf Carts = G/C   Pull Carts = P/C   Golf shop = G/S

MANNAN CASTLE GOLF CLUB
No. of holes: 18

Carrickmacross, Co. Monaghan.
T: 042-9663308
F: 042-9663195
E: mannancastlegc@eircom.net
Contact Name: Dennis McArdle
Secretary\Manager
Captain 2003: Derek Murnaghan
Green Fees Weekdays: €20
Weekends: €30
G/C: Y   P/C : Y   G/S : N
Course Distance C'ship: 5,442m
Ladies: 4,551m

MANOR GOLF CLUB
No. of holes: 9

69 Bridge Street, Kilrea, Coleraine
Co. Derry BT51 5RR.
T: 028-29540205
F: 028-29540134
Contact Name: Charlie Hasson
Hon\Secretary
Captain 2003: Gerald Donaghy
Green Fees Weekdays: Stg £9
Weekends: Stg £10
G/C: N   P/C : Y   G/S : N
Course Distance C'ship: 4,174m
Ladies: 3,607m

MASSEREENE GOLF CLUB
No. of holes: 18

51 Lough Road, Antrim BT41 4DQ.
T: 028-94428096
F: 028-94487661
E: massereenegc@utvinternet.com
W: www.massereenegolfclub.com
Contact Name: Kevin Stevenson
Manager
Captain 2003: George Houston
Green Fees Weekdays: Stg £25
Weekends: Stg £30
G/C: N   P/C : Y   G/S : Y
Course Distance C'ship: 5,936m
Ladies: 5,048m

MILLICENT GOLF CLUB
No. of holes: 18

Millicent, Clane, Co. Kildare.
T/F: 045-893279

Contact Name: Daniel Killian – Director
Captain 2003: Peter Kenny
Green Fees Weekdays: €30
Weekends: €40
G/C: Y   P/C : Y   G/S : Y
Course Distance C'ship: 6,405m
Ladies: 4,962m

MILLTOWN GOLF CLUB
No. of holes: 18

Lower Churchtown Road, Dublin 14.
T: 01-4976090
F: 01-4976008
E: info@milltowngolfclub.ie
W: www.milltowngolfclub.com
Contact Name: Eamonn Lawless
General Manager
Captain 2003: Gerry Coleman
Green Fees Weekdays: €80
Weekends: N\A
G/C: Y   P/C : Y   G/S : Y
Course Distance C'ship: 5,638m
Ladies: 5,198m

MITCHELSTOWN GOLF CLUB
No. of holes: 21

Gurrane, Mitchelstown, Co. Cork.
T: 025-24072
F: 025-85997
W: www.mitchelstown-golf.com

Contact Name: Dennis Gorey
Secretary\Manager
Captain 2003: Sean Buckley
Green Fees Weekdays: €20
Weekends: €25
G/C: N   P/C : Y   G/S : N
Course Distance C'ship: 5,160m
Ladies: 4,489m

Golf Carts = G/C   **Pull Carts = P/C**   **Golf shop = G/S**

MOATE GOLF CLUB
No. of holes: 18

Aghanargit, Moate, Co. Westmeath.
T: 0902-81271
F: 0902-81267
E: moategolfclub@eircom.net
W: Under construction
Contact Name: P.J. Higgins
Secretary\Manager
Captain 2003: Seamus Buckley
Green Fees Weekdays: €25
Weekends: €30
G/C: Y   P/C : Y   G/S : Y
Course Distance C'ship: 5,742m
Ladies: 5,446m

MONKSTOWN GOLF CLUB
No. of holes: 18

Parkgariffe, Monkstown, Co. Cork.
T: 021-4841376
F: 021-4841722
E: office@monkstowngolfclub.com
W: www.monkstowngolfclub.com
Contact Name: Hilary Madden
Secretary\Manager
Captain 2003: Ted Scriven
Green Fees Weekdays: €37
Weekends: €44
G/C: N   P/C : Y   G/S : Y
Course Distance C'ship: 5,669m
Ladies: 4,862m

MOOR PARK GOLF CLUB
No. of holes: 18

Moortown, Navan, Co. Meath.
T/F: 046-27661

Contact Name: Martin Fagan
Secretary\Manager
Captain 2003: Tom Grimes
Green Fees Weekdays: €20
Weekends: €25
G/C: N   P/C : Y   G/S : Y
Course Distance C'ship: 5,607m
Ladies: 4,777m

MOUNT JULIET GOLF CLUB
No. of holes: 18

Thomastown, Co. Kilkenny.
T: 056-73000
F: 056-73019
E: info@mountjuliet.ie
W: www.mountjuliet.com
Contact Name: Deirdre Brennan
Director of Golf
Captain 2003: Pat Heffernan
Green Fees Weekdays: €140
Weekends: €155
G/C: Y   P/C : Y   G/S : Y
Course Distance C'ship: 6,545m
Ladies: 5,802m

MOUNT OBER GOLF CLUB
No. of holes: 18

24 Ballymanconaghy Road,
Belfast BT8 4SB.
T: 028-90401811 **F:** 028-90705862
E: mtober@ukonline.co.uk
W: www.mountober.com
Contact Name: Don McNamara
Secretary\Manager
Captain 2003: Bob McCrossan
Green Fees Weekdays: Stg £14.50
Weekends: Stg £16.50
G/C: N   P/C : Y   G/S : Y
Course Distance C'ship: 4,953m
Ladies: 4,597m

MOUNT TEMPLE GOLF CLUB
No. of holes: 18

Mount Temple Village, Moate, Co.
Westmeath.
T: 0902-81841
F: 0902-81957
E: mounttemple@tinet.ie
W: www.mounttemplegolfclub.com
Contact Name: Michael Dolan – Director
Captain 2003: Sean Donaghy
Green Fees Weekdays: €30
Weekends: €35
G/C: Y   P/C : Y   G/S : Y
Course Distance C'ship: 5,927m
Ladies: 4,804m

Golf Carts = G/C   **Pull Carts = P/C**   **Golf shop = G/S**

MOUNT WOLSELEY GOLF CLUB
No. of holes: 18

Tullow, Co. Carlow.
T: 059-9151674
F: 059-9152123
E: info@mountwolseley.ie
W: www.mountwolseley.ie
Contact Name: Stephen Anderson
                  Secretary\Manager
Captain 2003: Declan Fogarty
Green Fees   Weekdays: €50
                 Weekends: €70
G/C: N   P/C : Y   G/S : Y
Course Distance C'ship: 6,533m
Ladies: 5,069m

MOUNTAIN VIEW GOLF CLUB
No. of holes: 18

Kiltorcan, Ballyhale, Co. Kilkenny.
T/F: 056-68122
E: info@mviewgolf.com
W: www.mviewgolf.com

Contact Name: Daneil O'Neill
                  Managing Director
Captain 2003: Jimmy Fitzpatrick
Green Fees   Weekdays: €20
                 Weekends: €25
G/C: Y   P/C : Y   G/S : Y
Course Distance C'ship: 5,425m
Ladies: 4,695m

MOUNTBELLEW GOLF CLUB
No. of holes: 9

Shankill, Mountbellew, Ballinasloe,
Co. Galway.
T: 0905-79274
F: 0905-79725

Contact Name: Michael Dolan
                  Secretary\Manager
Captain 2003: Des Cheeves
Green Fees   Weekdays: €15
                 Weekends: €15
G/C: N   P/C : Y   G/S : Y
Course Distance C'ship: 5,214m
Ladies: 4,469m

MOUNTRATH GOLF CLUB
No. of holes: 18

Knockinina, Mountrath, Co. Laois.
T: 0502-32643
F: 0502-56735

Contact Name: Dinah Kingsley
                  Secretary\Manager
Captain 2003: Liam Fitzpatrick
Green Fees   Weekdays: €20
                 Weekends: €20
G/C: Y   P/C : Y   G/S : Y
Course Distance C'ship: 5,643m
Ladies: 4,944m

MOURNE GOLF CLUB
No. of holes: 36

36 Golf Links Road, Newcastle,
Co. Down BT33 0AN.
T: 028-43723314   **F:** 028-43723847
E: secretary@mournegcfreeservice.co.uk
W: www.mournegc.freeserve.co.uk
Contact Name: Eleanor Walsh
                  Secretary\Manager
Captain 2003: Raymond Small
Green Fees   Weekdays: Stg £95
                 Weekends: Stg £105
G/C: N   P/C : Y   G/S : Y
Course Distance C'ship: 6,460m
Ladies: 5,660m

MOYOLA PARK GOLF CLUB
No. of holes: 18

15 Curran Road, Castledawson
BT45 8DG, Derry.
T: 028-79468468
F: 028-79468626

Contact Name: Tony McGuire
                  Secretary\Manager
Captain 2003: Charlie Murphy
Green Fees   Weekdays: Stg £20
                 Weekends: Stg £30
G/C: Y   P/C : Y   G/S : Y
Course Distance C'ship: 5,926m
Ladies: 5,144m

Golf Carts = G/C   Pull Carts = P/C   Golf shop = G/S

MULLINGAR GOLF CLUB
No. of holes: 18

Belvedere, Mulligar, Co. Westmeath.
T: 044-48366
F: 044-41499
E: mullingargolfclub@hotmail.com

Contact Name: Ann Scully
Secretary\Manager
Captain 2003: Colm Maguire
Green Fees Weekdays: €32
Weekends: €40
G/C: Y   P/C : Y   G/S : Y
Course Distance C'ship: 5,913m
Ladies: 4,991m

MULRANNY GOLF CLUB
No. of holes: 9

Mulranny, Co. Mayo.
T: 098-36262

Contact Name: Ciaran Moran
Secretary\Manager
Captain 2003: Tom Gallagher
Green Fees Weekdays: €15
Weekends: €20
G/C: Y   P/C : Y   G/S : Y
Course Distance C'ship: 5,810m
Ladies: 4,368m

MUSKERRY GOLF CLUB
No. of holes: 18

Carrigrohane, Co. Cork.

T: 021-4385297
F: 021-4516860

Contact Name: Hugo Gallagher
Secretary\Manager
Captain 2003: Feidhlim O'Suilleabhain
Green Fees Weekdays: €35
Weekends: €40
G/C: Y   P/C : Y   G/S : Y
Course Distance C'ship: 5,786m
Ladies: 4,972m

NAAS GOLF CLUB
No. of holes: 18

Kerdiffstown, Naas, Co. Kildare.
T: 045-897509
F: 045-896019
E: naasgolfclub@eircom.net
W: www.naasgolfclub.ie
Contact Name: Denis Mullins
Hon\Secretary
Captain 2003: Johnny O'Brien
Green Fees Weekdays: €27
Weekends: €35
G/C: Y   P/C : Y   G/S : Y
Course Distance C'ship: 5,700m
Ladies: 5,180m

NARIN & PORTNOO GOLF CLUB
No. of holes: 18

Narin Portnoo, Co. Donegal.
T/F: 075-45107
E: narinportnoo@eircom.net

Contact Name: Sean Murphy - Manager
Captain 2003: Harry Reid
Green Fees Weekdays: €26
Weekends: €32
G/C: Y   P/C : Y   G/S : Y
Course Distance C'ship: 5,396m
Ladies: 5,249m

NAVAN GOLF CLUB
No. of holes: 18

Proudstown Road, Navan, Co. Meath.
T: 046-72888
F: 046-76722
E: francis@navangolfclub.ie
W: www.navangolfclub.ie
Contact Name: Francis Duffy
Secretary\Manager
Captain 2003: Donal Geraghty
Green Fees Weekdays: €25
Weekends: €30
G/C: Y   P/C : Y   G/S : Y
Course Distance C'ship: 6,132m
Ladies: 5,138m

Golf Carts = G/C   Pull Carts = P/C   Golf shop = G/S

NENAGH GOLF CLUB
No. of holes: 18

Beechwood, Nenagh, Co. Tipperary.
T: 067-31476
F: 067-34808
E: nenaghgolfclub@eircom.net
W: www.nenaghgolfclub.com
Contact Name: Tony Prendergast
Hon\Secretary
Captain 2003: Noel Cleary
Green Fees Weekdays: €30
Weekends: €30
G/C: Y   P/C : Y   G/S : Y
Course Distance C'ship: 6,009m
Ladies: 5,110m

NEW ROSS GOLF CLUB
No. of holes: 18

Tinneranny, New Ross, Co. Wexford.
T: 051-421433
F: 051-420098
E: golfnewross@eircom.net

Contact Name: Kathleen Daly
Secretary\Manager
Captain 2003: John Moran
Green Fees Weekdays: €20
Weekends: €30
G/C: N   P/C : Y   G/S : N
Course Distance C'ship: 5,751m
Ladies: 5,167m

NEWBRIDGE GOLF CLUB
No. of holes: 18

Tankardsgarden, Newbridge, Co. Kildare.
T: 045-486110
W: www.newbridgegolfclub.com

Contact Name: Jamie Stafford
Secretary\Manager
Captain 2003: Ray Kenny
Green Fees Weekdays: €19
Weekends: €25
G/C: Y   P/C : Y   G/S : N
Course Distance C'ship: 5,960m
Ladies: 4,534m

NEWCASTLEWEST GOLF CLUB
No. of holes: 18

Ardagh, Co. Limerick.
T: 069-76500
F: 069-76511
E: ncw@eircom.net

Contact Name: Eamonn Cregan
Secretary\Manager
Captain 2003: Joe White
Green Fees Weekdays: €30
Weekends: €35
G/C: N   P/C : Y   G/S : Y
Course Distance C'ship: 5,858m
Ladies: 4,395m

NEWLANDS GOLF CLUB
No. of holes: 18

Clondalkin, Dublin 22.
T: 01-4593157
F: 01-4593498

Contact Name: Tony O'Neill
Secretary\Manager
Captain 2003: Des Binley
Green Fees Weekdays: €55
Weekends: €55
G/C: Y   P/C : Y   G/S : Y
Course Distance C'ship: 5,897m
Ladies: 5,095m

NEWTOWNSTEWART GOLF CLUB
No. of holes: 18

38 Golf Course Road, Newtownstewart,
Omagh, Co. Tyrone BT78 4HU.
T: 028-81661466
F: 028-81662506
E: newtown.stewart@lineout.net
Contact Name: Diane Cooke
Secretary\Manager
Captain 2003: Tom Graham
Green Fees Weekdays: Stg £12
Weekends: Stg £17
G/C: N   P/C : Y   G/S : Y
Course Distance C'ship: 5,341m
Ladies: 4,603m

Golf Carts = G/C   Pull Carts = P/C   Golf shop = G/S

NORTH WEST GOLF CLUB
No. of holes: 18

Lisfannon, Fahan, Co. Donegal.
T: 077-61027
F: 077-63284
E: nwgc@tinet.ie

Contact Name: Dudley Coyle
Secretary\Manager
Captain 2003: Sean Gleeson
Green Fees Weekdays: €25
Weekends: €30
G/C: N   P/C : Y   G/S : Y
Course Distance C'ship: 5,759m
Ladies: 4,982m

NUREMORE GOLF CLUB
No. of holes: 18

Carrickmacross, Co. Monaghan.
T: 042-9664016
F: 042-9661853
E: nuremore@eircom.net
W: www.nuremore.com
Contact Name: Maurice Cassidy
Professional
Captain 2003: Charles Dolan
Green Fees Weekdays: €33
Weekends: €40
G/C: Y   P/C : Y   G/S : Y
Course Distance C'ship: 5,870m
Ladies: 4,690m

OLD CONNA GOLF CLUB
No. of holes: 18

Ferndale, Bray, Co. Wicklow.
T: 01-2826055
F: 01-2825611
E: info@oldconna.com
W: www.oldconna.com
Contact Name: Tom Sheridan
General Manager
Captain 2003: Michael Kilkenny
Green Fees Weekdays: €45
Weekends: €60
G/C: Y   P/C : Y   G/S : Y
Course Distance C'ship: 6,553m
Ladies: 5,473m

OLD HEAD GOLF LINKS
No. of holes: 18

Old Head of Kinsale, Kinsale, Co. Cork.
T: 021-4778444
F: 021-4778022
E: info@oldheadgolflinks.com
W: www.oldheadgolflinks.com

Contact Name: Jim O'Brien
General Manager
Green Fees Weekdays: €250
Weekends: €250
G/C: Y   P/C : N   G/S : N
Course Distance C'ship: 6,559m
Ladies: 4,665m

OMAGH GOLF CLUB
No. of holes: 18

83a Dublin Road, Omagh
Co. Tyrone BT78 1HQ.
T: 028-82241442
F: 028-82243160
E: omaghgolfclub@tiscali.co.uk
Contact Name: Joseph A. McElholm
Hon\Secretary
Captain 2003: Gerard Harte
Green Fees Weekdays: Stg £15
Weekends: Stg £20
G/C: N   P/C : Y   G/S : N
Course Distance C'ship: 5,650m
Ladies: 4,749m

ORMEAU GOLF CLUB
No. of holes: 18

50 Park Road, Belfast BT7 2FX.
T: 028-90640700
F: 028-90646250
E: ormeaugolfclub@utvinternet.com
W: www.ormeaugolfclub.co.uk

Contact Name: R. Barnes – Hon\Secretary
Captain 2003: Steve Martin
Green Fees Weekdays: Stg £14
Weekends: Stg £16.50
G/C: N   P/C : Y   G/S : N
Course Distance C'ship: 5,400m
Ladies: 5,100m

Golf Carts = G/C   Pull Carts = P/C   Golf shop = G/S

OTWAY GOLF CLUB
No. of holes: 9

Saltpans, Rathmullan, Co. Donegal.
T: 074-9158319
E: gmgivern@ntworld.com

Contact Name: Gerry McGivern
Secretary\Manager
Captain 2003: Gerry Gallagher
Green Fees Weekdays: €15
Weekends: €15
G/C: N   P/C : Y   G/S : N
Course Distance C'ship: 4,234m
Ladies: 3,350m

OUGHTERARD GOLF CLUB
No. of holes: 18

Gortreevagh, Oughterard, Co. Galway.
T: 091-552131
F: 091-552733
E: oughterardgc@eircom.net

Contact Name: John Waters
Secretary\Manager
Captain 2003: Denis O'Connor
Green Fees Weekdays: €30
Weekends: €30
G/C: Y   P/C : Y   G/S : Y
Course Distance C'ship: 5,876m
Ladies: 4,857m

PARKNASILLA GOLF CLUB
No. of holes: 12

Sneem, Co. Kerry.
T: 064-45122

Contact Name: Maurice Walsh
Secretary\Manager
Captain 2003: Michael Kinsella
Green Fees Weekdays: €30
Weekends: N\A
G/C: N   P/C : Y   G/S : N
Course Distance C'ship: 5,284m
Ladies: 4,792m

PORTADOWN GOLF CLUB
No. of holes: 18

192 Gilford Road, Portadown, Co. Armagh
BT63 5LF.
T: 028-38355356
F: 028-38392214

Contact Name: Lillie Holloway
Secretary\Manager
Captain 2003: William Nixon
Green Fees Weekdays: Stg £18
Weekends: Stg £23
G/C: N   P/C : Y   G/S : Y
Course Distance C'ship: 6,130m
Ladies: 5,618m

PORTARLINGTON GOLF CLUB
No. of holes: 18

Garryhinch, Portarlington, Co. Laois.
T: 0502-23115
F: 0502-23044
E: portarlingtongc@eircom.net
W: www.portarlingtongolf.com
Contact Name: Jim Cannon
Secretary\Manager
Captain 2003: PJ Dempsey
Green Fees Weekdays: €20
Weekends: €25
G/C: N   P/C : Y   G/S : Y
Course Distance C'ship: 5,906m
Ladies: 5,152m

PORTMARNOCK HOTEL & GOLF CLUB
No. of holes: 18

Starnd Road, Portmarnock, Co. Dublin.
T: 01-8461800
F: 01-8461077
E: golfres@portmarnock.com
W: www.portmarnock.com

Contact: Reservations
Green Fees Weekdays: €110
Weekends: €110
G/C: Y   P/C : Y   G/S : Y
Course Distance C'ship: 6,255m
Ladies: 5,051m

Golf Carts = G/C   **Pull Carts = P/C**   **Golf shop = G/S**

PORTMARNOCK GOLF CLUB
No. of holes: 27

Portmarnock, Co. Dublin.
T: 01-8462968
F: 01-8462601
E: secretary@portmarnockgolfclub.ie
W: www.portmarnockgolfclub.ie
Contact Name: John Quigley
                 Secretary\Manager
Captain 2003: Bruce Mitchell
Green Fees Weekdays: €165
              Weekends: €190
G/C: N   P/C: Y   G/S: Y
Course Distance C'ship: 6,656m
Ladies: 5,304m

PORTSALON GOLF CLUB
No. of holes: 18

Portsalon, Fanad, Co. Donegal.
T: 074-9159459
F: 074-9159919
E: portsalongolfclub@eircom.net
Contact Name: Peter Doherty
                 Secretary\Manager
Captain 2003: Jack Barrett
Green Fees Weekdays: €30
              Weekends: €35
G/C: Y   P/C: Y   G/S: Y
Course Distance C'ship: 6,185m
Ladies: 5,185m

PORTSTEWART GOLF CLUB
No. of holes: 45

Strand Head, Portstewart, Co. Londonderry.
T: 028-70832601
F: 028-70832015
E: bill@portstewartgc.co.uk
W: www.portstewartgc.co.uk
Contact Name: Michael Moss
                 Secretary\Manager
Captain 2003: Adrian Wreath
Green Fees Weekdays: Stg £60
              Weekends: Stg £80
G/C: Y   P/C: Y   G/S: Y
Course Distance C'ship: 6,172m
Ladies: 5,319m

PORTUMNA GOLF CLUB
No. of holes: 18

Ennis Road, Portumna, Co. Galway.
T: 0509-41059
F: 0509-4178
E: portumnagc@eircom.net
Contact Name: John Harte
                 Hon\Secretary
Captain 2003: Gene Claffey
Green Fees Weekdays: €30
              Weekends: €30
G/C: Y   P/C: Y   G/S: Y
Course Distance C'ship: 6,222m
Ladies: 5,415m

POWERSCOURT GOLF CLUB
No. of holes: 18

Enniskerry, Co. Wicklow.
T: 01-2046033
F: 01-2761303
E: golfclub@powerscourt.ie
W: www.powerscourt.ie
Contact Name: Bernard Gibbons
                 Manager
Captain 2003: Marcus Magner
Green Fees Weekdays: €100
              Weekends: €100
G/C: Y   P/C: Y   G/S: Y
Course Distance C'ship: 6,241m
Ladies: 5,349m

RAFFEEN CREEK GOLF CLUB
No. of holes: 9

Ringaskiddy, Co. Cork.
T: 021-4378430
Contact Name: Frank Wiley
                 Hon\Secretary
Captain 2003: Michael O'Brien
Green Fees Weekdays: €22
              Weekends: €27
G/C: N   P/C: Y   G/S: N
Course Distance C'ship: 5,146m
Ladies: 4,412m

Golf Carts = G/C   Pull Carts = P/C   Golf shop = G/S

RATHBANE GOLF CLUB
No. of holes: 18

Rathbane, Crossagalla, Limerick.
T/F: 061-313655
E: info@rathbanegolf.com
W: www.rathbanegolf.com

Contact Name: John O'Sullivan
Secretary\Manager
Captain 2003: Leonard Fitzgerald
Green Fees Weekdays: €17
Weekends: €20
G/C: N   P/C : Y   G/S : N
Course Distance C'ship: 5,671m
Ladies: 4,933m

RATHDOWNEY GOLF CLUB
No. of holes: 18

Coolnaboul West, Rathdowney, Co. Laois.
T: 0506-46170
F: 0506-46065
E: rathdowneygolf@eircom.net

Contact Name: Myles Munro
Secretary\Manager
Captain 2003: Christy Jones
Green Fees Weekdays: €20
Weekends: €25
G/C: N   P/C : Y   G/S : Y
Course Distance C'ship: 5,864m
Ladies: 5,139m

RATHFARNHAM GOLF CLUB
No. of holes: 18

Newtown, Rathfarnham, Dublin 16.
T: 01-4931201
F: 01-4931561
E: rgc@oceanfree.net

Contact Name: Colin McInerney
Secretary\Manager
Captain 2003: Alan Cole
Green Fees Weekdays: €38
Weekends: €48
G/C: N   P/C : Y   G/S : Y
Course Distance C'ship: 5,4242m
Ladies: 4,863m

RATHMORE GOLF CLUB
No. of holes: 18

Bushmills Road, Portrush,
Co. Antrim BT56 8JG.
T/F: 028-70822996
E: dwilliamson555@btconnect.com

Contact Name: Derek Williamson
Secretary\Manager
Captain 2003: Jackson Taggart
Green Fees Weekdays: £30
Weekends: £35
Golf Carts: Y   Pull Carts: Y Golf shop: N
Course Distance C'ship: 5,864m
Ladies: 5,057m

RATHSALLAGH GOLF CLUB
No. of holes: 18

Dunlavin, Co. Wicklow.
T: 045-403316
F: 045-403295
E: info@rathsallagh.com
W: www.rathsallagh.com

Contact Name: Joe O'Flynn - CEO
Captain 2003: Paul Mullen
Green Fees Weekdays: €60
Weekends: €75
G/C: Y   P/C : Y   G/S : Y
Course Distance C'ship: 6,259m
Ladies: 4,985m

REDCASTLE GOLF CLUB
No. of holes: 18

Redcastle Hotel, Redcastle, Co. Donegal.
T: 077-82073
F: 077-82214
E: redcastle.hotel@oceanfree.net

Contact Name: Mark Wilson
Secretary\Manager
Captain 2003: C. Donnelly
Green Fees Weekdays: €18
Weekends: €22
G/C: N   P/C : Y   G/S : Y
Course Distance C'ship: 5,593m
Ladies: 4,705m

Golf Carts = G/C   Pull Carts = P/C   Golf shop = G/S

RING OF KERRY GOLF CLUB
No. of holes: 18

Templenoe, Kenmare, Co. Kerry.
T: 064-42000
F: 064-42533
E: reservations@ringofkerrygolf.com
W: www.ringofkerrygolf.com
Contact Name: Ed Edwards
Golf Manager
Captain 2003: Brendan Breslin
Green Fees Weekdays: €70
Weekends: €70
G/C: Y   P/C : Y   G/S : Y
Course Distance C'ship: 6,245m
Ladies: 4,960m

RINGDUFFERIN GOLF CLUB
No. of holes: 18

36 Ringdufferin Road, Toye, Downpatrick,
Co. Down BT30 9PH.
T: 028-44828812

Contact Name: Mike Dallas
Secretary\Manager
Captain 2003: Darren Tate
Green Fees Weekdays: Stg £10
Weekends: Stg £12
G/C: N   P/C : Y   G/S : Y
Course Distance C'ship: 4,648m
Ladies: 4,437m

ROCKMOUNT GOLF CLUB
No. of holes: 18

28 Drumalig Road, Carryduff, Belfast BT8
8EQ.
T: 028-90812279
F: 028-90815851
E: info@rockmountgolfclub.co.uk
W: www.rockmountgolfclub.co.uk
Contact Name: Diane Patterson - Director
Captain 2003: Jack Bloomer
Green Fees Weekdays: Stg £21
Weekends: Stg £25
G/C: Y   P/C : Y   G/S : Y
Course Distance C'ship: 5,827m
Ladies: 5,022m

ROE PARK GOLF CLUB
No. of holes: 18

Radisson Roe Park Hotel, Limavady,
Co. Derry BT49 9LB.
T: 028-77760105 **F:** 028-77722313
E: golf@radissonroepark.com
W: www.radissonroepark.com
Contact Name: Don Brockerton
Secretary\Manager
Captain 2003: Phil Hendrick
Green Fees Weekdays: Stg £20
Weekends: Stg £25
G/C: Y   P/C : Y   G/S : Y
Course Distance C'ship: 5,749m
Ladies: 4,576m

ROGANSTOWN GOLF & COUNTRY CLUB
No. of holes: 18

Roganstown, Swords, Co. Dublin.
T: 01-8433118
E: info@roganstown.com
W: www.roganstown.com

Contact Name: Ian McGuinness
Director of Golf
Green Fees Weekdays: Opening 2004
Weekends: Opening 2004
G/C: Y   P/C : Y   G/S : Y
Course Distance C'ship: 6,364m

ROSAPENNA GOLF CLUB
No. of holes: 27

Downings, Co. Donegal.
T: 074-55301
F: 074-55128

Contact Name: John Sweeney
Hon\Secretary
Captain 2003: Fr. Charlie Byrne
Green Fees Weekdays: €40
Weekends: €45
G/C: N   P/C : Y   G/S : Y
Course Distance C'ship: 5,734m
Ladies: 5,061m

ROSCOMMON GOLF CLUB
No. of holes: 18

Mote Park, Roscommon.
T: 0903-26382
F: 0903-26043
E: rosgolfclub@eircom.net

Contact Name: Noreen O'Grady
Hon\Secretary
Captain 2003: Gerry O'Dowd
Green Fees   Weekdays: €20
Weekends: €25
G/C: Y   P/C : Y   G/S : Y
Course Distance C'ship: 6,059m
Ladies: 5,045m

ROSCREA GOLF CLUB
No. of holes: 18

Derryvale, Roscrea, Co. Tipperary.
T: 0505-21130
F: 0505-23410
E: roscreagolfclub@eircom.net

Contact Name: Steve Crofton
Hon\Secretary
Captain 2003: John Ryan
Green Fees   Weekdays: €20
Weekends: €25
G/C: Y   P/C : Y   G/S : Y
Course Distance C'ship: 5,782m
Ladies: 4,841m

ROSS GOLF CLUB
No. of holes: 9

Ross Road, Killarney, Co. Kerry.
T: 064-31125
F: 064-31860
E: info@rossgolfclub.com
W: www.rossgolfclub.com
Contact Name: Alan O'Meara
Professional
Captain 2003: Mossie Cremin
Green Fees   Weekdays: €25
Weekends: €25
G/C: N   P/C : Y   G/S : Y
Course Distance C'ship: 3,225m
Ladies: 2,642m

ROSSLARE GOLF CLUB
No. of holes: 18

Rosslare Strand, Co. Wexford.
T: 053-32203
F: 053-32263
E: office@rosslaregolf.com
W: www.rosslaregolf.com

Contact Name: J.F. Hall - Manager
Captain 2003: Dr. Paddy MacKiernan
Green Fees   Weekdays: €35
Weekends: €50
G/C: Y   P/C : Y   G/S : Y
Course Distance C'ship: 6,165m
Ladies: 5,145m

ROSSMORE GOLF CLUB
No. of holes: 18

Cootehill, Monaghan.
T: 047-81316

Contact Name: Jimmy McKenna
Secretary\Manager
Captain 2003: Vincent Lee
Green Fees   Weekdays: €25
Weekends: €32
G/C: N   P/C : Y   G/S : Y
Course Distance C'ship: 5,590m
Ladies: 4,677m

ROUNDWOOD GOLF CLUB
No. of holes: 18

Ballinahinch, Newtownmountkennedy,
Co. Wicklow.
T: :01-2818488
F: 01-2843642
E: rwood@indigo.ie
W: www.roundwoodgolf.com
Contact Name: Angela Brady Administrator
Captain 2003: Barry O'Keeffe
Green Fees   Weekdays: €35
Weekends: €50
G/C: Y   P/C : Y   G/S : Y
Course Distance C'ship: 6,035m
Ladies: 4,916m

Golf Carts = G/C   Pull Carts = P/C   Golf shop = G/S

ROYAL DUBLIN GOLF CLUB
No. of holes: 18

North Bull Island, Dollymount, Dublin 3.
T: 01-8336346
F: 01-8336504
E: info@theroyaldublingolfclub.com
W: www.theroyaldublingolfclub.com
Contact Name: John Lambe
                Secretary\Manager
Captain 2003: Bill Wallace
Green Fees   Weekdays: €100
                Weekends: €115
G/C: Y   P/C : Y   G/S : Y
Course Distance C'ship: 6,309m
Ladies: 5,432m

ROYAL BELFAST GOLF CLUB
No. of holes: 18

Station Road, Craigavad, Holywood,
Co.Down BT18 0BP.
T: 028-90428165   **F:** 028-90421404
E: royalbelfastgc@btclick.com
W: www.royalbelfast.com
Contact Name: Susanna Morrison
                Secretary\Manager
Captain 2003: T.A. Burgess
Green Fees   Weekdays: Stg £40
                Weekends: Stg £50
G/C: Y   P/C : Y   G/S : Y
Course Distance C'ship: 5,733m
Ladies: 5,036m

ROYAL COUNTY DOWN GOLF CLUB
No. of holes: 36

Newcastle, Co. Down BT33 0AN.
T: 028-43723314
F: 028-43726281
E: golf@royalcountydown.org
W: www.royalcountydown.org

Contact Name: J.H. Laibler
                Secretary\Manager
Green Fees   Weekdays: Stg £95
                Weekends: Stg £105
G/C: N   P/C : Y   G/S : Y
Course Distance C'ship: 6,460m
Ladies: 5,660m

ROYAL PORTRUSH GOLF CLUB
No. of holes: 45

Dunluce Road, Portrush,
Co. Antrim BT56 8JQ.
T: 028-70822311
F: 028-70823139
E: rpgc@dnet.co.uk
W: www.royalportrushgolfclub.com
Contact Name: F.J. Trufelli
                Hon\Secretary
Captain 2003: Ian Bamford
Green Fees   Weekdays: £85
                Weekends: £95
G/C: Y   P/C : Y   G/S : Y
Course Distance C'ship: 6,137m

ROYAL TARA GOLF CLUB
No. of holes: 18

Bellinter, Navan, Co. Meath.
T/F: 046-25508
E: info@royaltaragolfclub.com
W: www.royaltaragolfclub.com

Contact Name: Larry Clarke
                General Manager
Captain 2003: Jim Banan
Green Fees   Weekdays: €35
                Weekends: €45
G/C: Y   P/C : Y   G/S : Y
Course Distance C'ship: 5,904m
Ladies: 4,939m

RUSH GOLF CLUB
No. of holes: 18

Rush, Co. Dublin.
T/F: 01-8438177
E: info@rushgolfclub.com
W: www.rushgolfclub.com

Contact Name: Noeline Quirke
                Secretary\Manager
Captain 2003: Gerry Masterson
Green Fees   Weekdays: €32
                Weekends: N\A
G/C: N   P/C : Y   G/S : Y
Course Distance C'ship: 5,639m
Ladies: 4,662m

Golf Carts = G/C   Pull Carts = P/C   Golf shop = G/S

SCRABO GOLF CLUB
No. of holes: 18

233 Scrabo Road, Newtownards, Co. Down BT23 4SL.
T: 028-91812355 **F:** 028-91822919
E: scrabogc@compuserve.com
W: www.scrabo-golf-club.org
Contact Name: Christine Hamill
Secretary\Manager
Captain 2003: John Hiles
Green Fees Weekdays: Stg £18
Weekends: Stg £23
G/C: N   P/C : Y   G/S : Y
Course Distance C'ship: 5,6601m
Ladies: 4,792m

SEAFIELD GOLF & COUNTRY CLUB
No. of holes: 18

Ballymoney, Gorey, Co. Wexford.
T: 055-24777
F: 055-24837
E: info@seafieldgolf.com
W: www.seafieldgolf.com
Contact Name: Darragh O'Neill
Secretary\Manager
Captain 2003: Peter O'Reilly
Green Fees Weekdays: €85
Weekends: €95
G/C: Y   P/C : Y   G/S : Y
Course Distance C'ship: 5,861m
Ladies: 4,680m

SEAPOINT GOLF CLUB
No. of holes: 18

Termonfeckin, Co. Louth.
T: 041-9822333
F: 041-9822331
E: golflinks@seapoint.ie
W: www.seapointgolfclub.com
Contact Name: Kevin Carrie
Secretary\Manager
Captain 2003: Charlie Brodigan
Green Fees Weekdays: €40
Weekends: €60
G/C: Y   P/C : Y   G/S : Y
Course Distance C'ship: 6,420m
Ladies: 5,119m

SHANDON PARK GOLF CLUB
No. of holes: 18

73 Shandon Park, Belfast BT5 6NY.
T: 028-90805030
F: 028-90805999

Contact Name: David Jenkins
Secretary\Manager
Captain 2003: Peter Young
Green Fees Weekdays: Stg £28
Weekends: Stg £37
G/C: Y   P/C : Y   G/S : Y
Course Distance C'ship: 5,727m
Ladies: 5,182m

SHANNON GOLF CLUB
No. of holes: 18

Shannon, Co. Clare.
T: 061-471849
F: 061-471507
E: shannongolfclub@eircom.net
W: www.shannongolf.com
Contact Name: Michael Corry
General Manager
Captain 2003: Oliver Doherty
Green Fees Weekdays: €35
Weekends: €45
G/C: Y   P/C : Y   G/S : Y
Course Distance C'ship: 6,184m
Ladies: 5,163m

SILVERWOOD GOLF CLUB
No. of holes: 18

Turmoyra Lane, Silverwood, Lurgan, Co. Armagh BT66 6NG.
T: 028-38326606
F: 028-38347272

Contact Name: Kieran Devlin
Hon\Secretary
Captain 2003: Eamon Nelson
Green Fees Weekdays: Stg £15
Weekends: Stg £17.50
G/C: N   P/C : Y   G/S : N
Course Distance C'ship: 5,912m
Ladies: 5,642m

Golf Carts = G/C   Pull Carts = P/C   Golf shop = G/S

SKERRIES GOLF CLUB
No. of holes: 18

Hacketstown, Skerris, Co. Dublin.
T: 01-8491567
F: 01-8491591
E: skerriesgolfclub@eircom.net
W: www.skerriesgolfclub.ie

Contact Name: Aiden Burns – Manager
Captain 2003: Peter Galligan
Green Fees Weekdays: €60
Weekends: €55
G/C: N   P/C : Y   G/S : Y
Course Distance C'ship: 6,107m
Ladies: 5,301m

SKIBBEREEN GOLF CLUB
No. of holes: 18

Licknavar, Skibbereen, Co. Cork.
T: 028-21227
F: 028-22994
E: bookings@skibgolf.com
W: www.skibgolf.com

Contact Name: Seamus Brett
Secretary\Manager
Captain 2003: Christy O'Donovan
Green Fees Weekdays: €35
Weekends: €35
G/C: Y   P/C : Y   G/S : N
Course Distance C'ship: 5,425m
Ladies: 4,614m

SLADE VALLEY GOLF CLUB
No. of holes: 18

Lynch Park, Brittas, Co.Dublin.
T: 01-4582183
F: 01-4582784
E: sladevalley@eircom.net

Contact Name: Dermot Clancy
Secretary\Manager
Captain 2003: Sean Farrell
Green Fees Weekdays: €30
Weekends: €40
G/C: Y   P/C : Y   G/S : Y
Course Distance C'ship: 5,457m
Ladies: 4,883m

SLIEVE RUSSELL GOLF CLUB
No. of holes: 18

Ballyconnell, Co. Cavan.
T: 049-9525093
F: 049-9526640
E: slieve-golf-club@quinn-hotels.com

Contact Name: Aine McCluskey
Administrator
Captain 2003: Packie McKiernan
Green Fees Weekdays: €55
Weekends: €70
G/C: Y   P/C : Y   G/S : Y
Course Distance C'ship: 6,055m
Ladies: 5,164m

SLIEVENAMON GOLF CLUB
No. of holes: 18

Clonacody, Lisronagh, Clonmel,
Co.Tipperary.
T: 052-32213   **F:** 052-30875
E: info@slievenamongolfclub.com
W: www.slievenamongolfclub.com
Contact Name: Brendan Kenny
Secretary\Manager
Captain 2003: Des Delahunty
Green Fees Weekdays: €10
Weekends: €15
G/C: N   P/C : Y   G/S : Y
Course Distance C'ship: 5,000m
Ladies: 4,800m

SOUTH COUNTY GOLF CLUB
No. of holes: 18

Lisheen Road, Brittas, Co. Dublin.
T: 01-4582965
F: 01-4582842
E: info@southcountygolf.ie
W: www.southcountygolf.ie
Contact Name: Joe O'Connor
Secretary\Manager
Captain 2003: Stuart Walker
Green Fees Weekdays: €65
Weekends: N\A
G/C: Y   P/C : Y   G/S : Y
Course Distance C'ship: 6,370m
Ladies: 5,812m

Golf Carts = G/C   Pull Carts = P/C   Golf shop = G/S

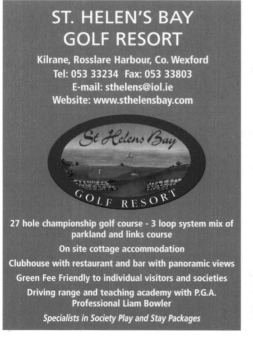

SOUTH MEATH GOLF CLUB
No. of holes: 9

Longwood, Trim, Co. Meath.
T: 046-31471

Contact Name: Brendan Breen
Hon\Secretary
Captain 2003: Terry Farrell
Green Fees Weekdays: €12
Weekends: €15
G/C: Y   P/C : Y   G/S : N
Course Distance C'ship: 5.312m
Ladies: 4,485m

SPA GOLF CLUB
No. of holes: 18

20 Grove Road, Ballynahinch BT24 8PN,
Down.
T: 028-97562365
F: 028-97564158
E: spagolfclub@btconnect.com
Contact Name: Terry Magee
Secretary\Manager
Captain 2003: Gordon Fitzpatrick
Green Fees Weekdays: Stg £16
Weekends: Stg £20
G/C: N   P/C : Y   G/S : N
Course Distance C'ship: 5,881m
Ladies: 4,883m

SPANISH POINT GOLF CLUB
No. of holes: 9

Spanish Point, Milltown Malbay, Co. Clare.
T: 065-7084196
E: info@spanish-point.com
W: www.spanish-point.com

Contact Name: David K. Fitzgerald
Secretary\Manager
Captain 2003: Gerry Talty
Green Fees Weekdays: €25
Weekends: €30
G/C: N   P/C : Y   G/S : N
Course Distance C'ship: 4,678m
Ladies: 3,908m

ST. HELENS BAY GOLF RESORT
No. of holes: 27

St. Helen's Bay, Rosslare Harbour,
Co. Wexford.
T: 053-33234 **F:** 053-33803
E: sthelens@iol.ie
W: www.sthelensbay.com
Contact Name: Barry Brennan
Operations Manager
Captain 2003: Eddie Barrett
Green Fees Weekdays: €38
Weekends: €45
G/C: Y   P/C : Y   G/S : Y
Course Distance C'ship: 6,091m
Ladies: 5,081m

ST. ANNES GOLF CLUB
No. of holes: 18

Bull Island Nature Reserve, North Bull
Island, Dollymount, Dublin 5.
T: 01-8336471 **F:** 01-8334618
E: info@stanneslinksgolf.com
W: www.stannesgolfclub.ie
Contact Name: Shirley Sleator
Secretary\Manager
Captain 2003: Philip Roche
Green Fees Weekdays: €50
Weekends: €70
G/C: Y   P/C : Y   G/S : Y
Course Distance C'ship: 5,669m
Ladies: 4,870m

ST. MARGARET'S GOLF & COUNTRY CLUB
No. of holes: 18

St. Margaret's, Co. Dublin.
T: 01-8640400
F: 01-8640289
E: sales@stmargaretsgolf.com
W: www.stmargaretsgolf.com
Contact Name: Arthur McKenna
Secretary\Manager
Captain 2003: Adrian O'Connell
Green Fees Weekdays: €65
Weekends: €80
G/C: Y   P/C : Y   G/S : Y
Course Distance C'ship: 6,326m
Ladies: 5,195m

Golf Carts = G/C   **Pull Carts = P/C**   **Golf shop = G/S**

STACKSTOWN GOLF CLUB
No. of holes: 18

Kellystown Road, Rathfarnham, Dublin 16.
T: 01-4941993
F: 01-4933934
E: stackstowngc@eircom.net
W: www.stackstowngolfclub.com
Contact Name: Paul Kennedy
Secretary\Manager
Captain 2003: Gerry Mullins
Green Fees Weekdays: €30
Weekends: €38
G/C: N   P/C : Y   G/S : Y
Course Distance C'ship: 5,623m
Ladies: 4,561m

STRABANE GOLF CLUB
No. of holes: 18

33 Ballycolman Road, Strabane,
Co. Tyrone BT82 9PH.
T: 028-71382007
F: 028-71886514
E: strabgc@aol.com
Contact Name: Gerald Glover
Hon\Secretary
Captain 2003: Danny Duffy
Green Fees Weekdays: Stg £15
Weekends: Stg £17
G/C: N   P/C : Y   G/S : N
Course Distance C'ship: 5,610m
Ladies: 4,844m

STRANDHILL GOLF CLUB
No. of holes: 18

Strandhill, Co. Sligo.
T: 071-68188

Contact Name: Sandra Corcoran
Administrator
Captain 2003: Leo Logan
Green Fees Weekdays: €40
Weekends: €50
G/C: Y   P/C : Y   G/S : Y
Course Distance C'ship: 5,675m
Ladies: 5,020m

STROKESTOWN GOLF CLUB
No. of holes: 9

Strokestown, Co. Roscommon.
T: 078-33528
E: silkemartin@eircom.net

Contact Name: Liam Glover
Hon\Secretary
Captain 2003: John Joe Cox
Green Fees Weekdays: €15
Weekends: €15
G/C: N   P/C : Y   G/S : N
Course Distance C'ship: 2,656m
Ladies: 2,293m

SUMMERHILL GOLF CLUB
No. of holes: 9

Agher, Rathmolyon, Co. Meath.
T: 0405-57557

Contact Name: Mark Nagle
Secretary\Manager
Captain 2003: Dennis O'Keeffe
Green Fees Weekdays: €15
Weekends: €20
G/C: N   P/C : Y   G/S : N
Course Distance C'ship: 5,837m
Ladies: 4,546m

SUTTON GOLF CLUB
No. of holes: 18

Cush Point, Sutton, Dublin 13.
T: 01-8322965
F: 01-8321603
E: info@suttongolfclub.com
W: www.suttongolfclub.org
Contact Name: Michael Healy
General Manager
Captain 2003: Colm Moriarty
Green Fees Weekdays: €35
Weekends: €45
G/C: N   P/C : Y   G/S : N
Course Distance C'ship: 5,252m
Ladies: 4,820m

Golf Carts = G/C   Pull Carts = P/C   Golf shop = G/S

SWINFORD GOLF CLUB
No. of holes: 18

Brabazon Park, Swinford, Co. Mayo.
T/F: 094-9251378
E: regantommy@eircom.net

Contact Name: Tom Regan
Hon\Secretary
Captain 2003: Kevin Quinn
Green Fees Weekdays: €15
Weekends: €15
G/C: N   P/C : Y   G/S : Y
Course Distance C'ship: 5,502m
Ladies: 4,462m

SWORDS GOLF CLUB
No. of holes: 18

Balheary Avenue, Swords, Co. Dublin.
T/F: 01-8409819
E: swordsgc@indigo.ie
W: www.swordsopengolfcourse.com

Contact Name: Orla McGuinness
Secretary\Manager
Captain 2003: Fintan Murray
Green Fees Weekdays: €15
Weekends: €22
G/C: N   P/C : Y   G/S : N
Course Distance C'ship: 5,631m
Ladies: 4,845m

THE EUROPEAN CLUB
No. of holes: 18

Brittas Bay, Co. Wicklow.
T: 0404-47415
F: 0404-47449
E: info@theeuropeanclub.com
W: www.theeuropeanclub.com

Contact Name: Sidon Ruddy - Manager
Captain 2003: Eddie Fallon
Green Fees Weekdays: €100
Weekends: €100
G/C: Y   P/C : Y   G/S : Y
Course Distance C'ship: 6,698m
Ladies: 5,276m

THE HEATH GOLF CLUB
No. of holes: 18

The Heath, Portlaoise, Co. Laois.
T: 0502-46045
F: 0502-46866
E: info@theheathgc.ie
W: www.theheathgc.ie
Contact Name: Christy Crawford
Hon\Secretary
Captain 2003: Michael Brody
Green Fees Weekdays: €16
Weekends: €30
G/C: Y   P/C : Y   G/S : Y
Course Distance C'ship: 6,120m
Ladies: 4,986m

THE HERITAGE GOLF & COUNTRY CLUB
No. of holes: 18

Killenard, Co. Laois.
T: 0502-61700
F: 0502-61704
E: info@theheritagegolf.com
W: www.theheritagegolf.com

Contact Name: Eddie Dunne
General Manager
Green Fees Weekdays: €80
Weekends: €100
G/C: Y   P/C : Y   G/S : Y
Course Distance C'ship: 6,714m
Ladies: 5,501m

THE ISLAND GOLF CLUB
No. of holes: 18

Corballis, Donabate, Co. Dublin.
T: 01-8436205
F: 01-8436860
E: islandgc@iol.ie
W: www.theislandgolfclub.com
Contact Name: Peter McDunphy
General Manager
Captain 2003: Humphrey Kelliher
Green Fees Weekdays: €110
Weekends: N\A
G/C: Y   P/C : Y   G/S : Y
Course Distance C'ship: 6,206m
Ladies: 5,403m

Golf Carts = G/C   Pull Carts = P/C   Golf shop = G/S

THE K CLUB
No. of holes: 18

Straffan, Co. Kildare.
T: 01-6017300
F: 01-6017399
E: golf@kclub.ie
W: www.kclub.ie
Contact Name: Paul Crowe
Director of Golf
Captain 2003: Joseph O'Grady
Green Fees Weekdays: €265
Weekends: €265
G/C: Y   P/C : Y   G/S : Y
Course Distance C'ship: 6,525m
Ladies: 4,963m

THURLES GOLF CLUB
No. of holes: 18

Turtulla, Thurles, Co. Tipperary.
T: 0504-21983
F: 0504-24647

Contact Name: Thomas Ryan
Hon\Secretary
Captain 2003: Eddie Clancy
Green Fees Weekdays: €25
Weekends: €30
G/C: N   P/C : Y   G/S : Y
Course Distance C'ship: 6,465m
Ladies: 5,364m

TANDRAGEE GOLF CLUB
No. of holes: 18

Markethill Road, Tandragee, Co.Armagh
BT62 2ER.
T: 028-38841272 **F:** 028-38840664
E: office@tandragee.co.uk
W: www.tandragee.co.uk
Contact Name: David Clayton
Secretary\Manager
Captain 2003: Tom Johnston
Green Fees Weekdays: Stg £15
Weekends: Stg £20
G/C: Y   P/C : Y   G/S : Y
Course Distance C'ship: 5,365m
Ladies: 4,930m

TARA GLEN GOLF CLUB
No. of holes: 9

Ballymoney, Gorey, Co. Wexford.
T: 055-25413
F: 055-25612

Contact Name: D. Popplewell
Secretary\Manager
Captain 2003: Brian Rogers
Green Fees Weekdays: €22
Weekends: €22
G/C: N   P/C : Y   G/S : N
Course Distance C'ship: 5,790m
Ladies: 4,859m

TEMPLE GOLF CLUB
No. of holes: 9

60 Church Road, Boardmills, Lisburn
BT27 6UP, Down.
T: 028-92639213 Fax: 028-92638637
E: david@templegolf.com

Contact Name: David Kinnear
Secretary\Manager
Captain 2003: Gary Coates
Green Fees Weekdays: Stg £10
Weekends: Stg £14
G/C: Y   P/C : Y   G/S : Y
Course Distance C'ship: 5,451m
Ladies: 5,121m

TEMPLEMORE GOLF CLUB
No. of holes: 18

Manna South, Templemore, Co. Tipperary.
T: 0504-32502

Contact Name: John Hackett
Hon\Secretary
Captain 2003: Denis Tuohy
Green Fees Weekdays: €15
Weekends: €20
G/C: N   P/C : Y   G/S : Y
Course Distance C'ship: 5,443m
Ladies: 4,541m

Golf Carts = G/C   Pull Carts = P/C   Golf shop = G/S

EXECUTIVE GOLF & LEISURE PLATINUM CLUB

Can you afford to miss out on "All-Year-Round" reductions at over 350 venues throughout Ireland including restaurants, hotels and golf courses?

PLATINUM CLUB MEMBER PRIVILIGES INCLUDE:

- 20% reduction for cardholder and up to three playing partners at more than 100 of Ireland's leading golf courses.
- Between 20% and 25% reduction for cardholder and three guests at up to 130 leading restaurants nationwide.
- Up to 50% discount at over 100, three, four and five star hotels nationwide and 5,000 worldwide.

In addition to the above main benefits members also receive a selection of vouchers for exclusive member packages at some of the world's leading golf resorts including: -

- The K-Club
  venue for the Ryder Cup 2006.
- The Belfry
  venue for the Ryder Cup 2003.
- St. Andrews
  venue for the British Open on many occasions.
- Glen Eagles
  host to the WPGA Championship of Europe.

Executive Golf and Leisure Platinum Club Membership is the perfect corporate gift for all occasions.

For further information on individual or corporate membership telephone 061-306200 or email egl@eircom.net.

Executive Golf & Leisure, Unit 1, Ballycummin Village, Raheen, Limerick
T: +353 61 306200
F: +353 61 306215
E: egl@eircom.net
Executive Golf & Leisure and **The Essential Golfers Guide** are part of the Vista Marketing Group.

EXECUTIVE GOLF & LEISURE PLATINUM CLUB CARD... THE ULTIMATE ACCESSORY FOR THE SERIOUS GOLFER

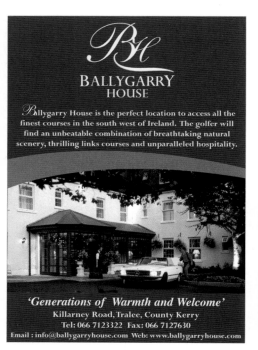

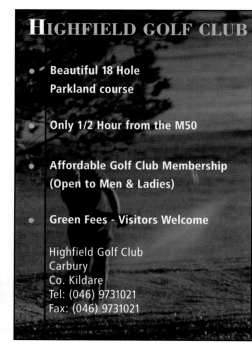

TIPPERARY GOLF CLUB
No. of holes: 18

Rathanny, Tipperary.
T: 062-51119
F: 062-52132
E: tipperarygolfclub@eircom.net

Contact Name: Joe Considine
Secretary\Manager
Captain 2003: Conor Carroll
Green Fees Weekdays: €25
Weekends: €30
G/C: Y   P/C : Y   G/S : Y
Course Distance C'ship: 5,843m
Ladies: 5,024m

TOWNLEY HALL GOLF CLUB
No. of holes: 9

Tullyallen, Drogheda, Co. Louth.
T: 041-9842229
F: 041-9873977
E: townleyhall@oceanfree.net

Contact Name: Michael Foley
Hon\Secretary
Captain 2003: Joe Coogan
Green Fees Weekdays: €12
Weekends: €15
G/C: N   P/C : Y   G/S : N
Course Distance C'ship: 5,331m
Ladies: 4,398m

TRAAD POINTS GOLF CLUB
No. of holes: 9

122a Shore Road, Magherafelt
BT45 6LR, Derry.
T: 028-79418865

Contact Name: B. Coleman
Hon\Secretary
Green Fees Weekdays: Stg £12
Weekends: Stg £12
G/C: N   P/C : Y   G/S : N
Course Distance C'ship: 4,888m
Ladies: 3,642m

TRALEE GOLF CLUB
No. of holes: 18

West Barrow, Ardfert, Co. Kerry.
T: 066-7136379
F: 066-7136008
E: info@traleegolfclub.com
W: www.traleegolfclub.com
Contact Name: Anthony Byrne
General Manager
Captain 2003: Philip O'Sullivan
Green Fees Weekdays: €130
Weekends: €130
G/C: N   P/C : Y   G/S : Y
Course Distance C'ship: 6,263m
Ladies: 4,921m

TRAMORE GOLF CLUB
No. of holes: 18

Newtown Hill, Tramore, Co. Waterford.
T: 051-386170
F: 051-390961
E: tragolf@iol.ie
W: www.tramoregolfclub.com
Contact Name: Ted Power
General Manager
Captain 2003: Michael Delany
Green Fees Weekdays: €40
Weekends: €55
G/C: Y   P/C : Y   G/S : Y
Course Distance C'ship: 6,055m
Ladies: 5,164m

TUAM GOLF CLUB
No. of holes: 18

Barnacurragh, Tuam, Co. Galway.
T: 093-28993
F: 093-26003
E: tuamgolfclub@eircom.net

Contact Name: Vincent Gaffney
Secretary\Manager
Captain 2003: Frank Biggins
Green Fees Weekdays: €25
Weekends: €25
G/C: Y   P/C : Y   G/S : Y
Course Distance C'ship: 6,045m
Ladies: 4,840m

Golf Carts = G/C   Pull Carts = P/C   Golf shop = G/S

TUBBERCURRY GOLF CLUB
No. of holes: 9

Ballymote Road, Tubbercurry, Co. Sligo.
T: 071-85849
E: tgc2002life@yahoo.co.uk
W: www.tubbercurrygolfclub.com

Contact Name: John F. Kelly
Secretary\Manager
Captain 2003: John Brennan
Green Fees Weekdays: €15
Weekends: €20
G/C: N   P/C : Y   G/S : Y
Course Distance C'ship: 5,531m
Ladies: 4,655m

TULFARRIS GOLF CLUB
No. of holes: 18

Blessington Lakes, Blessington,
Co. Wicklow.
E: 045-867644   **F:** 045-867600
E: info@tulfarris.com
W: www.tulfarris.com
Contact Name: Brian Begley
Secretary\Manager
Captain 2003: Padraig Whelan
Green Fees Weekdays: €55
Weekends: €75
G/C: Y   P/C : Y   G/S : Y
Course Distance C'ship: 6,506m
Ladies: 5,687m

TULLAMORE GOLF CLUB
No. of holes: 18

Brookfield, Tullamore, Co. Offaly.
T: 0506-21439
F: 0506-41439
E: tullamoregolfclub@iol.ie
W: www.tullamoregolfclub.ie
Contact Name: Jo Barber-Loughlin
Secretary\Manager
Captain 2003: Brendan Walsh
Green Fees Weekdays: €35
Weekends: €40
G/C: Y   P/C : Y   G/S : Y
Course Distance C'ship: 5,844m
Ladies: 4,913m

TURVEY GOLF CLUB
No. of holes: 18

Turvey Avenue, Donabate, Co. Dublin.
T: 01-8435169
F: 01-8435179

Contact Name: Derek McNally
Secretary\Manager
Captain 2003: John Timmins
Green Fees Weekdays: €25
Weekends: €31
G/C: N   P/C : Y   G/S : N
Course Distance C'ship: 6,068m
Ladies: 5,407m

VARTRY LAKES GOLF CLUB
No. of holes: 9

Roundwood, Co. Wicklow.
T/F: 01-2817006
E: vartrylakes@hotmail.com

Contact Name: Ann McDonald
Secretary\Manager
Captain 2003: John McCormack
Green Fees Weekdays: €22
Weekends: €22
G/C:N   P/C : Y   G/S : N
Course Distance C'ship: 5,276m
Ladies: 4,478m

VIRGINIA GOLF CLUB
No. of holes: 9

Park Hotel, Virginia, Co. Cavan.
T: 049-8548066

Contact Name: Tom Hutchison
Hon\Secretary
Captain 2003: Pat O'Reilly
Green Fees Weekdays: €15
Weekends: €15
G/C:N   P/C : Y   G/S : N
Course Distance C'ship: 4,139m
Ladies: 4,139m

Golf Carts = G/C   Pull Carts = P/C   Golf shop = G/S

WARRENPOINT GOLF CLUB
No. of holes: 18

Lower Dromore Road, Warrenpoint
BT34 3LN, Down.
T: 028-41753695 **F:** 028-41752918
E: warrenpointgolfclub@talk21.com
W: Under Construction
Contact Name: Marina Trainor
Secretary\Manager
Captain 2003: Brian McKee
Green Fees Weekdays: £28
Weekends: £29
G/C: N   P/C : Y   G/S : Y
Course Distance C'ship: 5,612m
Ladies: 4,888m

WATERFORD GOLF CLUB
No. of holes: 18

Newrath, Waterford.
T: 051-876748
F: 051-853405
E: inf@waterfordgolfclub.com

Contact Name: Joe Condon
Secretary\Manager
Captain 2003: Eamon Keane
Green Fees Weekdays: €49
Weekends: €59
G/C: Y   P/C : Y   G/S : Y
Course Distance C'ship: 6,231m
Ladies: 5,103m

WATERFORD CASTLE GOLF CLUB
No. of holes: 18

The Island, Ballinakill, Waterford.
T: 051-871633
F: 051-871634
E: golf@waterfordcastle.com
W: www.waterfordcastle.com
Contact Name: Michael Garland
Secretary\Manager
Captain 2003: Cormac Aherne
Green Fees Weekdays: €49
Weekends: €59
G/C: Y   P/C : Y   G/S : Y
Course Distance C'ship: 6,231m
Ladies: 5,103m

WATERVILLE GOLF LINKS
No. of holes: 18

Waterville, Co. Kerry.
T: 066-9474102
F: 066-9474482
E: wvgolf@iol.ie
W: www.watervillegolflinks.com
Contact Name: Noel Cronin
Secretary\Manager
Captain 2003: Sean O'Shea
Green Fees Weekdays: €125
Weekends: €125
G/C: Y   P/C : Y   G/S : Y
Course Distance C'ship: 6,568m
Ladies: 4,789m

WEST WATERFORD GOLF CLUB
No. of holes: 18

Dungarvan, Co. Waterford.
T: 058-43216
F: 058-44343
E: info@westwaterfordgolf.com
W: www.westwaterfordgolf.com
Contact Name: Tom Whelan
Secretary\Manager
Captain 2003: Dr. Terry O'Callaghan
Green Fees Weekdays: €28
Weekends: €36
G/C: Y   P/C : Y   G/S : Y
Course Distance C'ship: 6,102m
Ladies: 4,731m

WESTMANSTOWN GOLF CLUB
No. of holes: 18

Clonsilla, Dublin 15.
T: 01-8205817
F: 01-8205858
E: info@westmanstowngolfclub.ie
W: www.westmanstowngolfclub.ie
Contact Name: Michael O'Shea
Secretary\Manager
Captain 2003: John Joyce
Green Fees Weekdays: €35
Weekends: €40
G/C: N   P/C : Y   G/S : Y
Course Distance C'ship: 5,826m
Ladies: 4,900m

Golf Carts = G/C   **Pull Carts = P/C**   **Golf shop = G/S**

WESTPORT GOLF CLUB
No. of holes: 18

Carrowholly, Wesport, Co. Mayo.
T: 098-28262
F: 098-27217
E: wpgolf@eircom.net
W: www.golfwestport.com
Contact Name: Paul O'Neill
General Manager
Captain 2003: Joe Giddons
Green Fees Weekdays: €40
Weekends: €50
G/C: Y   P/C : Y   G/S : Y
Course Distance C'ship: 6,670m
Ladies: 5,615m

WEXFORD GOLF CLUB
No. of holes: 18

Mulgannon, Wexford.
T: 053-42238
F: 053-42243
E: info@wexfordgolfclub.ie
W: www.wexfordgolfclub.ie
Contact Name: Pat Daly
Manager
Captain 2003: Larry Burn
Green Fees Weekdays: €30
Weekends: €35
G/C: N   P/C : Y   G/S : Y
Course Distance C'ship: 5,734m
Ladies: 4,922m

WHITEHEAD GOLF CLUB
No. of holes: 18

McCrea's Brae, Whitehead, Carrickfergus
BT38 9NZ, Antrim.
T: 028-93370820
F: 028-93370825
E: robin@whitegc.fsnet.co.uk
Contact Name: Dr. R. Patrick
Hon\Secretary
Captain 2003: Joe McKernon
Green Fees Weekdays: Stg £12
Weekends: Stg £16
G/C: N   P/C : Y   G/S : Y
Course Distance C'ship: 5,532m
Ladies: 4,929m

WICKLOW GOLF CLUB
No. of holes: 18

Dunbur Road, Wicklow.
T: 0404-67379
F: 0404-66122
W: www.wicklowgolfclub.ie

Contact Name: Joe Kelly – Hon\Secretary
Captain 2003: Keith Clarke
Green Fees Weekdays: €35
Weekends: €35
G/C: N   P/C : Y   G/S : Y
Course Distance C'ship: 5,442m
Ladies: 4,677m

WILLIAMSTOWN GOLF CLUB
No. of holes: 18

Airport Road, Williamstown, Co. Waterford.
T: 051-853131
F: 051-843690

Contact Name: Margaret Murray
Secretary\Manager
Captain 2003: Jack Morrissey
Green Fees Weekdays: €18
Weekends: €22
G/C: N   P/C : Y   G/S : Y
Course Distance C'ship: 6,053m
Ladies: 5,694m

WOODBROOK GOLF CLUB
No. of holes: 18

Dublin Road, Bray, Co. Wicklow.
T: 01-2824799
F: 01-2821950
E: woodbrook@internet-ireland.ie
W: www.woodbrook.ie
Contact Name: Patrick F. Byrne
General Manager
Captain 2003: Noel Dwyer
Green Fees Weekdays: €80
Weekends: €90
G/C: Y   P/C : Y   G/S : Y
Course Distance C'ship: 6,342m
Ladies: 5,539m

Golf Carts = G/C   Pull Carts = P/C   Golf shop = G/S

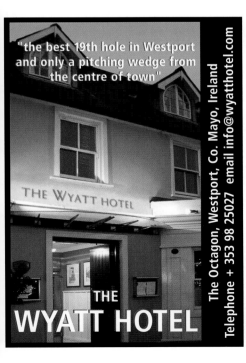

WOODENBRIDGE GOLF CLUB
No. of holes: 18

Vale of Avoca, Arklow, Co. Wicklow.
T: 0402-35202
F: 0402-35754
E: wgc@eircom.net
W: www.globalgolf.com
Contact Name: Ronan Smyth
General Manager
Captain 2003: Frank Duffy
Green Fees Weekdays: €51
Weekends: €63
G/C: Y   P/C : Y   G/S : Y
Course Distance C'ship: 5,852m
Ladies: 5,042m

WOODLANDS GOLF CLUB
No. of holes: 18

Coill Dubh, Naas, Co. Kildare.
T: 045-860777
F: 045-860988
E: woodlandsgolf@eircom.net

Contact Name: Kieran Savage
Secretary\Manager
Captain 2003: Dermot McCabe
Green Fees Weekdays: €20
Weekends: €25
G/C: N   P/C : Y   G/S : Y
Course Distance C'ship: 5,924m
Ladies: 5,079m

WOODSTOCK GOLF CLUB
No. of holes: 18

Shanaway Road, Ennis, Co. Clare.
T: 065-6829463
F: 065-6820304
E: woodstock.ennis@eircom.net
W: www.woodstockgolfclub.ie
Contact Name: Seamus Kelly
Sales & Marketing
Captain 2003: Gerry Sadlier
Green Fees Weekdays: €37
Weekends: €42
G/C: Y   P/C : Y   G/S : Y
Course Distance C'ship: 5,864m
Ladies: 5,045m

YOUGHAL GOLF CLUB
No. of holes: 18

Knockaverry, Youghal, Co. Cork.
T: 024-92787
F: 024-92641
E: youghalgolfclub@eircom.net
W: www.youghalgolfclub.net
Contact Name: Margaret O'Sullivan
Secretary\Manager
Captain 2003: Peter Murray
Green Fees Weekdays: €25
Weekends: €32
G/C: N   P/C : Y   G/S : Y
Course Distance C'ship: 5,640m
Ladies: 4,948m

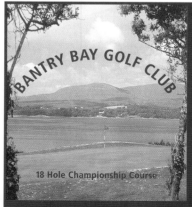
Golf Carts = G/C   Pull Carts = P/C   Golf shop = G/S

Who'd have thought so many news items could be compressed into this Special Edition?

The new Mercedes-Benz C180 Kompressor SE

Take the enhanced 1.8L 4 cylinder engines with supercharging and intercooling.

That's a story all its own.

As is the 11% lower fuel consumption. And this Special Edition car comes to the Irish market with airconditioning and special alloys as standard - that's certainly worth a word or two.

Not to mention over 20 premium class innovations. But these are just the headlines.

For a full analysis, turn to your authorised Mercedes-Benz dealer.

CO_2 emissions 202 - 216 g/km. Fuel Economy Combined 8.4 - 9.2 lts/100km

Mercedes-Benz

The Future of the Automobile

Tel: 01 409 4444

www.mercedes-benz.ie

The Irish and the Ryder Cup

Paul McGinley celebrates in 2002

From Samuel Ryder's point of view the best moment in the famous contest named after him probably took place at Royal Birkdale in 1969 when Jack Nicklaus graciously conceded a short putt of about 30 inches on the final green to his opponent, Tony Jacklin. Nicklaus is reported to have said to Jacklin afterwards that he felt sure the putt would have been holed but that he was not prepared to give him the opportunity of missing it. Marvellous sportsmanship, Mr. Ryder would definitely have approved. Big Jack's gesture meant the overall match result between the USA and Great Britain and Ireland was tied for the first time. It was not an universally popular thing for Nicklaus to do. Some of his fellow countrymen were mildly aggrieved but Sam Ryder, who died in 1936, would surely have applauded. Mr. Ryder had intended that "his competition" should foster friendly relations between the professional golfers of Britain and the USA

He never envisaged the matches turning into the mega, over-hyped event bordering on an "inter-continental war" that it has become. As the cup holders, the USA retained the beautiful trophy in 1969 but it felt more like a victory to the home team who had suffered so many embarrassing defeats by wide margins.

Eamonn Darcy holes the match winning putt in 1987.

Nicklaus was the dominant player in World golf in 1969 but his concession to Jacklin caused such a fierce debate that the Golden Bear, as Jack was known, was inspired to apply his considerable intellect to finding a way to make the Ryder Cup more competitive. Eventually an acceptable solution emerged. Big Jack put forward the suggestion that the best players from Europe instead of being confined to British and Irish players only should supply the USA's opposition. The European players were invited to join in 1979 and it did not take long for the Americans to find themselves up against far tougher opposition than they might have bargained for. Almost as soon as the likes of Seve Ballesteros and Bernhard Langer became involved, the walkover attitude of the USA team changed dramatically. The result of every Ryder Cup since 1983 has been balanced on a knife-edge.

Ironically, it is only since the Continental Europeans were invited to take part for the first time in 1979 that some of the greatest moments in Ryder Cup history from an Irish point of view have taken place. Fred Daly became our first Ryder Cup representative in 1947. He played in four series but never featured on a winning side. Daly had his greatest Ryder Cup moment in 1953 when in foursome's partnership with Harry Bradshaw they combined to chip and putt from about sixty yards short of the eighteenth green at Wentworth, to secure a winning birdie and victory in their match with Walter Burkemo and Cary Middlecoff. The Brad used to tell a story about the final moments of that particular match. Faced with the tricky shot into the green, Harry was unsure what to do and asked Fred whether he should "pitch it or run it?" "I do not care what you do because I will hole the putt anyway!" was the confident reply. He did too. Fred was even more outstanding in the singles on the following day when he beat one-time leading money winner, Ted Kroll, by 9 and 7 over 36 holes. Fred's magnificent effort was in vain as the GB&I team lost narrowly.

From 1927 until 1959, all Ryder Cup matches were two-day affairs with all of the head-to-head games played over 36 holes. There were four alternate shot foursomes matches played on the first day followed by eight singles matches on the second day. In 1961 the matches were reduced to 18 holes with two series of foursomes and two series of singles played each day. In 1963 it became a three-day affair for the first time when better-ball four ball matches were introduced. In 1977 the final day programme of morning and afternoon singles matches was reduced to one series of matches only. With only minor amendments to the sequence of the pairs or "team" matches the Cup has been played by this formula ever since.

Harry Bradshaw's biggest Ryder Cup moment came at Lindrick in 1957 when he was a member of a rare winning GB&I side. Left out of the foursome's matches, Harry halved his singles match with the US Open champion of that same year, Dick Mayer, one of the most stylish players the game has known. Christy O'Connor Senior was also in that winning team at Lindrick having made his debut in 1955. Christy Senior has played in ten Ryder Cup series and 36 matches in all. Only Nick Faldo has played more often. Christy's 7/6 hammering of Dow Finsterwald at Lindrick was a big factor in that famous victory.

Norman Drew (1959) became the first former Walker Cup golfer to appear on a GB&I Ryder Cup team when he played at Eldorado CC in California. His uncompromising team captain, Dai Rees, selected the Ulsterman for only one match. He did not let the side down, halving the top singles match with two-time US Major winner, Doug Ford.

The next four Irishmen to join Ryder Cup action, Jimmy Martin (1965), Hugh Boyle (1967), Eddie Polland (1973) and John

O'Leary (1975), did not set the world on fire or manage to win any points between them but they can be proud that they were part of a great tradition.

Eamon Darcy and Christy O'Connor Junior joined O'Leary in the outplayed 1975 team that lost by 21/11 at Arnold Palmer's home course of Laurel Valley CC in Pennsylvania. The Darce and Junior's moments of fame were still ahead of them.

Des Smyth made his Ryder debut alongside Seve Ballesteros and Antonio Garrido on the first European side in 1979 at the Greenbrier in West Virginia. The addition of the two Spaniards to the normal British and Irish cocktail did not change the pattern of USA victories. Smyth was once again the lone Irishman selected to play at Walton Heath in 1981. Seve Ballesteros was ignored and left out due to a row over appearance money. The County Louth man won both of his games in fine style on the opening day but he and his team mates were steamrolled out of existence on days two and three by what is widely regarded as the "best ever" American side.

There was no more Irish involvement until 1987 at Muirfield Village, Ohio. Eamon Darcy had withstood incredible competition and pressure throughout the entire European tournament season to make the side. The trials and tribulations endured stood "Aimin", as the American crowds named him, in good stead when he had to face the most difficult of downhill, side-hill putts imaginable on the 18th green. He holed it to secure a vital one-hole victory over Ben Crenshaw. The putt gave Darcy his only win in 11 Ryder Cup matches but it also wrapped up victory for his team. Darcy picked the right moment to apply his personal stamp. It was the first time that the USA had been beaten on home soil by golfers from across the pond.

Who can forget the way Christy O'Connor Junior played the Belfry's infamous 18th hole against Freddie Couples in 1989? Couples certainly won't. A majestic approach over the lake by Christy had such an effect on the laconic American that he, in turn, missed the green by a country mile with a simple nine iron shot and was eventually forced to concede the hole in a whimper. Not only did they make up ballads about that famous shot but also one Englishman present insisted that when he died his ashes should be spread on the very spot from where Junior had played that famous two-iron stroke. In due course the man's wish was carried out.

Surprisingly for such a once dominant player, Ronan Rafferty made only one Ryder Cup appearance. He made it a winning one for both the team and himself with a one hole singles victory over Mark Calcavecchia at the Belfry in 1989.

Christy Junior gives thanks on the final green in 1989.

The Ryder Cup match that would have least pleased Mr. Ryder was without doubt the "War on the Shore" at Kiawah Island in 1991. The American Captain, Dave Stockton, seemed to over-react to Europe's emergence as golfing equals. Emotions of national pride inflamed by the Desert Storm War with Iraq did not help. The home crowd atmosphere that the Europeans faced at Kiawah was extremely hostile. It was a difficult place to make one's debut. However, good humour and an unconventional way of looking at things buoyed Ireland's only representative that year in David Feherty. David came away with an excellent 50% record from three outings, including a brilliant singles win over Payne Stewart.

There were no Irishmen on the losing European side at the Belfry in 1993 that was out played and out thought by USA Captain Tom Watson and his team after another close battle. Watson not only led his team to victory but he did so in an admirable manner and spirit.

Philip Walton had a magnificent season in 1995 and was the only Irishman to make the team selected to go to Oak Hill in Rochester, New York. The final day of singles play featured the most amazing, tension packed scenes. Malahide's Walton was in the thick of it all the way and was almost inevitably and reluctantly forced onto centre stage as the climax was reached. Three up and three to go on Jay Haas, Philip knew at that stage that a win by him would almost certainly mean that the cup would be going back across the Atlantic by Concorde. After a few scares, he managed to get the job done by playing a great 5-wood second shot out of thick rough to the front edge of the 18th green and then chipping close enough to ensure a famous victory. There were copious tears of joy from so-called hard men like Nick Faldo, Seve Ballesteros and Team Captain, Bernard Gallacher at the greenside. Walton was lifted high and shouldered off the green by his highly delighted teammates.

The Ryder Cup matches went to Spain for the first time in 1997. Valderamma was the venue. Europe had to face the awesome Tiger Woods who making his debut for the USA. The unique difficulties and requirements of team golf found Tiger wanting and with the golf course blatantly set up to nullify Tiger's great length, Europe, under the captaincy of Seve Ballesteros won again. Irish debutant Darren Clarke was frustrated to be on the bench for all of the first day's play. On the second morning, he was sprung into action like a caged lion to form a brilliant, winning four-ball partnership with Colin Montgomerie. Going head to head with Phil Mickelson in the singles, Clarke eventually had to give best to a torrent of birdies, losing by 2/1. The priceless point gained with Monty over one of America's most successful ever pairings of Couples and Love proved vital in the final winning margin of one single point.

American pride was so severely hurt in Spain that the 1999 US Team Captain, Ben Crenshaw decided to go all out for revenge at Brookline, Boston. He called on former US President George Bush, an avid golfer, to make an inspiring motivational breakfast speech to the USA team on the final morning. The USA was three points behind and needed all the inspiration they could get. The European side was cock-a-hoop but a few questionable tactical decisions by the team captain, Mark James conspired to throw away the advantage and lose the momentum. Darren Clarke, at this stage regarded as one of Europe's strongmen and debutant, Padraig Harrington were the Irishmen involved. Padraig with the experience of three Walker Cup matches behind him knew all about team golf at the highest level, performed superbly. A heroic foursome's partnership with Jimenez of Spain yielded only a half point despite some terrific play by Padraig. In the cauldron of the final day's singles, Harrington's magnificent one-hole victory over Mark O'Meara marked his arrival as

Focus.   Supported by Allianz.

If you want to be a winner you have to be focused. Totally committed and always striving to be the best. At Allianz we focus on one thing only, providing world class insurance for our customers - nothing less will do. That's why we're proud to support Paul McGinley, because we know, like us, he's focused on one thing only ... being the best.

Allianz (Ⅲ)
The Power On Your Side

a world-class player. Clarke was an ever present this time, gaining two points in partnership with Lee Westwood before losing his singles match to the "on-course leader" of the USA side, Hal Sutton.

The Ryder Cup of 2001 was postponed for a year for reasons we do not have to go into here. Clarke and Harrington qualified for selection as numbers one and two on the points system, a unique feat. For only the second time in history a third Irishman made the side. Only one Englishman and one Scot were in the team that contained six Continental Europeans which shows how much things had changed since 1979. Jack Nicklaus's gentle suggestion to include "a few Europeans" had come of age whereas such an increase in the Irish representation was hardly considered.

Paul McGinley had the unnerving experience of having to wait for over a year to make his debut. During the long build up his game suffered. However, once the contest got underway, he re-found his form and was ready and willing to become a hero. Only minutes before McGinley's moment of destiny, Jim Furyk (USA) had come mighty close to a heart stopping

moment of his own, almost holing out the bravest of greenside bunker shots. Up stepped Paul to put his team's points total beyond the reach of the Americans by unerringly drilling an 11-foot putt right into the heart of the cup. The crowd of many thousands, not to mention the millions of TV watchers, looked on breathlessly. Clarke and Harrington had earlier achieved heroics of their own. Clarke chipped superbly from the bank beside the 18th green to halve a torrid, seesaw match with David Duval. Harrington had outclassed the normally tough Calcavecchia by 5/4. Almost as soon as his ball hit the bottom of the hole, McGinley was engulfed and unceremoniously pushed into the lake beside the Belfry's 18th green in celebration while fittingly wrapped in the Irish tricolour. It was a moment in Ryder Cup history that will live in Irish memories forever.

In 2006, Ireland and The K-Club will host the Ryder Cup for the first time. We look forward to more great moments at this wonderful venue from our Irish Golfing heroes.

Paul McGinley reacts to his match winning putt 2003

Ryder Cup Results

1927	at Worcester CC. Mass.	USA 9½	GB 2½.
1929	at Moortown, Leeds.	GB 7	USA 5.
1931	at Scioto, Ohio.	USA 9	GB 3.
1933	at Southport & Ainsdale, Lancs.	GB 6½	USA 5½.
1935	at Ridgewood, NJ.	USA 9	GB 3.
1937	at Southport & Ainsdale, Lancs.	USA 8	GB 4.
1947	at Portland, Oregon.*(First Irish participation)*.	USA 11	GB&I 1.
1949	at Ganton, Yorks.	USA 7	GB&I 5.
1951	at Pinehurst, NC.	USA 9½	GB&I 2½.
1953	at Wentworth, Surrey.	USA 6½	GB&I 5½.
1955	at Thunderbird CC, Cal.	USA 8	GB&I 4.
1957	at Lindrick, Lincs.	GB&I 7½	USA 4½.
1959	at Eldorado CC., Cal.	USA 8½	GB&I 3½.
1961	at Royal Lytham, Lancs.	USA 14½	GB&I 9½.
1963	at Atlanta CC, Georgia.	USA 23	GB&I 9.
1965	at Royal Birkdale, Lancs.	USA 19½	GB&I 12½.
1967	at Champions CC., Texas.	USA 23½	GB&I 8½.
1969	at Royal Birkdale, Lancs.	USA 16	GB&I 16.
1971	at St. Louis, Missouri.	USA 18½	GB&I 13½.
1973	at Muirfield, Scotland.	USA 19	GB&I 13.
1975	at Laurel Valley, Pa.	USA 21	GB&I 11.
1977	at Royal Lytham, Lancs.	USA 12½	GB&I 7½.
1979	at Greenbrier, WV. *(1st European participation)*.	USA 17	Europe 11.
1981	at Walton Heath, Surrey.	USA 18½	Europe 9½.
1983	at PGA National, Fla.	USA 14½	Europe 13½.
1985	at The Belfry, England.	Europe 16½	USA 11½.
1987	at Muirfield Village, Ohio.	Europe 15	USA 13.
1989	at The Belfry, England.	Europe 14	USA 14.
1991	at Kiawah Island, S.C.	USA 14½	Europe 13½.
1993	at The Belfry, England.	USA 15	Europe 13.
1995	at Oak Hill, NY.	Europe 14½	USA 13½.
1997	at Valderrama, Spain.	Europe 14½	USA 13½.
1999	at Brookline, Mass.	USA 14½	Europe 13½.
2002	at The Belfry, England.	Europe 15½	USA 12½.

Irish Ryder Cup players

Fred Daly	(1947 – 1953)	(3½pts out of 8)
Harry Bradshaw	(1953- 1957)	(2½pts out of 5)
Christy O'Connor Senior	(1955- 1973)	(13 pts out of 36)
Norman Drew	(1959)	(½ pts out of 1)
Jimmy Martin	(1965)	(0 pts out of 1)
Hugh Boyle	(1967)	(0 pts out of 3)
Eddie Polland	(1973)	(0 pts out of 2)
John O'Leary	(1975)	(0 pts out of 4)
Christy O'Connor Junior	(1975, 1989)	(1 pts out of 4)
Eamon Darcy	(1975, 1977, 1987)	(2 pts out of 11)
Des Smyth	(1979-1981)	(2 pts out of 5)
Ronan Rafferty	(1989)	(1 pts out of 3)
David Feherty	(1991)	(1½pts out of 3)
Philip Walton	(1995)	(1 pts out of 2)
Darren Clarke	(1997, 1999, 2002)	(5 pts out of 12)
Padraig Harrington	(1999, 2002)	(3½pts out of 7)
Paul McGinley	(2002)	(1 pts out of 3)

ROYAL JORDANIAN AIRLINES

Return fares from

Amman	from €424.00
Dubai/Bahrain	from €546.00
Cairo	from €581.00
Bangkok	from €598.00
Kuala Lumpur	from €634.00
Bombay	from €590.00
Karachi	from €458.00
Colombo	from €581.00

All above fares are valid for departures ex London Heathrow and exclude tax.

Conditions apply

PLEASE RING RESERVATIONS ON 1 800 481 049

South Course - The K Club
STRAFFAN, CO. KILDARE, IRELAND

The construction of the South Course at The K Club was completed in October 2002. Work began in February 2001 and during the first year of construction all 18 Greens were planted, seeded and grown-in in order to ensure optimum maturity as it opens in July, 2003.

One of the characteristics this course shares with the North Course is the challenge of water hazards. Spanning a total area of 180 acres, a tenth is accounted for by water features. Apart from this aquatic emphasis, it has all the appearance and feel of an inland links, with high undulating fairways, large difficult greens and treacherous rough. Bunkering is also a major aspect of the Golf Course.

The course has many truly great holes, the most dramatic of which will most certainly be the 7th Quarry Hole – all will be revealed in due course.

With a length from the back tees of 7,300 yards, this will be a true test of golf. However, it will accommodate all levels of player, with four or five tees on each hole so that the overall length can be considerably reduced.

The K Club is the first Resort in Europe to develop two bona fide Championship courses side by side, each offering a distinctive and different experience for the golfer.

HOTEL

Tel: 01 6017200   Fax: 01 6017299

GOLF

Tel: 01 6017300   Fax: 01 6017399

Email: golf@kclub.ie   Web: www.kclub.ie

*Home of The Smurfit European Open &
The Venue for The 2006 Ryder Cup Matches*

Three Lady Golfers who took on the Men

Having won thirteen tournaments in the 2002 golf season, the Swede Annika Sorenstam needed an incentive to drive her onto a higher level of play. Having had a year like that, she wanted a new challenge to make the game more interesting. After much thought she has decided to give herself a huge task, taking on the men at level terms. It will not be the first time that a woman played in a male tour event but it is nevertheless brave. Nick Price, one the game's best male professionals over the past twenty years certainly thinks so. He said,

"I admire her courage. I don't think I'd have the guts to do it if I were in her shoes".

Annika's outstanding performances in recent years has tempted certain pundits to declare that she is perhaps the best lady golfer of all time. Playing in a men's event will neither prove nor disprove that. It is an impossible comparison to make because a player can only be the best in his or her own era. Besides the game is changing all the time due to technology and the level of competition.

"It is going to attract a lot of interest," Jack Nicklaus said from his home in Florida. *"I have played golf with Annika. She hits the ball long and straight but she will have to be at her best to compete with the men. I wonder how she will cope with the deeper rough on the men's tour but then; of course, she might never be in it! It will be very good for the game of golf, it cannot be anything but."*

"Ball striking is my strength", Annika is quoted as saying but what is going on in her head and tummy when she steps up to the tee is going to have a greater effect on her than anything she has encountered before. Her nerves will be jangling and the men who are paired with her will feel likewise. The interest worldwide will be enormous. As I see it, hitting a lower trajectory ball into firm greens could be the biggest problem for Annika. Although Annika can hardly believe that she will beat the boys, she is entitled to give herself the challenge of facing the toughest opposition available if she wants to.

George Zaharias wrestled alligators for a living in Florida but his wife Mildred "Babe" Didrickson never backed away from a fair fight at any time in her life, least of all with any man whether it was her husband or not. She was brave enough to file an entry for the British Open in 1947 when she was still an amateur but it was politely declined. Two years earlier she had managed to compete on equal terms with men in the LA Open without setting the world on fire. To be fair, she was no more than a raw, albeit big hitting rookie in 1945 and with her brash over-confident personality expected too much. She would have loved to have been allowed another go when her game had matured but her colleagues in the LPGA discouraged her believing that another poor performance would be detrimental to the ladies' game.

Famous for once saying, "When I want to hit an extra long tee-shot, I just loosen my girdle and if it weren't for "these things" (mammary glands) I could hit the ball another twenty yards!" the Babe was the world's greatest ever all-round woman athlete, if not quite the greatest ever lady golfer. A multiple Olympic champion in Track and Field, Zaharias only took up golf when her more active sports career ended prematurely due to a ridiculous amateur status suspension. Realising that golf could be her best means of earning a legitimate living from sports into middle-age, Babe Zaharias resolved to become a professional lady golfer as soon as she could master the basics of the game.

The superb form of Mickey Wright

Ever since she was a young girl in a Texas High School, Mildred Didrickson competed on equal terms with boys on the athletics track, basketball court and baseball diamond. Later, she regularly played in exhibition baseball games with major leaguers during springtime training in Florida. When she eventually targeted golf, she tackled it in a brash, determined manner that the establishment considered unladylike. Babe's super confident personality was certainly something new in ladies' golf. She practiced for hours and hours every day until her hands bled. She shunned lady golfers and played with men all the time. As in the other sports she played, playing with the boys exclusively toughened her up and gave her higher standards to measure herself against. Her natural talent and absolute dedication soon helped to fast track her to brilliant triumphs in the US and British Women's Amateur Championships in 1946 and 1947 respectively. Her apprenticeship successfully completed, she turned pro and became an instant marketing asset for the fledgling LPGA Tour. Babe's long hitting and devil-may-care attitude helped to make ladies golf exciting, newsworthy and attractive.

As I said already, it is a pointless exercise to say that one player rather than another, male or female, is or was the greatest of all-time. One thing is certain, in her day Mickey Wright was head and shoulders above any other lady golfer in her era and, like Babe Zaharias, possibly as good as many of the men too. Wright dominated more than Zaharias and Nancy Lopez ever did. Annika Sorenstam is the only lady to come close to Mickey Wright's record. In the early 1960s Wright was untouchable; her record of 82 tournament victories including 13 majors during an eighteen-year spell speaks for itself. She ceased playing because of fairly bizarre ailments. She was allergic to sunlight and could not wear conventional golf shoes due to a foot ailment. She finally quit for good in 1973 after a final, brief comeback during which she won the Colgate Dinah Shore Tournament, considered a major for the LPGA. Mickey's rate of success if she were playing for today's purses would have won her many millions of dollars instead of a paltry $368,770.

If ever there was a woman capable of playing with the best men in her time it was Mickey Wright. Tall, superbly athletic and balanced, Mickey attacked the ball with grace, style and power. She could consistently hit the ball over 240 yards. By today's standards that might not sound impressive but it was about the same distance the average male professional was achieving with far inferior golf balls and the persimmon woodenheaded equipment of that time. Crucially, she could also hit the ball as high as the men and this rare ability separated her from her female competition and put her in a different class altogether. She was far too shy a personality to have ever considered competing against men in public and apart from the occasional tension free exhibition game did not do so.

Many knowledgeable students of the golf swing say that Mickey Wright had the most attractive and technically correct golf swing action of all-time, male or female. Even the normally impossible to impress Ben Hogan said that she had the "most perfect golf swing" he ever saw. A blue-eyed 5' 9" blonde with a gentle femininity about her off the course, Mickey Wright was extraordinarily modest and self-effacing with no interest in fame or publicity as can be seen by the way she "disappeared" from the spotlight once she retired from playing in tournaments.

If Annika Sorenstam manages to make it through the halfway cut at Forth Worth it will have been a fabulous achievement. But nothing can be judged on one tournament performance. Some chauvinists say she should not be allowed to play. "Why not?" Annika is only testing herself and satisfying her curiosity. It is a free country. It is not like other sports. Golf is an individual game. She will play her own ball. Nobody will body-check her or knock her over. What the opposition do or do not do will not effect her directly. Golf is a self-contained game. Most of the action takes place inside the player's own head.

That is where the biggest challenges are. It is always the player versus herself first and then the golf course and last and least the opposition. Any misgivings that Annika might feel will be due to her own emotional reaction to what will be an unique psychological experience. Playing her normal game will be out of the question. We know that Annika Sorenstam can hit golf shots but the unfamiliar circumstances that she will face at Colonial CC, will be akin to playing on the moon.

If you want to take long walks, take long walks. If you want to hit things with a stick, hit things with a stick. But there's no excuse for combining the two and putting the results on TV.
National Lampoon

When Two Irish Lady Golfers Were The Best In The World

One hundred years ago the two best lady golfers in the world were both Irish. In 1899 May Hezlet, a slip of a girl only seventeen years old, won the British Ladies Amateur Championship for the first of three times. To all intents and purposes it was the championship of the world for ladies at that time. Over the next twelve years Irish players figured in nine finals and were victorious five times, surely the golden era of Irish ladies golf.

May Hezlet with the tropies she won as a seventeen year old, the British and Irish Ladies Championships of 1899.

May Hezlet was acclaimed as the "most finished" golfer of her day, male or female. Miss Hezlet used to cycle a 24-mile round trip to get in a game of golf at their home club, Royal Portrush, where she once sported a domestic handicap of +7.

Rhona Adair from Killymoon was also just seventeen years of age when she won the British Ladies Championship in 1900. Miss Adair won again in 1903 and also won the Irish Ladies Close Championship four years running, 1900 to 1903. Adair and Hezlet were club mates and friends but their rivalry dominated Irish and British ladies golf for the first decade of the twentieth century.

In 1899, Miss Adair created quite a stir by bravely taking on Old Tom Morris in a 36-hole challenge match at St. Andrews. Old Tom was 77 years old and Rhona, only sixteen but the old man expressed "no wish to be licked by a lassie". Only one hole up at halfway, Morris dragged himself to a three holes lead with nine holes to go but then had to hold on grimly as youthful stamina began to make a difference. Tom just managed to hang on to win by a single hole margin. Miss Adair was renowned as a long hitter and this ability more than anything else was the cause of her being invited to make a wide-ranging tour of the United States in the autumn of 1903. In a letter, May Hezlet wrote about her friend as follows, "Rhona's USA trip was certainly a wonderful success. She carried off sixteen trophies from the different courses she visited. Only once during the time she was there was she defeated by an American lady golfer and when it is taken into consideration that she was in a strange land and climate and playing on unfamiliar turf, after a great deal of travelling and rushing about, her success appears something marvellous. No other lady in the world could have performed such wonders or given the American people such a splendid exhibition of play. The visit made a tremendous sensation and will probably arouse fresh interest in the game of golf, enlisting many new members into the already large ranks of enthusiasts."

Rhonda Adair
Irish Champion
1900, 1901, 1902, 1903,
British Champion
1900 and 1903

The famous British player, Harold Hilton, said of Rhona, "She stands up to the ball in a manner quite worthy of the sterner sex. There is determination and firmness in her address. Lady golfers as a general rule appear to persuade the ball on its way; Miss Adair, on the contrary, hits very hard indeed." Her power play astonished her American hosts. After her marriage Rhona retired from competitive golf but took an active interest ILGU affairs being President in 1931-1933 and thereafter Honorary Vice-President until her death in 1961. Since that golden era we have had the occasional British champion - Kitty McCann (1951), Philomena Garvey (1957), Maureen Madill (1979), Lillian Behan (1985). While Irish winners of the slightly less prestigious British Ladies Stroke Play Championship were Mary McKenna (1979), Maureen Madill (1980) and Claire Hourihane (1986). Unlike their male colleagues, Irish lady professionals have been few and far between, none of them has ever to make an impact or come anywhere near the success achieved by our men.

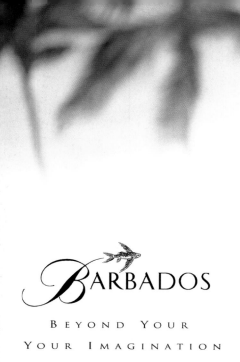

BARBADOS

BEYOND YOUR YOUR IMAGINATION

$\mathscr{T}$he original Barbados Golf and Country Club was designed and built in 1974 by notable architect Col J Harris . For more than 20 years it has laid sleeping and awaiting its rebirth. In August 2000 the redesigned and completely reconstructed Barbados Golf Club reopened as Barbados first Championship golf course open to visitors.

The 6,805 yards par 72 courses is an official destination of the PGA European Tour, magnificent trees strategically planted 25 years ago give the course a mature ambience. Two lakes intrude and enhance play on five holes and create a dramatic Amen Corner on holes 15 and 16 . A series of coral waste bunkers carved through 4 holes adds to the excitement and personality of the course. Ron Kirby one of the most respected and experienced golf course architects in the world, redesigned the course to be fair , challenging and a pleasurable walk amidst tropical surroundings

COURSE RATING

USGA Slope rating Blue 124
USGA Course rating Blue 71.0

FACTS AND FACILITIES

18 Hole Championship golf course
6805 Yards Par 72
Clubhouse Bar and Restaurant
Tax free merchandising and pro shop
Club rentals (Cobras)
Warm up nets Pre book able tee times
Cart, electric trolley and pull cart rentals

www.barbadosgolfclub.com

Now fly to your dream golfing destination in the hands of the Caribbean experts BWIA,
With over 60 years experience in flying golfers to more parts of the Caribbean than any other airline. We fly direct from London with great connections from Ireland to Barbados and onward to over 20 destinations within the Caribbean. Relax onboard our new state of the art Airbus aircraft knowing you will receive your Caribbean warmth from the moment you start to fly with us . We have the best fares available on flights to your dream golfing holidays through our partners in Ireland Castle Transport, call 01 201-3915 for further details.

Castle Transport
&Marketing Service

ACCOMMODATION GUIDE

The Hotels and Guest Houses listed in this section are all you need to find the accommodation you require for Golf travel or Business reservations. You should always use your Essential Golfers Guide Ireland when making your choice of accommodation.

THE ESSENTIAL

GOLFERS GUIDE

IRELAND 2003

CARNSIDE
23 Causeway Road, Giants Causeway, Bushmills, Co. Antrim BT57 8SU.

Contact: Alice Trufelli

T: 028-20731337/0077-647395
F: 028-70825761
E: carnsideguests-gaintscauseway@hotmail.com

Bushfoot Golf Club 2miles.

COLLIERS HALL
50 Cushendall Road, Ballycastle, Co. Antrim BT54 6QR.

Contact: Maurren McCarry

T: 028-20762531
E: reservations@colliershall.com
W: www.colliershall.com

Ballycastle Golf Club 2 miles.

CRAIGALAPPIN COUNTRY HOUSE
26 Craigalappin Road, Co. Antrim BT57 8X4.

Contact: A Matthews

T: 028-20732027

Rathmore Golf Club 10miles.

GALGORM HOUSE
117 Eglington Street, Portrush, Co. Antrim BT56 8D2.

Contact: Drew & Ann Semple

T: 028-70823787
E: semple/ann@hotmail.com
W: www.galgormhse.co.uk

Royal Portrush Golf Club 0.5 miles.

HARBOUR HEIGHTS
17 Kerr Street, Portrush, Co. Antrim BT56 8DG.

Contact: Ann Rossborough

T: 028-70822765   F: 028-70822558
E: info@harbourheightsportrush.com
W: www.harbourheightsportrush.com

Royal Portrush Golf Club 0.5miles.

MALONE HOUSE
79 Malone Road, Belfast, Co Antrim BT9 6SH.

Contact: Ruby Millar

T: 028-90669565
F: 028-90375090

Balmoral Golf Club 1mile.

OAKFIELD
9 Crumlin Road, Lower Ballinderry, Lisburn, Co. Antrim BT28 2JU.

Contact: Rosaleen Faloon

T: 028-92651307

Antrim Golf Club 2miles.

PORTCAMPLEY
8 Harbour Road, Ballintoy, Ballycastle, Co. Antrim BT54 6NA.

Contact: Megan Donnelly

T: 028-20768200
E: m.donnelly@btclick.com

Ballycastle Golf Club 4miles.

WARREN GUEST HOUSE
10 Thornhill Road, Kingsway, Dunmurr, Belfast, Co Antrim BT17 9EJ.

Contact: Mary Hughes

T: 024-90611702   F: 028-90620654
E: info@warrenhouseni.com
W: www.warrenhouseni.com

Dunmurry Golf Club 1mile.

CHERRYVILLE HOUSE
180 Dungannon Road, Portadown, Co. Armagh.

Contact: Stephen & Claire Trouton

T: 028-38852323
E: claire@cherryvillehouse.fs.net.co.uk
W: www.cherryvillehouse.com

Portadown Golf Club 5miles.

GERALDINE HOUSE
CARLOW

Aghade, Kilbride, Carlow.

Contact: Anne & John Fitzgerald

T: 0503-55642
E: gerhouse@iol.ie

Mount Wolseley Golf Club 1mile.

MCHUGHS COURTHOUSE HOTEL
CARLOW

38/39 Dublin Street, Carlow.

Contact: Richard McHugh

T   059-9133243
E: info@mchughscourthousehotel.com
W: www.mchughscourthousehotel.com

Carlow Golf Club 1.5miles.

EONISH LODGE
CAVAN

Eonish, Killeshandra, Co. Cavan.

Contact: Geraldine O'Reilly

T: 049-4334487
E: eonishlodge@eircom.net

Slieve Russell Golf Club 9miles.

OAK LODGE
CAVAN

Corranierna, Ballyconnell, Co. Cavan.

Contact: Eugene & Caroline Burns

T: 049-9526047

Slieve Russell Golf Club 1mile.

ROCKWOOD HOUSE
CAVAN

Cloverhill, Belturbet, Co. Cavan.

Contact: James & Susan McCauley

T: 047-55351
F: 047-55373
E: jbmac@eircom.net

Belturbet Golf Club 4miles.

AVALON
CLARE

11 Ballycaseymore Hill, Shannon, Co. Clare.

Contact: Mary O'Loughlin

T: 061-362032
E: avalonbnb@eircom.net

Shannon Golf Club 3.5miles.

CHURCHFIELD HOUSE
CLARE

Inch, Ennis, Co Clare.

Contact: Ann Talty

T: 065-6839167
E: churchfieldinch@eircom.net

Woodstock Golf Club 4miles.

CLAREVILLE HOUSE
CLARE

Tuamgraney, Scariff, Co. Clare.

Contact: Teresa Browne

T: 061-922925/087-6867548
W: www.clarevillehouse.com

Kilkee Golf Club 10miles.

GORTEEN FARM HOUSE
CLARE

Tulla, Co Clare.

Contact: Mary Hoey

T: 065-6835140

East Clare Golf Club 1mile.

LE BORD DE MER
CLARE

Miltown Malbay Road, Lahinch, Co. Clare.

Contact: Annie O'Brien

T: 065-7081454
E: annieobrien@boinet.ie

Lahinch Golf Club 1mile.

LIG DO SCITH
Ogonnelloe, Scariff, Co Clare

Contact: Kathleen Flannery

T: 061-923172
E: ligdoscithbandb@eircom.net

Kilrush Golf Club 4miles.

BANTRY HOUSE
Bantry, Co. Cork.

Contact: Mr. & Mrs. Shellswell-White

T: 027-50047
E: info@bantryhouse.ie

Bantry Bay Golf Club 1mile.

CASTLE ISLAND VIEW
Dereenatra, Schull, Co. Cork.

Contact: Eileen Whelton

T: 028-28102
E: eileenwhelton@hotmail.com

Coosheen Schull Golf Club 1mile.

GOLDEN GARDEN
Cappagh, Kinsale, Co. Cork.

Contact: Bernie Godkin

T: 021-4772490

Kinsale Golf Club 2miles.

HARBOUR LODGE & VINTAGE RESTAURANT
Scilly, Kinsale, Co. Cork.

Contact: Raoul & Seiko De Gendre

T: 021-4772376
F: 021-4772675
E: relax@harbourlodge.com

Old Head Golf Links 7miles.

KILBOLANE HOUSE
Milford, Charleville, Co. Cork.

Contact: Patricia Bourke

T: 063-80171
E: kilbolanehse@msn.com

Charleville Golf Club 5miles.

ST. MARTINS
Greencloyne, Youghal, Co Cork.

Contact: Margôt Barry

T: 024-92992

Youghal Golf Club 1mile.

THE OLD IMPERIAL HOTEL
27 North Main Street, Youghal, Co Cork.

Contact: James & Mary Browne

T: 024-92435 F: 024-90268
E: theoldimperialhotel@eircom.net
W: www.theoldimperialhotel.com
Youghal Golf Club 1mile.
See our display advert page 104

ARKLE HOUSE
2 Coshquin Road, Derry.

Contact: Terry Cassidy

T: 028-71271156
E: arklehse@tinyonline.co.uk

Ballyliffin Golf Club 16 miles.

BREEZEMOUNT HOUSE
26 Castlerock Road, Coleraine,
Co. Derry BT51 3HP.

Contact: Winston Wallace

T: 028-70344615
E: breezemounthouse@csi.com

Castlerock Golf Club 4miles.

COOLBEG
2E Grange Road, Coleraine, Derry.

Contact: Dorothy Chandler

T: 028-70344961
E: dorothy@coolbeg.totalserve.co.uk

Portstewart Golf Club 4miles.

DRUMCOVITT HOUSE & BARN
304 Feeny Road, Feeny, Co. Derry BT47 4SU.

Contact: Florence & Frank Sloan

T/F: 028-77781224
E: drumcovitt.feeny@btinternet.com

Radisson Roe Golf Club 8miles.

ARDEEN HOUSE
Ardeen, Ramelton, Co. Donegal.

Contact: Anne Campbell

T: 074-51243
E: ardeenbandb@eircom.net

Portsalon Golf Club 10miles.

CALDRA
Lisnakelly, Buncrana, Co. Donegal.
Contact: Marie Vaughan

T: 074-9363703
F: 074-9363759

Ballyliffin Golf Club 9miles.

CARNAWEEN HOUSE
Narin-Portnoo, Co. Donegal.

Contact: Nora Shovlin

T: 075-45122

Narin-Portnoo Golf Club 0.5miles.

COVE HILL HOUSE
Port Road, Letterkenny, Co. Donegal.

Contact: Jo McGlinchey

T: 074-21038

Letterkenny Golf Club 2miles.

GARTON
(Outdoor Education Centre)
Church Hill, Letterkenny, Co. Donegal.

Contact: Reservations

T: 074-9137032   F: 074-9137254
E: office@garton.com
W: www.garton.com
Letterkenny Golf Club 10miles
See our display advert page 45

JACKSONS HOTEL
Ballybofey, Co. Donegal.

Contact: Barry Jackson

T: 074-31021
E: bjackson@iol.ie

Ballybofey & Stanorlar Golf Club 2miles.

LOGUES
Kincasslagh, Co. Donegal.

Contact: Dermot & Mary Logue

T: 075-43134
E: loguers@yahoo.com

Cruit Island Golf Club 4miles.

VIKING HOUSE HOTEL
Belcruit, Kincasslagh,Co Donegal.

Contact: May Carey

T: 075-43295
F: 075-43931
E: careyvikinghouse@eircom.net

Cruit Island Golf Club 2miles.

WESTBROOK HOUSE
Buncrana, Co. Donegal.

Contact: Margaret Grant

T: 077-61067
E: mgwest@eircom.net

Ballyliffin Golf Club 8miles.

ADAIRS
22 The Square, Portaferry, Newtownards,
Co. Down BT22 1LW.

Contact: Marie Adair

T: 028-42728412

Kirkistown Castle Golf Club 1mile.

ARDSEEIN
10 Golf Road, Helen's Bay, Co. Down BT19 1TL.

Contact: Rosie Campbell-Whyte

T: 028-91853443
E: ardseein@hotmail.com

Kirkistown Castle Golf Club 1mile.

MOUNT PLEASANT
38 Banbridge Road, Gilford,
Co. Down BT63 6DJ.

Contact: Margaret Gamble

T: 028-38831522
F: 028-38882555
E: contact@mountpleasantgilford.com

Banbridge Golf Club 1mile.

RAYANNE HOUSE
60 Demesne Road, Holywood,
Co. Down BT18 9EX.

Contact: Conor & Bernadette McClelland

T\F: 028-90425859

Holywood Golf Club 1mile.

THE MILL AT BALLYDUGAN
Drumcullen Road, Downpatrick, Co Down
BT30 8HZ.

Contact: Nicola Heyneke

T: 028-44613654 F: 028-44839754
E: info@ballyduganmill.com
W: www.ballyduganmill.com

Ardglass Golf Club 1mile.

ASHLING GUESTHOUSE
168 Upper Drumcondra Road, Dublin 9.

Contact: Michele Bonner

T\F: 01-8375432

Malahide Golf Club 2miles.

CLADDAGH HOUSE
Posey Row, Kinsealy, Co Dublin.

Contact: Elaine Connellan

T/F: 01-8461361

Portmarnock Links 1mile.

STILLORGAN PARK HOTEL
Stillorgan Road, Dublin.

Contact: Reservations

T: 01-2881621
F: 01-2831610
E: sales@stillorganpark.com

Foxrock Golf Club 1mile.

SUNTRAP
Carrslane, Balgriffin, Co. Dublin.

Contact: Tina Lynch

T: 01-8484351
F: 01-8484380
E: suntrapbb@eircom.net

Portmarnock Golf Club 3miles.

DONEGAL

DOWN

DOWN

DOWN

DOWN

DOWN

DUBLIN

DUBLIN

DUBLIN

DUBLIN

THE HOLIDAY INN

99-107 Pearce Street, Dublin 2.

Contact: Reservations

T: 01-6703666
E   infor@holidayinndublin.ie
W: www.holidayinndublincitycentre.ie
The Royal Dublin Golf Club 5miles.
See our display advert page 98

THE REEFS

Balbriggan Coast Road, Skerries, Co. Dublin.

Contact: Violet Clinton

T/F: 01-8491574

Skerries Golf Club 2miles.

WILLOW BANK HOUSE

60 Bellevue Road, Enniskillen, Co. Fermanagh
BT44 4JH.

Contact: Joan Foster

T: 028-66328582
E: joan@willowbankhouse.com

Castle Hume Golf Club 1mile.

ANACH CUIN HOUSE

36 Wellpark Grove, Galway City.

Contact: Mary O'Brien

T: 091-755120

Galway Bay Golf & Country Club 4miles.

CAPPA VEAGH

76 Dalysfort Road, Salthill, Galway.

Contact: Catherine Quinlan

T: 091-526518
E: cappaghveaghbandb@eircom.net

Galway Golf Club 1.5miles.

DUN LIOS

Parkwest, Spiddal, Co. Galway.

Contact: Alice Canconnan

T: 091-553165
E: concass@indigo.ie

Barna Golf Club 5miles.

ERRISEASK HOUSE HOTEL

Ballyconneely, Clifden, Co. Galway.

Contact: Reservations

T: 095-23553
E: info@erriseask.com

Connemara Golf Club 2.5miles.

FERMOYLE LODGE

Costello, Co. Galway.

Contact: Nicola Stronach

T: 091-786111   F: 091-786154
E: fermoylelodge@eircom.net
W: www.fermoylelodge.com

Connemara Golf Club 10miles.

**GALWAY BAY GOLF &
COUNTRY CLUB**

Renville, Oranmore, Galway.

Contact: Reservations

T: 091-790503   F: 091-792510
E: gbay@iol.ie
W: www.gbaygolf.com
At Galway Bay Golf & Country Golf.
See our display advert page 68

OLDTHORT HOUSE

Oldthort, Tynagh Road, Portumna, Co. Galway.

Contact: Martin & Dympna Donoghue

T: 0509-41666
E: donoghuesoldthort@eircom.net

Portumna Golf Club 0.5miles.

RADISSON SAS HOTEL
Lough Atalia Road, Galway.

Contact: Reservations

T: 091-538300
F: 091-538506
W: www.RadissonSAS.com
Galway Golf Club 2miles.
*See our display advert page 69

RIVERWALK HOUSE
Riverside, Oughterard, Co. Galway.

Contact: Patrick & Ann Kelleher

T: 091-552788
E: riverwalk@eircom.net

Oughterard Golf Club 0.5miles.

TEACH AN GHARRAIN
Ballygaraun South, Athenry, Co. Galway.

Contact: Marion McDonagh

T: 091-844579
F: 091-845390
E: mcdhaus@eircom.net

Athenry Golf Club 2.5miles.

TEACH AN EASARD
Ballyconneely, Connemara, Co. Galway.

Contact: Carmel Joyce

T: 095-23560
E: joycejt@eircom.net

Connemara Golf Club 1mile.

AN SPÉICE
Ballyferriter West, Dingle, Co. Kerry.

Contact: Alice Hannafin

T: 066-9156254

Ceann Sibéal Golf Links 1.5miles.

BALLYGARRY HOUSE
Killarney Road, Tralee, Co Kerry.

Contact: Reservations

T: 066-7123322 F: 066-7127630
E: info@ballygarryhouse.com
W: www.ballygarryhouse.com
Tralee Golf Club 1mile.
*See our display advert page 104

CASHEN COURSE HOUSE
Golf Links Road, Ballybunion, Co. Kerry.

Contact: Deirdre O'Brien

T: 068-27351
E: golfstay@eircom.net
W: www.playballybunion.com
Ballybunion Golf Club (Cashen Course) 0.5Miles.

CASTLE VIEW HOUSE
Carrig Island, Ballylongford, Co. Kerry.

Contact: Patricia & Garrett Dee

T: 068-43304
E: castleviewhouse@eircom.net

Ballybunion Golf Club 2miles.

CLIFFORDS
Main Street, Waterville, Co. Kerry.

Contact: Abbie Clifford

T: 066-9474283
E: cliffordbandb@eircom.net

Waterville Golf Club 1mile.

FERRITERS COVE
Ballyoughtra, Ballyferriter, Tralee, Co. Kerry.

Contact: Padraig & Marguerite Ferriter

T: 066-9156295
E: fcove@gofree.indigo.ie

Ceann Sibéal Golf Links 0.5miles.

Side labels: GALWAY, GALWAY, GALWAY, GALWAY, KERRY, KERRY, KERRY, KERRY, KERRY, KERRY

KILBURN HOUSE
Miltown, Killarney, Co. Kerry.

Contact: Mr. & Mrs. Podge

KERRY

T: 066-9767364
E: info@stayatkilburn.com
W: www.stayatkilburn.com

Dooks Golf Club 8miles.

NASHVILLE
Tralee Road, Killarney, Co. Kerry.

Contact: David Nash

KERRY

T: 064-32924
E: nashville@tinet.ie

Killarney Golf & Fishing Club 3miles.

RONNOCO
Knockanish, Spa, Tralee, Co. Kerry.

Contact: Majella Griffin

KERRY

T: 066-7136436
E: ligriffin@eircom.net

Tralee Golf Club 4miles.

ROSSMORE HOUSE
8 Ross Road, Killarney, Co. Kerry.

Contact: Maura & Michael McCarthy

KERRY

T: 064-34141
E: rossmorehousekly@hotmail.com

Ross Golf Club 0.5miles.

SEANOR HOUSE
Listowel Road, Ballybunion, Co. Kerry.

Contact: Sean & Nora Stack

KERRY

T: 068-27055
E: bed@eircom.net

Ballybunion Golf Club 1mile.

STRAND VIEW HOUSE
Kilcummin, Conor Pass Road, Castlegregory,
Co Kerry.

Contact: Mary Lynch

KERRY

T: 066-7138131   F: 066-7138386
E: strandview@eircom.net
W: www.strandview.com

Castlegregory Golf Club 1.5miles.

BELLA VISTA
105 Moorefield Park, Newbridge, Co. Kildare.

Contact: Breda Kelly

KILDARE

T: 045-431047
E: belavista@eircom.net

Curragh Golf Club 1.5mile.

STRAFFAN
Baybush, Straffan, Co Kildare.

Contact: Una Healy

KILDARE

T: 01-6272386
E: judj@glfree.indigo.ie
W: www.townandcourntry.ie

K-Club 1mile.

ANNA-VILLA
4 College Road, Kilkenny, Co. Kilkenny.

Contact: Sean Flynn

KILKENNY

T: 056-62680
F: 056- 62680
E: anna-villa@eircom.net

Kilkenny Golf Club 0.5miles.

ARAS MUIRE
21 Glendine Heights, Kilkenny.

KILKENNY

T/F: 056-51982

Kilkenny Golf Club 1mile.

BALLYOGAN HOUSE
New Ross Road, Graiguenamanagh,
Co. Kilkenny.

Contact: Fran Durie

T: 059-9725969
E: info@ballyoganhouse.com
W: www.ballyoganhouse.com

Mount Juliet Golf Club 10miles.

CHESTNUT LODGE
Kellsgrange, Kells, Co. Kilkenny.

Contact: Sean Behan

T: 056-28077

Mountainview Golf Club 4.5miles.

DAMERSTOWN FARM HOUSE
Damerstown, Castlecomer, Co. Kilkenny.

Contact: Liam & Mary Farrell

T: 056-41337

Castlecomer Golf Club 1.5miles.

FLOODHALL HOUSE
Floodhall, Knocktopher, Co. Kilkenny.

Contact: Mary Cummins

T: 056-68652 (087) 9536664

Mount Juliet Golf Club 1.5miles.

MOONARCH
Mullinahone Road, Callan, Co. Kilkenny.

Contact: Margaret Treacy

T: 056-25810
E: moonarch@indigo.ie
W: www.moonarch.com

Callan Golf Club 1.5miles.

ABBEYLEIX MANOR HOTEL
Abbeyleix, Co. Laois.

Contact: Reservations

T: 0502-30111
F: 0502-30220
E: info@abbeyleixmanorhotel.com

Abbeyleix Golf Club 0.5miles.

LANLEY
Mountsalem, Coolrain, Portlaoise, Co. Laois.

Contact: Janet Dooley

T: 0502-35013

Mountrath Golf Club 4miles.

TULLAMOY HOUSE
Tullamoy, Stradbally, Co. Laois.

Contact: Pat & Caroline Farrell

T: 0507-27111
E: tullamoy@indigo.ie

Heath Golf Club 6miles.

VILLA FLORA
Station Road, Carrick-on-Shannon,
Co. Leitrim.

Contact: Breedge Nolan

T: 078-20338

Carrick-on-Shannon Golf Club 3miles.

ABBEYVILLA
Station Road, Adare, Co. Limerick.

Contact: Elizabeth Jordan

T: 061-396113
E: abbeyvilla@eircom.net

Adare Manor Hotel & Golf Resort 0.5miles.

AVONA HOUSE	T:	061-396323
Kildimo Road, Adare, Co. Limerick.	E:	avona@eircom.net
Contact: Anna Harrington		
	Adare Manor Golf Club 0.5miles.	

LIMERICK

BERKELEY LODGE	T:	061-396857
Station Road, Adare, Co. Limerick.	E:	berlodge@iol.ie
	W:	www.adare.org
Contact: Pat & Bridie Donegan		
	Adare Manor Golf Club 0.5miles.	

LIMERICK

COURTENAY LODGE HOTEL	T:	069-62244
Newcastle West, Co. Limerick.	F:	069-77184
	E:	res@courtenaylodge.iol.ie
Contact: Marie Hayes		
	Newcastle West Golf Club 1mile.	

LIMERICK

RATHKEALE HOUSE HOTEL	T:	069-63333
Lower Main Street, Rathkeale, Co. Limerick.	F:	069-63300
	E:	rhh@iol.ie
Contact: Gerry O'Connor		
	Newcastle West Golf Club 3miles.	

LIMERICK

TWIN OAKS	T:	061-311633
Singland, Dublin Road, Limerick.		
Contact: Madeline Kelly		
	Castletroy Golf Club 1mile.	

LIMERICK

WOODFIELD HOUSE HOTEL	T:	061-453022 F: 061-326755
Ennis Road, Limerick.	E:	woodfieldhotel@eircom.net
	W:	www.woodfieldhousehotel.com
Contact: Austin Gibbons		
	Shannon Golf Club 7miles.	

LIMERICK

HARWOOD HEIGHTS	T:	042-9373379
Mountain Park, Carlingford, Co. Louth.	E:	harwoodheights@hotmail.com
Contact: Nuala Harold		
	Greenore Golf Club 3miles.	

LOUTH

INNISFREE GUEST HOUSE	T:	042-9334912
Carrick Road, Dundalk, Co. Louth.	E:	info@innisfreeguesthouse.com
Contact: Rosie Bell		
	Dundalk Golf Club 3miles.	

LOUTH

SALLYWELL HOUSE	T:	041-9834816
Hill of Rath, Drogheda, Co. Louth.	E:	sallywellhouse@eircom.net
	W:	www.sallywell.com
Contact: Mona Dunne		
	Seapoint Golf Club 7.5miles.	

LOUTH

SETANTA HOUSE	T:	041-6853319
7 Castle Street, Ardee, Co. Louth.	F:	041-6853413
Contact: Declan & Úna Taaffe		
	Ardee Golf Club 1.5miles.	

LOUTH

CARRICKHILL HOUSE
Breaffy, Castlebar, Co. Mayo.

Contact: Eileen Barrett

MAYO

T: 094-24046
E: jwbarrett@eircom.net

Castlebar Golf Club 3miles

DANAGHERS HOTEL
Cong, Co Mayo.

Contact: Harry & Helena Byrne

MAYO

T: 092-46028 / 48948
E: danaghers@hotmail.com

Close to Connemara Golf Club.
*See our display advert page 57

NEW LODGE
Station Road, Ballina, Co. Mayo.

Contact: Séan & Phil Henry

MAYO

T: 096-72693

Enniscrone Golf Club 5miles.

RIVER LODGE
River Lodge, Cong, Co. Mayo.

Contact: Breege Ryan

MAYO

T: 092-46057
E: bridryan1@eircom.net

Ballinrobe Golf Club 7.5miles.

ROCKSBERRY
Westport Road, Castlebar, Co. Mayo.

Contact: Bernadette Walsh

MAYO

T: 094-27254

Castlebar Golf Club 3miles.

THE WYATT HOTEL
The Octagon, Westport, Co Mayo.

Contact: Reservations

MAYO

T: 098-25027
E: info@wyatthotel.com

Westport Golf Club 1mile.
*See our display advert page 109

AVALON
5 Headfort Park, Kells, Co. Meath.

Contact: Terry Nolan

MEATH

T: 046-41536

Headfort Golf Club 2.5miles.

LIS-MAURA
Bettystown, Co. Meath.

Contact: Charlotte Lyons

MEATH

T: 041-9828387
F: 041-9887288

Laytown & Bettystown Golf Club 1mile.

MAHERFIELD HOUSE
Ross, Tara, Co. Meath.

Contact: Gloria Goggins

MEATH

T: 046-25784
E: mgoggins@gofree.indigo.ie

Royal Tara Golf Club 2miles.

ARRADALE HOUSE
Kingscourt Road, Carrickmacross,
Co Monaghan.

Contact: Christine McMahon

MONAGHAN

T: 042-9661941

Cabra Castle Golf Club 3miles.

CASTLE LESLIE
Glaslough, Co. Monaghan.

Contact: Reservations

T: 047-88109 F: 047-88256
E: info@castleleslie.com
W: www.castleleslie.com
Rossmore Golf Club 6miles.
*See our display advert page 150

GRANGEVIEW HOUSE
Mullinderg, Emyvale, Co. Monaghan.

Contact: Maureen Treanor

T: 047-87358

Rossmore Golf Club 7miles.

PINE LODGE
Ross, Screggan, Tullamore, Co. Offaly.

Contact: Claudia Krygel

T: 0506-51927

Tullamore Golf Club 1mile.

RAHAN LODGE
Tullamore, Co. Offaly.

Contact: Carole McDermott

T: 0506-55796
F: 0506-55606
E: info@rahanlodge.com

Esker Hills Golf Club 4miles.

FOREST PARK HOUSE
Carrick Road, Boyle, Co. Roscommon.

Contact: Eileen Kelly

T: 079-62227
E: forestparkhse@hotmail.com
W: www.bed-and-breakfast-boyle.com

Boyle Golf Club 0.5miles.

THE VILLA
Galway Road, Roscommon, Co. Roscommon.

Contact: Noreen O'Grady

T: 0906-625998
E: thevilla@oceanfree.net
W: www.ebookireland.com

Roscommon Golf Club 0.5miles.

PARK HOUSE
Pearse Road, Sligo.

Contact: Peter McManamy

T: 071-70333
E: parkhousebandb@eircom.net

Rosses Point Golf Club 3miles.

ST. ANNES
Pearse Road, Sligo Town, Co. Sligo.

Contact: Patricia Sheridan

T: 071-43188

County Sligo Golf Club 3miles.

ABBEYVALE HOUSE
Cashel Road, Holycross, Thurles, Co. Tipperary.

For reservations contact: Ed & Mary Hunt

T: 0504-43032
E: abbeyval@gofree.indigo.ie

County Tipperary Golf & Country Club 1mile.

ASHLEY PARK HOUSE
Ashley, Ardcrony, Nenagh, Co. Tipperary.

Contact: PJ & Margaret Mounsey

T: 067-38233
F: 067-38013
E: margaret@ashleypark.com

Nenagh Golf Club 2miles.

TIPPERARY

DUNDRUM HOUSE HOTEL
Dundrum, Cashel, Co. Tipperary.

Contact: Reservations

T: 062-71116   F: 062-71366
E: dundrumh@iol.ie
W: www.dundrumhousehotel.com
At County Tipperary Golf & Country Club.
See our display advert page page 34

TIPPERARY

KYLENOE
Ballinderry, Nenagh, Co Tipperary.

Contact: Virginia Moeran

T: 067-22015 / 086-2756000
F: 067-22275

Portumna Golf Club 9miles.

TIPPERARY

MONAINCHA HOUSE & FITNESS CLUB
Dublin Road, Roscrea, Co. Tipperary.
Contact: Carmel Moore

T: 0505-23181
E: info@monainchahouse.com

Roscrea Golf Club 0.5miles.

TIPPERARY

THE CASTLE
Two Mile Borris, Thurles, Co. Tipperary.

Contact: Pierce & Joan Duggan

T: 0504-44324
E: bandb@thecastletmb.com
W: www.thecastletmb.com

Thurles Golf Club 3miles.

TYRONE

FORTVIEW
36 Tullyboy Road, Cookstown, Co. Tyrone
BT45 7YE.

Contact: Joan Davison

T: 028-86762640
E: b-bfortview@talk21.com

Killymoon Golf Club 3miles.

OMAGH

MCGUIRES COUNTRY INN
115 Baronscourt Road, Drumquin, Omagh,
Co. Tyrone BT78 4TB.

Contact: Eithne McGuire

T/F: 028-81662029

Omagh Golf Club 1mile.

TYRONE

STANGMORE COUNTRY HOUSE
65 Moy Road, Dungannon,
Co Tyrone BT71 7DT.

Contact: Anne & Andy Brace

T: 028-87725600
F: 028-87726644
E: info@stangmorecountryhouse.com
W: www.stangmorecountryhouse.com
Royal Dungannon Golf Club 3miles.

WATERFORD

CLONEEN
Love Lane, Tramore, Co. Waterford.

Contact: Maria Skedd

T/F: 051-381264
E: cloneen@iol.ie

Tramore Golf Club 1mile.

WATERFORD

LISMORE HOTEL
Lismore, Co. Waterford.

Contact: Sean Read

T: 058-54555
F: 058-53068
E: lismorehotel@eircom.net

Lismore Golf Club 1mile.

WATERFORD

PINETREE HOUSE
Ballyanchor, Lismore, Co. Waterford.

Contact: Daphne & Shaun Power

T: 058-53282
E: pinetreehouse@oceanfree.net
W: www.pinetreehouselismore.com

Lismore Golf Club 0.5miles.

READES FARMHOUSE & BAR	T: 051-898430 / 086-2754298
Hillview, Lukeswell, Mullinavatt, Co. Waterford.	
Contact: Margaret Reade	
	Faithlegg Golf Club 15miles.

WATERFORD

WATERFORD CASTLE	T: 051-878203 F: 051-878342
The Island Ballinakill, Waterford.	E: info@waterfordcastle.com
	W: www.waterfordcastle.com
Contact: Reservations	*At Waterford Castle Hotel & Golf Club.*
	*See our display advert page 109

WATERFORD

CATSTONE LODGE FARMHOUSE	T: 044-56494
Mullenmeehan, Ballymore, Co. Westmeath.	E: info@catstone.net
Contact: Evelyn & Klaus Filsinger	
	Moate Golf Club 3miles.

WESTMEATH

HODSON BAY HOTEL	T: 0902-80500 F: 0902-80587
(Conference & Leisure Centre)	E: info@hodsonbayhotel.com
Athlone, Co Westmeath.	W: www.hodsonbayhotel.com
	Athlone Golf Club 1mile.
Contact: Reservations	**See our display advert page 37*

WESTMEATH

INNY BAY	T: 0902-85284 / 087-6370237
Annagh, The Pigeons, Athlone,	E: foxed@eircom.net
Co. Westmeath.	
Contact: Paul & Deirdre Foxe	
	Nearest Club: Glasson Golf Club 5miles

WESTMEATH

MULLINGAR EQUESTRIAN CENTRE	T: 044-48331
Athlone Road, Mullingar, Co. Westmeath.	E: info@mullingarequestrian.com
Contact: Margaret Fagan	
	Mullingar Golf Club 1mile.

WESTMEATH

BALLYDUFF HOUSE	T: 054-88512
Ballycarney, Enniscorthy, Co Wexford.	F: 054-88131
	E: adpmurphy@hotmail.com
Contact: Yvonne Jordan & Donal Murphy	
	Enniscorthy 6.5miles.

WEXFORD

O'LEARYS FARM	T: 053-33134
Killilane, Rosslare Harbour, Co Wexford.	E: poleary@eircom.net
Contact: Philomena & Kathleen O'Leary	
	St. Helens Bay Golf Resort 0.5miles.

WEXFORD

STATION HOUSE	T: 053-32363
Station Road, Rosslare, Co. Wexford.	
Contact: Debbie Aherne	
	Rosslare Golf Club 1mile.

WEXFORD

STONELODGE	T: 055-25765 / 087-2378776
Riverchaple, Courtown, Gorey, Co. Wexford.	F: 055-20467
Contact: Claire Mullins	
	Courtown Golf Club 1mile.

WEXFORD

TOWNPARKS HOUSE
Coolcotts, Wexford.

Contact: Angela Doocey

T: 053-45191

Wexford Golf Club 1mile.

BALLYKILTY HOUSE
Coolgreany, Arklow, Co. Wicklow.

Contact: A Nuzum

T: 0402-37111
E: ballykiltyfarmhouse@eircom.net

Arklow Golf Club 1mile.

DOIRE COILLE HOUSE
Glendalough Cullentragh, Rathdrum,
Co. Wicklow.

Contact: Mary Byrne

T: 0404- 45131
E: marybyrne@esatclear.ie

Glenmalure Golf Club 3miles.

DRUIDS HOUSE
Kilmacullagh, Newtownmountkennedy, Co.
Wicklow.

Contact: Catherine Tierney

T: 01-2819477

Druids Glen Golf Club 1mile.

GLANDORE
St. Vincent Road, Burnaby Estate, Greystones,
Co. Wicklow.

Contact: Malcolm & Penny Hall

T: 01-2874364
E: glandorepennyhall@eircom.net

Greystones Golf Club 1mile.

LARNOR
Ballynerrin Lower, Wicklow.

Contact: Mary Larkin

T: 0404-69266
E: larkinmick@hotmail.com

Wicklow Golf Club 2miles.

PLATTENSTOWN HOUSE
Coolgreaney Road, Arklow, Co. Wicklow.

Contact: Margaret McDowell

T: 0402-37822
E: mcdpr@indigo.ie

Arklow Golf Club 3miles.

RATHMORE COUNTRY HOUSE
Rathmore, Ashford, Co. Wicklow.

Contact: Belinda Cullen

T: 086-8858127
E: rathmorecountryhouse@indigo.ie
W: www.rathmorecountryhouse.com

The European Club 9miles.

TULFARRIS HOTEL & GOLF RESORT
Blessington Lakes, Co. Wicklow.

Contact: Reservations

T: 045-867600 F: 045-867565
E: info@tulfarris.com
W: www.tulfarris.com
At Tulfarris Golf Resort
See our display advert page 161

---

*If a lot of people gripped a knife and fork the way they do a golf club,
they'd starve to death.*
Sam Snead

DINING
GUIDE

Whilst on your travels of the
Great Golf Courses of Ireland we
can recommend the following
restaurants and eateries to enjoy
some "Fine Irish Dining". All the
establishments listed in this section
welcome groups and corporate
outings.

THE ESSENTIAL
GOLFERS GUIDE
IRELAND 2003

TEDFORDS RESTAURANT
5 Donegall Quay, Belfast BT1 3EF.
Co Antrim.

Contact: Aidan Small.

T: 028-90434000
F: 028-90248889

Royal Belfast Golf Club 4 Miles.

THE PAVILLON RESTAURANT
Galgorm Castle, Galgorm Road,
Ballymena, Co. Antrim BT42 1HL.

Contact: Sean McCollun

T: 028-25650220
F: 028-25630173

Ballymena Golf Club 3 Miles.

WATER MARGIN RESTAURANT
159-161 Donegal Pass, Belfast,
Co. Antrim.

Contact: Elizabeth Tuman.

T: 028-90326888
F: 028-90327333
E: water.margin@btconnect.com

Fortwilliam Golf Club 2 Miles.

MONTAGU ARMS
9-19 Church Street, Tandragee,
Co. Armagh BT62 7AF.

Contact: Gary Rogerson

T: 028-38840219

Tandragee Golf Club 0.5 Miles.

PALACE STABLE RESTAURANT
& Outside Catering
The Palace, Demense,
Armagh BT60 4EL.
Contact: Craig Lee.

T: 028-37529634

Armagh Golf Club 1 Mile.

THE GREEN DRAKE INN
Borris, Co. Carlow.

Contact: Annette Walsh.

T: 0503-73116

Borris Golf Club 1 Mile.

LITTLE SICILY RESTAURANT
18, Newcourt Centre, Church Street,
Cavan.
Contact: Ibrahim Shalabi or
             Sophie Hamilton.

T: 049-4362558
F: 049-4362530
E: manager@little-siciliy.com

Cavan Golf Club 2 Miles.

THE OLD POST INN
Clover Hill, Co. Cavan.

Contact: Tara McCann.

T: 047-55555
F: 047-55111

Slieve Russell Golf Club 8 Miles.

BLACK OAK RESTAURANT
Rineen, Miltown Malbay, Co. Clare.

Contact: Bernie & Tom Hamilton .

T: 065-7084403

Lahinch Golf Club 4 Miles.

CLARE

GALLOPING HOGANS
Ballina, Killaloe, Co. Clare.

Contact: John White.

T: 061-376162
F: 061-375492

East Clare Golf Club 2 Miles.

CLARE

THE BALI ROOM RESTAURANT
Main Street, Newmarket-on-Fergus,
Co. Clare.

Contact: Paul or Neneng Higgins.

T: 061-368114

Dromoland Golf Club 1.5 Miles.

CLARE

BANNA THAI
15 Maylor Street, Cork.

Contact: Sulesri Pisanvaioert.

T: 021-4251571
F: 021-4251583

Cork Golf Club 2 Miles.

CORK

CRACKPOTS RESTAURANT
3 Cork Street, Kinsale, Co. Cork.

Contact: Carole Norman.

T: 021-4772847
E: crackpots@iol.ie

Old Head Golf Links 7 Miles.

CORK

ISAACS RESTAURANT
48 MacCurtain Street, Cork.

Contact: Michael Ryan.

T: 021-4503805
F: 021-4557348
E: isaacs@iol.ie

Fota Island Golf Club 2 Miles.

CORK

LARCHWOOD
Pearsons Bridge, Bantry, Co Cork

Contact: Sheila Vaughan.

T: 027-66181

Bantry Bay Golf Club 1 Mile.

CORK

NAKON THAI
Tramway House, Douglas, Cork.

Contact: Dave McGreal.

T: 021-4369900
F: 021-4888002
W: www.nakonthai.com

Fota Island Golf Club 6 Miles.

CORK

CORK

OVERDRAUGHT BAR & RESTAURANT
Tracton, Minane Bridge, Co. Cork.

Contact: Margaret Murray.

T: 021-4887136

Kinsale Golf Club 10 Miles.

CORK

PI RESTAURANT & WINE BAR
Washington Street, Cork.

Contact: Robert O'Leary.

T: 021-4222860
W: www.pirestaurant.com

Fota Island Golf Club 5 Miles.

CORK

PROBYS RESTAURANT
Proby's Quay, Crosses Green, Cork.

Contact: Michael Condon.

T: 021-4316531
F: 021-4975882
E: info@probysbistro.com

Harbour Point Golf Club 5 Miles.

CORK

SAVANNAH WATERFRONT RESTAURANT & Wharf Tavern
Trident Hotel, World's End, Kinsale, Co. Cork.
Contact: Hal McElroy (Managing

Director).   T: 021-4772301
E: info@tridenthotel.com

Old Head Golf Links 7 Miles.

CORK

THE PINEWOOD INN
Main Street, Charleville, Co. Cork.

Contact: Noel O'Toole.

T: 063-81551
E: thepinewoodinn@hotmail.com

Charleville Golf Club 2 Miles.

CORK

THE WHITE DEER
Bridge Street, Mallow, Co. Cork.

Contact: Pat Mannix.

T: 022-51299/51952

Mallow Golf Club 2 Miles.

DERRY

KAM HOUSE CHINESE RESTAURANT
14/16 William Street, Derry BT4 8ES.

Contact: Joe Kam.

T: 028-71372166
F: 028-71372252

Foyle Golf Club 1 Mile.

DONEGAL

CASTLE INN
Greencastle, Co. Donegal.

Contact: Kevin McGowan.

T: 077-81426
F: 077-81427

Greencastle Golf Club 0.5 Miles.

DONEGAL

COXTOWN MANOR RESTAURANT
Belgian Gourmet Restaurant &
Accommodation
Laghey, Co. Donegal.
Contact: Edward Dewael.

T: 073-34575
F: 073-34576
E: coxtownmanor@oceanfree.net

Donegal Golf Club 2 Miles.

DUBLIN

CAFÉ TOPOLIS
37 Parliament Street, Temple Bar,
Dublin 2.

Contact: Azad Shirazi.

T: 01-6704961
E: saidamirkamvar@msn.com

Royal Dublin Golf Club 6 Miles.

DUBLIN

ELIZA BLUE
23/24 Wellington Quay, Dublin 2.

Contact: Danny Byrne.

T: 01-6719114
F: 01-6719113
W: www.elizablues.com

Sutton Golf Club 8 Miles.

DUBLIN

NICOS RESTAURANT
53 Dame Street, Dublin 2.

Contact: Emilio Cirillo & Graziano
Romeri.

T: 01-6773062

Elm Park Golf Club 5 Miles.

DUBLIN

THE BLUE ORCHID
Newtown Park Avenue, Blackrock,
Dublin.

Contact: Nader Gholizadeh.

T: 01-2831767
F: 01-2880478
E: info@blueorchid.ie

Dun Laoghaire Golf Club 2 Miles.

GALWAY

DRUID LANE RESTAURANT
9 Quay Street, Galway.

Contact: Camilla Cutlan.

T / F: 091-563015

Galway Golf Club 3 Miles.

GALWAY

ODOWDS SEAFOOD BAR &
RESTAURANT
Roundstone, Connemara, Co. Galway.

Contact: Nicholas Griffin.

T: 095-35809
F: 095-35907
E: odowds@indigo.ie
W: www.odowdsrestaurant.com

Connemara Golf Club 1 Mile.

KERRY

FINNEGANS RESTAURANT
17 Denny Street, Tralee, Co. Kerry.

Contact: Bernard Cassidy.

T: 066-7181400
F: 066-7186756

Tralee Golf Club 7 Miles.

HARMONY RESTAURANT
Mill Road, Killorglin, Co. Kerry.

Contact: Jimmy Lei.

KERRY

T/F: 066-9790823

Killorglin Golf Club 2 Miles.

KIRBYS BROGUE INN & STEAKHOUSE
Rock Street, Tralee, Co. Kerry.

Contact: Bill & Mary Kirby.

KERRY

T: 066-23221
F: 066-28977

Tralee Golf Club 2 Miles.

PACKIES RESTAURANT
Henry Street, Kenmare, Co. Kerry.

Contact: Martin.

KERRY

T: 087-6593431

Kenmare Golf Club 1 Mile.

PADDYS RESTAURANT
35 Main Street, Killarney, Co. Kerry.

Contact: Paddy O'Donoghue.

KERRY

T: 064-36600
E: paddysrestaurant@eircom.net

*Killarney Golf &
Fishing Club 4 Miles.*

RESTAURANT DAVID NORRIS
Ivy House, Ivy Terrace, Tralee,
Co. Kerry.

Contact: David Norris.

KERRY

T: 066-7185654
F: 066-7126600

Tralee Golf Club 6 Miles.

THE BLIND PIPER
Caherdaniel, Co. Kerry.

Contact: Sandra O'Farrell.

KERRY

T: 066-9475126
E: blindpiper@indigo.ie

Waterville Golf Club 9 Miles.

THE THREE MERMAIDS
William Street, Listowel, Co. Kerry.

Contact: Pat Mahony.

KERRY

T: 068-21184

Ballybunion Golf Club 8 Miles.

THE LIME TREE BISTRO
The Square, Castlecomer,
Co. Kilkenny.

Contact: Maggie Brennan.

KILKENNY

T/F: 056-40966

Castlecomer Golf Club 0.5 Miles.

TAO TAO RESTAURANT
Main Street, Patrickswell, Co. Limerick.

Contact: Yang Jian.

T: 061-355999

Limerick Golf Club 3 Miles.

THE OLD BAKE HOUSE RESTAURANT
Main Street, Bruff, Co. Limerick.

Contact: Eric or Mary Lye.

T\F: 061-382797
E: barry.lye@tinet.ie

Limerick County Golf Club 1 Mile.

THE WILD GEESE RESTAURANT
Main Street, Adare, Co. Limerick.

Contact: Julie Randles.

T\F: 061-396451
E: wildgeese@indigo.ie

*Adare Manor Golf
Resort 0.5 Miles.*

BROADWAY BAR & RESTAURANT
Euston Street, Greenore, Co. Louth.

Contact: Eamonn & Maria Sheridan.

T: 042-9373209

Greenore Golf Club 0.5 Miles.

LYNCHS FERDIA ARMS
Castle Street, Ardee, Co. Louth.

Contact: Frank Lynch.

T: 041-6853331
F: 041-6853675

Ardee Golf Club 1 Mile.

SPORTSMANS BAR & RESTAURANT
Newry Road, Dundalk, Co. Louth.

Contact: Paul Keane.

T: 042-9371537
W:
www.sportsmansroadhouse.com

Dundalk Golf Club 1 Mile.

GRANDSTAND RESTAURANT
Ratoath Village, Co. Meath.

Contact: Colm Norton & Justine Fanning.

T: 01-8256880

Ashbourne Golf Club 2 Miles.

ANATOLIA RESTAURANT
Harbour Street, Tullamore, Co. Offaly.

Contact: Haluk Barut.

T/F: 0506-23669
E: service@anatolia.ie
W : www.anatolia.ie

Tullamore Golf Club 1 Mile.

LIMERICK LIMERICK LIMERICK LOUTH LOUTH LOUTH MEATH OFFALY

OFFALY

RIVERBANK RESTAURANT
Riverstown, Birr, Co. Offaly.

Contact: Declan Leonard & Des O'Connor.

T: 0509-21528
E: riverbankrest@msn.com

Birr Golf Club 1.5 Miles.

ROSCOMMON

DALYS TAVERN
Kiltoom, Athlone, Co. Roscommon.

Contact: Kevin Daly.

T/F: 0902-89082
E: dalystavern@eircom.net

Athlone Golf Club 1.5 Miles.

SLIGO

LECAN LODGE & WALSHES PUB
Main Street, Enniscrone, Co Sligo.

Contact: Eamonn & Catherine Walshe

T: 096-36110
F: 096-36574
E: epwalshe@iol.ie

Enniscrone Golf Club 0.5 Miles.

WATERFORD

CHEZ K'S RESTAURANT
20-22 William Street, Waterford.

Contact: Nessa Gaffney.

T: 051-844180
F: 051-856924

Waterford Golf Club 2 Miles.

WESTMEATH

GLASSON VILLAGE RESTAURANT
Glasson, Athlone, Co. Westmeath.

Contact: Michael Brooks.

T: 0902-85001
E: michaelbrooks@oceanfree.net
W: www.glassonvillagerestaurant.com

Glasson Golf Club 1 Mile.

WEXFORD

THE UPPER DECK SEAFOOD RESTAURANT
Kilmore Quay, Co. Wexford.

Contact: Deirdre Brady.

T: 053-48966
F: 053-48925

Rosslare Golf Club 7 Miles.

WICKLOW

KITTYS RESTAURANT
56 Main Street, Arklow, Co. Wicklow.

Contact: Conor Lawlor.

T: 0402-31669
F: 0402-31553

The European Club 3 Miles.

WICKLOW

MADELINES RESTAURANT & GUEST ACCOMMODATION
Tinahely, Arklow, Co. Wicklow.

Contact: Madeline Menton.

T\F: 0402-38166

Coollattin Golf Club 5 Miles.

OUGHTERARD GOLF CLUB

Founded as a nine-hole course in 1974, it was upgraded to 18 in 1982. Oughterard enjoys a reputation for being a friendly and progressive Club embracing all of the best qualities that golf can offer, a testing challenge, excellent food, a hospitable bar and welcoming members. Located beside Lough Corrib at the edge of Connemara, Oughterard is the ideal place to golf in the West of Ireland.

The course from the Medal Tees measures 6426 Yards, but a choice of teeing areas offers golfers of all abilities an opportunity to test themselves against lesser or greater distances, but whatever the choice, careful shot planning is essential to avoid the multiplicity of hazards abounding the course.

OUGHTERARD GOLF CLUB
Oughterard, Co. Galway
Tel 091 552131   Fax 091 552733
e-mail oughterardgc@eircom.net
Club Professional: Michael Ryan
Club Secretary: John Waters (086 2739933)

The Ball

In my hand I hold a ball,
white and dimpled, rather small
oh, how bland it does appear
this harmless looking little sphere.

By it's size I could not guess,
the awesome strength it does possess.
But since I fell beneath its spell,
I've wandered through the fires of hell.

My life has not been quite the same,
since I chose to play this game.
It rules my mind for hours on end,
a fortune it has made me spend.

It has made me curse and cry,
I hate myself and want to die.
It promises a thing called par,
if I can hit it straight and far.

To master such a tiny ball,
should not be very hard at all.
But my desires the ball refuses,
and does exactly as it chooses.

It hooks and slices, dribbles and dies,
or disappears before my eyes.
Often it will have a whim,
to hit a tree or take a swim.

With miles of grass on which to land,
it finds a tiny patch of sand.
Then has me offering up my soul,
if only it would find the hole.

It's made me whimper like a pup,
and swear that I will give it up.
And take to drink to ease my sorrow,
but the ball knows...

I'll be back tomorrow

IVAN MORRIS

CARTON HOUSE

GOLF CLUB

The Mark O'Meara

Located at Carton House, Maynooth, just 30 minutes drive from Dublin's city centre, is one of Ireland's greatest estates, providing the golfer today with two great courses and a choice of parkland or "inland links" style golf.

The O'Meara
"The course is demure rather than showy but with an overwhelming feel of subtle class..."
The Montgomerie
"It has grace as with many of the great links of which it deliberately shares some characteristics - head high pot bunkers, run offs into cavernous swales, incredible contouring on and around the greens...Enjoy"
Steve Carr, Golf World
Carton...one of Ireland's best kept secrets

Vistors always welcome. Limited membership available.

T 01 6286271 | **E** golf@carton.ie
F 01 6286555 | **W** www.carton.ie

Carton House Golf Club Plc, Carton House, Maynooth, Co. Kildare, Ireland

eARLy IRIsh GoLf

So, where, why and how did golf begin in Ireland? It is known that as early as 1606 a primitive form of golf was being played on the Ards peninsula, south of Belfast, having been imported across the Irish Sea from Scotland by Hugh Montgomery, the Laird of Braidstane, near Ayr and Capt. James Hamilton. As a reward for services rendered to King James VI of Scotland when he became King James I of Great Britain and Ireland in 1603 on the death of Elizabeth I, both of these Scottish military adventurers were allowed to buy up huge tracts of land in Ireland cheaply. King James was a golfing Stuart just like his mother, Mary, Queen of Scots. It is quite possible but unproven that James may well have played golf at Ards with his two friends on a visit to Ulster.

By the middle of the eighteenth century some people with British military connections in the Co. Wicklow town of Bray, were dabbling in their own form of "rough golf" but it was not until 1851; four hundred years after golf first began on the east coast of Scotland that a committed golfing missionary migrated from there to Ireland bringing with him the "one true faith". David Ritchie was the zealous golfing messiah, who became the prime mover and shaker in the establishment of Ireland's first properly laid out golf course at the Curragh in County Kildare. Although Ritchie wasted no time in getting things up and running in the correct manner, infecting a small, exclusive band of close Irish associates with the golf bug, he neglected to get his Club legally constituted and therefore the Curragh is not recognised as the oldest Golf Club in Ireland which in reality it is. The official honour goes to Royal Belfast Golf Club, founded in 1881.

Before going any further it is important to point out that images of modern multi-million dollar golf start-ups should be put clean out of our minds when imagining the way that the business of laying out a golf course was undertaken back then. The only requirements were to find a piece of underused land and a man skilled in the use of the scythe. The scythe man had to be mighty skilled to be able to virtually shave the designated putting surfaces down to the required height. No easy task. A mere thirty acres was considered sufficient to begin with and, of course, some basic knowledge of the game. Holes were rarely longer than 250 yards and new golf courses almost always consisted of six or nine holes at the start up stage.

DAVID RITCHIE (1824-1910)
Founder of first golf course at the Curragh in 1852.

Courtesy of Bill Gibson

A major part of the Irish jigsaw fell into place in 1852 when the Earl of Eglinton was appointed First Lord Lieutenant of Ireland. Eglinton was a founder member of the trail-blazing, highly significant Prestwick Club in Scotland and a most enthusiastic golfer. He was so dedicated to the promotion of the game that whenever he could get away from his onerous duties at Dublin Castle, he would go down to the Curragh to encourage David Ritchie's endeavours and to play a round of golf or two with him. Eglinton was obviously a committed golfer, prepared to suffer to get in a game because in 1852 a 30-miles journey was of no little inconvenience.

During Eglinton's short political tenure in Ireland he became the fulcrum of the sudden surge of interest in golf by the Irish upper classes. This may have been down to their wish to keep up with the Joneses, so to speak, as much as any genuine interest in a new activity that would provide them with healthy exercise and a pleasurable challenge. When he went back home to Scotland, Lord Eglinton continued to play a major and quite historic part in the development of the game. He personally presented the Open Championship belt that was to be won outright by Young Tom Morris in 1870 and is now on display in the R&A Museum at St. Andrews.

The Blackwatch Regiment

In the summer of 1886 the famous Blackwatch Regiment from Scotland was dispatched to Ireland to perform routine garrison duties. Although the political climate in Ireland was far from calm the men of the Blackwatch seemed to have plenty of leisure time available to them. Those Blackwatch fellows were good golfers, good organisers and good proselytisers. Everywhere they went, every town in which they were based for only the briefest time, golf erupted. Very soon golf, which had been extremely slow to cross the sea from Scotland and England, was expanding like wildfire all over the country.

The Irish quickly saw the benefits of having the game centrally organised so that the rules governing the game would be consistent and respected. In 1891, the first national golf association in the world was founded in Ireland as the Golfing Union of Ireland. At the date of its inception, twenty-eight *"greens"*, as golf courses were called back then, were in play in various parts of the 32 counties of Ireland. Not surprisingly, due to its close Scottish affiliations, the major proportion of golfing activity took place in Ulster, where there were nine Greens. Golf was also played in places that had *"enjoyed"* the presence of the Blackwatch as far away as Limerick, Kerry and Cork.

The South of Ireland Amateur Championship

The oldest provincial championship in Ireland reflects perfectly the way the social scene surrounding golf in Ireland has changed over the years. In 1895 golf balls cost two shillings each which, hard to believe, was the same price being paid for a much better quality ball after the Second World War, fifty years later. Two shillings was also the price of a five-course meal in a top class hotel. Put simply, the wealth required to be able to play golf in 1895 would be equivalent to what polo players need to pursue their sport these days.

Lahinch Golf Club was founded in 1892 with the almost inevitable assistance of the Blackwatch Regiment, stationed in Limerick. At the 1894 annual general meeting of the members, club founder, president and prime mover of the project, the far seeing Mr. Alex Shaw, who was head of a well-known bacon factory in Limerick city, proposed that some of the members should consider financing the building of a top class hotel to attract visiting golfers to the tiny, remote west Clare village. Shaw got his way. The new hotel - a stunning example of nineteenth century luxury was built in Norwegian style and it featured hot seawater baths as one of its attractions. The seawater was pumped straight from the Atlantic, up and over the formidable cliff edge to be discharged into every bedroom, having been heated on the way. The presence of the Golf Links Hotel, as it was named, underpinned the viability of Lahinch Golf Club and village for many years. Shaw must have been quite an operator because in 1894 he also managed to persuade Old Tom Morris, to come over from Scotland to layout and oversee the building of a first class course.

In 1927, Alister Mackenzie the architectural genius who designed Augusta and Cypress Point re-did Morris's work. Those of you have been to Lahinch, will understand if I say that Mackenzie basically moved the holes that were literally on the far side of the road across the street into the dunes. Lahinch, these days, is very much a Mackenzie monument having been extensively and brilliantly re-furbished in that vein under the supervision of the highly thought of English architect, Martin Hawtree during the course of the past three years.

The first *"South"* in 1895 was a gala affair. In attendance was the Chief Secretary of Ireland, John Balfour, an excellent player, who was Captain of the R&A the year previously and whose brother, James, became Prime Minister of Great Britain seven years later. The Irish Times newspaper reported that the Chief Secretary (in effect the Prime Minister of Ireland) *"had gone to the country to be amongst the people to ascertain for himself what they think to be best for their welfare."* The irony was, of course, that the Chief Secretary would not have ascertained an awful lot about his subjects welfare or otherwise at a golf meeting, as it was called back then. The *"ordinary"* Irish were more than likely in their fields tending to their animals and crops blissfully unaware of the existence of the sport and Balfour's presence nearby. I am also quite sure that the people with whom he was associating at the golf club would have been horrified if it was thought that their *"welfare"* was in need of being assessed in any way.

Courtesy of Bill Gibson

William Montgomery, the Earl of Eglington, 1st Lieutentant of Ireland 1851-2. Became Captain of the R and A in 1853

Lord Balfour and his wife, Elizabeth, arrived at the front door of Sherry's Hotel on Main Street, Lahinch in their horse-drawn carriage, and spectacularly scattering dust in all directions. Their four horses were covered in foam and froth after the 200-mile journey from Dublin that must have taken several days to complete.

Because of the harsh justice Balfour meted out from time to time, he became known throughout Ireland as *"Bloody"* Balfour. But the guy could not have been all that bad; he was a keen and expert golfing exponent who made a major contribution to the propagation of the game and once said:

"A tolerable day, a tolerable green and a tolerable opponent supply all that any reasonably constituted human being should require in the way of entertainment. With a fine sea view in front of him, the golfer may be excused if he regards golf, even though it be indifferent golf, as the true and adequate end of man's existence".
What true golfer could disagree with those sentiments?

In 1896, Alex Shaw placed an advertisement in the London Times newspaper offering overnight trips from Euston Station in London via Liverpool by boat and train to Lahinch for the sum of 2 guineas each way. Shaw persuaded the Railway Companies to arrange cheap excursion fares to attract golfers to come to Lahinch just as the owners of hotels in Florida and North Carolina were to do some years later. The gimmick was a roaring success until the Great War intervened and the fortunes of the hotel began to dwindle.

One hundred and seven years later the Golf Links Hotel is long gone (its Norwegian wooden frame burnt to a cinder in 1937) but the South of Ireland Championship and Lahinch seaside village and its thriving golf resort are all more popular than ever. In 1906, Alex Shaw was rewarded for his hospitality to the Balfours at Lahinch by being made a Knight of the Realm.

Golf is a game in which one endeavours to control a ball with implements ill adapted for the purpose
Woodrow Wilson

MEN'S FIXTURES 2003

DATE	EVENT	VENUE
April 4-6	Munster Youths Amateur Open	Killarney G&FC
April 10-13	US Masters	Augusta National
April 11-13	Connaught Youths Amateur Open	Connemara GC
April 18-22	West of Ireland Amateur Open	County Sligo GC
April 25	Irish Youths vs. Welsh Youths	Ashburnham GC
May 9-11	Irish Amateur Open	Royal Dublin GC
May 21-22	Munster Seniors' Amateur Open	Ballybunion GC
May 23-25	St. Andrews Links Trophy	St. Andrews
May 31- June 2	East of Ireland Amateur Open	County Louth GC
June 2-7	British Amateur Championship	Royal Troon GC
June 5&6	Irish Seniors Amateur Open	Mullingar GC
June 5-7	European Mid-Amateur	Mosjo GC, Sweden
June 8	Ulster Foursomes Open	Malone GC
June 9-10	Leinster Youths Amateur Open	The Island GC
June 12-14	European Seniors' & Nations Cup	Chantaco, France
June 12-15	US Open	Olympia Fields CC
June 14-18	Irish Amateur Close	Tramore GC
June 14	Munster Country Clubs Cup	Glengarriff, Listowel, Ardfert Templemore, Listowel, Cobh
June 17-18	Connaught Seniors' Amateur Open	Castlebar GC
June 26-27	Irish Youths Amateru	Cork Golf Club
July 3-6	Smurfit European Club	The K Club
July 8-12	European Boys Team Champhionship	Karlovy Vary GC, Sweden
July 1-5	European Team Amateur Championship	Royal Hague GC, Holland
July 11&12	Munster Mid-Amateur Open	Limerick GC
July 14-18	North of Ireland Amateur Open	Royal Portrush GC
July 17-20	British Open	Royal St. George's GC
July 24-27	Irish Open	Portmarnock GC
July 26-30	South of Ireland Amateur Championship	Lahinch GC
August 5-8	Boys Home Internationals	Royal St. David's
August 6-8	Ulster Youths Amateur Open	Royal County Down GC
August 6-8	British Seniors' Amateur Championship	Blairgowrie GC
August 13-15	Interprovincial Championship	Ballybunion GC
August 13-17	British Mid-Amateur Championship	St. Andrews (Jubilee Course)
August 14-17	USPGA Championship	Oak Hill Country Club
August 19-20	Connaught Veterans' Amateur Open	Tuam Golf Club
August 20-23	European Mens' Individual Championship	Nairn GC, Scotland
August 21&22	Ulster Seniors' Amateur Open	Bangor GC
August 25	Irish Club Youths Team Championship	Portumna GC
August 29 & 30	Jacques Legalise Trophy	Lahinch GC
September 1 & 2	Leinster Seniors' Amateur Open	Woodenbridge GC
September 6 & 7	Walker Cup	Ganton GC
September 11-13	Senior Cup National Finals	Lisburn GC

September 11-13	Barton Shield National Finals	Lisburn GC
September 11-13	Junior Cup National Finals	Lisburn GC
September 11-13	Jimmy Bruen National Finals	Lisburn GC
September 11-13	Pierce Purcell National Finals	Lisburn GC
September 24-26	Youth Interprovincial Championship	Lahnich GC
Sept 30 – Oct 2	Seniors' Home Internationals	Seaton Crew GC
October 3	All-Ireland Medal Championship	TBA
October 4&5	East of Ireland Open Mixed Foursomes	Luttrellstown G&CC
October 7-9	MGA v GUI	Quaker Ridge, USA
Oct 30 – Nov 2	European Club Cup Trophy	National GC, Turkey
November 13-16	World Cup of Golf	Kiawah Island

JUNIOR FIXTURES 2003

DATE	EVENT	VENUE
Feb 20&21	Irish Schools Strokeplay Qualifying	Beech Park & Donabate GC
April 7	Irish Schools Championship (Munster Section)	Monkstown & Limerick GC
April 23&24	Irish Boys vs. Welsh Boys	Rosslare GC
April 28	Irish Schools Golf Ch'ship (Munster Section)	Harbour Point GC
May 1	Irish Schools Golf Championship (Munster Final)	Newcastle West & Mitchelstown GC
May 6th	Irish Schools Golf Championship (Munster Final)	Kenmare GC
May 12th	Irish Schools Golf Championship (Munster Final)	Charleville GC
July 1-4	Ulster Boys Amateur Open Championship	Donaghadee GC
July 8-10	Connaught Boys Amateur Open Championship	Oughterard GC
July 16-18	Munster Boys Amateur Opean Championship	Tipperary GC
July 22-24	Leinster Boys Amateur Open Championship	Malahide GC
August 11-16	British Boys Championship	Royal Liverpool GC
August 18	Irish Junior Foursomes Trophy	Lucan GC
August 19	Fred Daly Trophy	Lucan GC
August 20-22	Irish Boys Amateur Close Championship	The Hermitage GC
August 25	Irish Schools Strokeplay Championship	Portumna GC
August 26	Irish Schools Matchplay Championship	Portumna GC
August 27-29	Boys Interprovincial Championship	Portumna GC
Sept 4&5	Irish Mixed Foursomes Challenge Cup	Galway GC
TBA	Irish Schools Matchplay Trophy	TBA

Golf appeals to the idiot in us and the child. Just how childlike golf players become is proven by their frequent inability to count past five.
John Updike

Golf is played by twenty million mature American men whose wives think they are out having fun.
Jim Bishop

LADIES FIXTURES 2003

DATE	EVENT	VENUE
April 15-17	Munster Ladies Championship	Waterville GC
April 23-25	Girls' Interprovincial Matches	Warrenpoint GC
April 28-30	Ladies' Leinster Junior Championship	Old Conna GC
May 5	Ladies Senior Cup (Leinster Qualifying)	Malahide GC
May 5&6	Irish Girls School Championship Final	Milltown GC
May 6-8	Ulster Ladies' Open Championship	Bangor GC
May 6-8	Ladies Senior Cup (Munster Qualifying)	East Clare GC
May 12&13	Ulster Meeting	Ringdufferin GC
May 22-24	Midland District Championship	The Heath GC
May 26	LGU Medals Final	Westmanstown\Lucan GC
May 26-27	Ladies Senior Cup (Ulster Qualifying)	Spa GC
May 28-30	Leinster Ladies' Championship	Glen of the Downs GC
June 2	ILGU Prizes (Country – Ulster)	Strabane GC
June 10-12	Connaught Ladies' Championship	County Sligo GC
June 10-14	Ladies' British Amateur Championship	Lindrick GC
June 14&15	Ladies' Intermediate Open Strokeplay	Laytown & Bettystown GC
June 15	Ladies District Matches	Kirkistown Castle GC
June 24-28	Irish Ladies' Close Championship	Donegal GC
July 2&3	North\West & Summer Meeting	Castlerock GC
July 2&3	ILGU Prizes (Town – Ulster)	Carnalea GC
July 4&5	Ladies Senior Cup (Connaught Qualifying)	Westport GC
July 8-12	Ladies' European Championship	Germany
July 15-18	Girls' Close & Intermediate Championship	Ardee GC
July 19-20	Irish Ladies' Open Strokeplay Championship	Rathsallagh GC
July 25-26	Vagliano Trophy	County Louth GC
July 28th	ILGU Prizes (Midland District)	New Ross\Mountrath GC
July 29th	Australian Spoons	Ballyclare GC
July 31-Aug3	Weetabix Women's British Open	Royal Lytham & St. Annes
August 4	Lady Veteran's Cup	Massereene GC
August 5-9	Girls' British Open Championship	Newport GC
August 6-8	Ladie's Interprovincial Matches	Galway GC
August 11	LGU Challenge Bowls	Moate GC
August 12-14	Girls' Home Internationals	Pyle & Kenfig GC
August 20-22	Ladies' Amateur British Open	Royal Portrush GC
August 25	ILGU Prizes (All-Ireland Final)	Gort GC
August 27-30	European Lades' Individual Championship	Shannon GC
September 1	Australian Spoons	Newcastle West GC
Sept 5&6	Ladies' Senior Cup Final	Blainroe GC
Sept 10-12	Ladies' Home Internationals	Cruden Bay GC
Sept 15-16	Irish Senior Ladies' Open Amateur Championship	South Staff GC
Nov 4-8	Commonwealth Tournament	Remeura GC, New Zealand

They say golf is like life, but don't believe them. Golf is more complicated than that.
Gardner Dickinson

**Tulfarris Hotel &
Golf Resort
Blessington Lakes
Co. Wicklow
Ireland**

**Tel:
+353 (0)45 867644 /
867655**

**Fax
+353 (0)45 867565 /
867561**

**Email
info@tulfarris.com**

**Web:
www.tulfarris.com**

The Tulfarris Golf Resort that wraps itself around the southern edge of Lake Blessington in County Wicklow is less than a one hours drive from Dublin city centre. The golf course, now five years old, has matured nicely and is one of the most scenic and challenging courses in Ireland.

A four-star luxury hotel, a walled holiday village and a golf course of championship standard plus a wide variety of leisure pursuits on the property and close by, make a long or short stay at this location extremely attractive for individuals or golfing groups.

In 2000 Tulfarris hosted The Irish Seniors Open with leading US Seniors player Bruce Fleischer emerging victorious. It is quite a compliment that the professionals were so high in their praises for a golf course on which only five players managed to beat par figures.

Designed by Paddy Merrigan, one of Ireland's foremost golf architects, the course is placed on three small peninsulas that jut into Lake Blessington.

No two holes are alike, the readymade integrity and natural beauty of the lake, rolling wooded landscape, environmentally friendly wetlands and indigenous stonework have all been cleverly preserved and exploited to provide a top class golfing challenge and restful environment to recharge one's batteries.

All golf bookings can be made through newly appointed Chief Executive, Brian Begley at 045-867644 or 086-8540804, a man who is highly experienced in the golfing world and knows how to present and maintain a golf course in tiptop condition.

OPEN COMPETITIONS 2003

DATE	EVENT	VENUE
March 31- April 1	Seniors' Open	Ceann Sibeal
April 5&6	Junior & Intermediate Scratch Cups	Castlegregory
April 21	Open Day	Kilkea Castle
April 24	Intermediate Scratch Cup	Blacklion
April 27	Intermediate Scratch	Wexford
April 28	Ladies Open	Lucan
May 3	Open Singles Stableford	Cloverhill
May 3	Club Classic	Cruit Island
May 3&4	Open Weekend	Connemara Isles
May 3-5	Open Mixed	Glenmalure
May 4	Bush Cup	Blacklion
May 4	Junior Scratch Cup	Blacklion
May 5	Open Day	Kilkea Castle
May 10&11	Intermediate\Junior Scratch Cup	Moate
May 10-17	Open Week	Lucan
May 17	Intermediate Scratch Cup	Corrstown
May 17&18	Intermediate & Junior Scratch Cups	Rathdowne
May 18	Intermediate Scratch Cup	Portartlington
May 18-25	Open Week	Dundalk
May 21&22	Senior Open Mixed	Courtown
May 22	Ladies Open Day	Hollystown
May 22	Senior Scratch Cup	Corrstown
May 22	Ladies Open 4-ball	Corrstown
May 22&23	Pro-Am	Monkstown
May 25	Ladies Open Day	Dunmore
May 25 – June 2	Open Week	Tipperary
May 30 – June 6	Open Week	Mitchelstown
May 31 – June 1	Open Weekend	Ceann Sibeal
May 31 – June 8	Open Week	Tullamore
June 1&2	Open Weekend	Carrick-on-Shannon
June 2	Open Day	Kilkea Castle
June 2	Open Mixed Foursomes	Newlands
June 4	Open Stableford	Dunmurry
June 6	Junior Scratch Cup	Youghal
June 7-15	Open Week	Mountrath
June 8	Senior Scratch	Strabane
June 8-14	Open Week	Clontarf
June 8-15	Open Week	Blainroe
June 9-13	Mini Open Festival of Food & Golf	St. Helens Bay
June 9-15	Open Week	Mullingar
June 13-23	Open Week	Portadown
June 14-22	Open Week	Connemara

DATE	EVENT	VENUE
June 14-22	Open Week	Curra West
June 15-22	Open Week	Gort
June 16-21	Open Week	Rafeen Creek
June 16-22	Open Week	Letterkenny
June 17-20	Celtic Classic	Omagh
June 20-22	Open Weekend	Bright Castle
June 20-26	Open Week	Bright Castle
June 20 – 29	Open Week	Goldcoast
June 21-27	Open Week	Carrcik-on-Shannon
June 21-29	Open Week	Coollattin
June 21-29	Open Week	Laytown & Bettystown
June 22	Open Stroke	Rathmore
June 23-28	Open Week	Knock
June 23-29	Open Week	Galway Bay
June 25-30	Open Week	Strabane
June 26&27	Open Stableford	Rathmore
June 26 – July 13	Open Fortnight	Dungarvan
June 27 – July 6	Open Week	Roscommon
June 27 – July 6	Open Week	Portsalon
June 28	Junior Scratch	Wexford
June 28 – July 6	Open Week	Portstewart
June 28 – July 6	Open Week	Boystown
June 29	Open Stroke	Rathmore
July 1-7	Open Week	Lee Valley
July 2-6	Open Festival	Skibbereen
July 4-13	Open Week	Greenore
July 4-13	Open Week	North West
July 4-13	Open Week	Moate
July 5-13	Open Week	Rossmore
July 5-13	Open Week	Mahee Island
July 5-13	Open Week	Ballinasloe
July 5-13	Open Week	Highfield
July 6	Junior Scratch	Tullamore
July 9	Junior Scratch Cup	Goldcoast
July 9-20	Open Week	Wexford
July 10-22	Open Week	Abbeyleix
July 11-18	Open Week	Kilkee
July 11-20	Open Week	St. Helens Bay
July 12-19	Open Week	Ballycastle
July 12-19	Open Week	Portstewart
July 13-19	Open Week	St. Helens Bay
July 13-20	Open Week	Dundalk
July 18-27	Open Week	East Cork
July 19-20	Open Week	Ceann Sibeal
July 19-26	Open Week	Shandon Park
July 19-27	Open Week	Strandhill
July 20-27	Open Week	Millicent
July 25-27	Jack Lynch Classic	Skibbereen

DATE	EVENT	VENUE
July 25 – August 10	Open Fortnight	Youghal
July 26&27	Junior, Intermediate & Minor Scratch	Rathbane
July 26 – august 2	Open Week	Carrickfergus
July 26 – August 3	Open Week	Lismore
July 26 – August 3	Open Week	Woodlands
July 26 – August 4	Open Week	Laytown & Bettystown
July 26 – August 4	Open Week	Dunmurry
July 26 – August 10	Open Fortnight	Waterford
July 28 – August 3	Open Week	Connemara Isles
July 28 – August 3	Open Week	West Waterford
August 1-4	Open Competitions	Cloverhill
August 1-10	Open Week	Dunmore
August 2-4	Open Fourball	Glenmalure
August 2-9	Open Week	Spa
August 2-10	Open Week	Strandhill
August 3	Minor Scratch Cup	Lee Valley
August 3&4	Open Weekend	Carrick-on- Shannon
August 3-12	Open Festival	Achill Island
August 4	Open Day	Kilkea Castle
August 9-17	Open Week	Blacklion
August 9-17	Open Week	Woodstock
August 10	Intermediate Scratch Cup	Boystown
August 10-14	Open Week	Hollystown
August 10-16	Lord Mayor's Cup	Clontarf
August 10-17	Open Week	Gort
August 11-17	Open Week	Galway Bay
August 15-18	Open Days	Kilkea Castle
August 17	Senior & Junior Scratch Cup	Greenore
August 17	John Dickson Trophy	Holywood
August 21	Ladies 4-ball	Corrstown
August 22-28	Open Week	Kerries
August 23-30	Open Week	Holywood
August 23-30	Open Week	Roscommon
August 24	Juvenile Open Day	Clontarf
August 24-31	Open Week	Newcastlewest
August 25-30	Open Week	Monkstown
August 30- Sept 5	Open Week	Carrick-on-Shannon
August 31	Senior Scratch Cup	Lee Valley
August 31	Junior Scratch Cup	Portarlington
September 6-14	Open Week	Connemara
September 13	Ladies Open Singles Stableford	Cloverhill
September 20&21	Senior Scratch Cup	Waterford
October 26	Open Day	Kilkea Castle
November 1	Open Fourball	Rathsallagh
November 15	Open Fourball	Rathsallagh
November 29	Open Fourball	Rathsallagh
December 13	Open Fourball	Rathsallagh

PROFESSION OF A LIFETIME
LEARN TO TEACH GOLF

Golf clubs, Driving Ranges and a variety of educational institutions throughout the world are crying out for personable Golf Teaching Professionals. By attending one of our Residential Diploma Courses, if successful, you will qualify to teach golf and in the past 12 months alone we have helped to place several hundred of our new professionals in all corners of the globe.

TIME FOR A CAREER CHANGE?

The European Golf Teachers Federation was established in 1992 with the aim of providing highly skilled and motivated teaching professionals. The world of professional golf in an open market, and competition is good for everyone, and we believe that people with a passion for teaching should not be denied the opportunity to fulfill their dreams.

The course that students attend is widely regarded as the most technically advanced and informative of its kind. In the golf profession, with the content continually being upgraded as new ideas and theories become available. We have over 2000 members throughout the world, with Head Professionals, Driving Range Owners, European Tour Players and Coaches,

and people from many walks of life, who have joined one of the fastest growing organisations in golf.

We have three levels of Diploma available: Teaching; Advanced and Masters, with it taking a minimum of 2 years to complete all levels. If you are looking for a career change, and have a passion to teach, try the EGTF, alternatively, if your game is suffering, try one of our professional in your local area, they are taught to analyse and cure individual faults with simple to understand ideas.

We believe our teachers are the best because they really want to teach and help people, to have more enjoyment form the game of golf.

EUROPEAN GOLF TEACHERS FEDERATION LTD
Leaders in the Field of Golf Instruction

"The EGTF is the most important development in world golf."
Bunkered Magazine
Scotland s Largest Golf Publication

For more information contact the EGTF Head Office on 0044-208-462-4120, or visit our website at www.egtf.co.uk.

For details of courses for 2003/2004 or Associate Membership call us on (020) 84624120 for a brochure e-mail: egtf@dial.pipex.com

DIPLOMA COURSES – NO AGE LIMIT BOTH MALE AND FEMALE!

MEMBERS OF THE COACHING FOUNDATION MEMBERS OF THE WORLD GOLF FEDERATION

Golfing Union of Ireland
Union Officers

GENERAL SECRETARY
Seamus Smith

PRESIDENT
Michael P. O'Donoghue
Galway Golf Club

HON.SECRETARY
J. Gerard O'Brien
Clontarf Golf Club

TREASURER
Rollo McClure
Malone Golf Club

GUI – HEAD OFFICE
Glencar House, 81 Eglinton Road, Donnybrook, Dublin 4.
Tel:01-2694111   Fax:01-2695368   email: gui@iol.ie

BRANCH CONTACTS:

GUI – LEINSTER BRANCH
Mr. Paul Smyth – Executive Officer
Unit 10, Block 8, Blanchardstown
Corporate Park, Dublin 15.
Tel: 01-8829789/8829798
Fax: 01-8829804
email: guilb@indigo.ie
www.gui.ie/Provinces/Leinster/index.htm

GUI – CONNACHT BRANCH
Mr. Enda Lonergan – General Secretary
2 Springfield Terrace, Castlebar, Co. Mayo.
Tel: 094-28141   Fax: 094-28143
email: guicb@eircom.net
www.gui.ie/Provinces/Connacht/index.htm

GUI – MUNSTER BRANCH
Ms. Karen Walsh - Administrator
6 Town View, Mallow, Co. Cork.
Tel: 022-21026   Fax: 022-42373
e-mail: guimb@iol.ie
www.gui.ie/Provinces/Munster/index.htm

GUI – ULSTER BRANCH
Mr. Brendan Edwards - Secretary
58a High Street, Holywood,
Co. Down BT18 9AE.
Tel: 028-90423708   Fax: 028-90426766
e-mail: ulster.gui@virgin.net
www.gui.ie/Provinces/Ulster/index.htm

IRISH LADIES GOLF UNION
1 Clonskeagh Square, Clonskeagh Road, Dublin 14
Secretary: *Ms. Teresa Thompson*
Tel: 00-353-1-2696244   Fax: 00-353-1-2838670

"Expensive colour documents?
Not in my office."

Smart use of Canon Colour will increase profitability — not costs.

Only Canon can help your company maximise the benefits of business colour. Why? With over 16 years' experience in business colour, we have more knowledge and experience than any other manufacturer. That's why so many companies rely on us.

Using Canon Colour smartly means you can control when, where and how you use it, so you can keep costs to a minimum whilst making the most of your investment in colour.

Make a smart business decision. Call **1850 220 320** or visit **www.canon.ie** today.

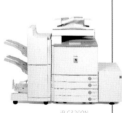

iR C3200N

you can
Canon

The Golfing Ducks

On their way home from a day out golfing, three keen golfing partners died in a car wreck and went to heaven. Upon arrival at the pearly gates, they discover to their great delight - the most beautiful golf course they had ever seen. St. Peter welcomes them and invites them to play the course, but he cautions them that there is one rule that must never be broken:

"Don't hit any of the ducks".

The men all have blank expressions, and finally one of them asks *"The ducks?"* *"Yes"*, St. Peter replies, *"There are thousands of ducks walking around the course and if one gets hit, he squawks then the one next to him squawks and soon they're all squawking to beat the band and it upsets the tranquility and drives the Boss mad! If you hit the ducks, you'll be penalised for sure. Don't do it. You have been warned. Otherwise everything is yours to enjoy."*

Upon teeing off the men soon noted that there were indeed lots of ducks wandering around the golf course and swimming in the many lakes. In no time at all one of the guys clobbers a duck. The duck lets out a loud squawk, the one next to it squawks too and soon there was a deafening caccophany of duck squawks upsetting the quietude.

St. Peter comes rushing up with an extremely homely-looking woman in tow and asks *"Who hit the duck?"* The guy who had done it owns up. *"I did."* Thinking he might be spotted a couple of shots. St. Peter immediately pulls out a pair of handcuffs and cuffs the man's right hand to the homely woman's left hand. *"I told you not to hit any of the ducks,"* he said. *"Now the two of you will be handcuffed together for eternity."*

The other two men continued their golf and were extremely careful about hitting another duck, but inevitably of few weeks later, one of them has a shank and accidentally strikes another duck. The squwaks are as deafening as before and within minutes St. Peter arrives with an even uglier woman. St.Peter determined who had hit the duck by the fear on the poor man's face and immediately cuffs the man's right hand to the ugly woman's left hand. *"I told you not to hit the ducks,"* he said. *"Now you'll be handcuffed together for eternity."*

The third man was the best golfer of the three, exerting extreme care and control over his golf ball he manages to avoid the ducks for some weeks but the pressure of it all begins to wear on his nerves and he is not enjoying his golf at all. Some days he cannot even move the clubhead for fear of nudging a duck. After three months of this "hell" he still hadn't hit a duck. Then, one day out of the blue, St. Peter walks up to him and he has with him a knock-out gorgeous woman, the most beautiful woman the man had ever seen in his entire life. St. Peter smiles and without saying a word, handcuffs the beautiful woman to the nerve - wrecked golfer and walks away.

The man, realising that he had just been handcuffed to this gorgeous creature for eternity, lets out a big sigh and says, *"What have I done to deserve this?"* The woman responds *"I don't know what you did, but I hit a duck"*.

Less than one hour from Dublin and Rosslare is one of the most unique golf course developments in Ireland.

On the Wicklow-Wexford border, just a few miles from Arklow, a stunning new golf course has been developed in the prosperous coastal village Ballymoney.

Designed to full USGA specifications, by renowned architect Peter McEvoy, the eighteen-hole championship layout is of the highest standard. Featuring a unique blend, of parkland, heathland and seaside holes this course will certainly challenge every level of golfer.

Seafield Golf & Country Club is now accepting applications for preferential shares, which entitle the holders to membership of this spectacular course.

SEAFIELD
GOLF & COUNTRY CLUB

Located in the Tara Hill/Ballymoney region, Seafield Golf & Country Club features a superb Peter McEvoy golf course offering homes and home sites with spectacular sea and golf course views. Our wide range of property options, from a turn-key townhouse to your ultimate architect dream home are priced from €250,000 to over €1,000,000. Whether you are seeking a permanent, holiday or retirement property Seafield Golf & Country club is sure to have something to meet your needs.

An absolute must play course for all golfers. Seafield will definitely keep you coming back again and again. There is no question that in time Seafield Golf & Country Club will be ranked alongside the leading golf courses in the world.

Whether you are visiting, looking for membership, booking your society or corporate outing, experience the unrivalled quality and service that Seafield Golf & Country Club has to offer.

Seafield Golf & Country Club, Ballymoney, Gorey, Co. Wexford.
www.seafieldgolf.com   e-mail: info@seafieldgolf.com
Tel: 055-24777   Fax: 055-24837

What will you do with your battery now that your watch doesn't need one?
The Citizen Eco-Drive Largo. Powered by light, it is the most technologically
advanced perpetual calendar chronograph in the world.
AND IT NEVER NEEDS A BATTERY.

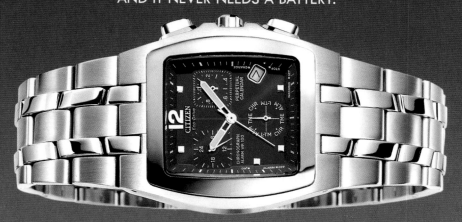

€395

CITIZEN.

Eco-Drive. A revolutionary watch.
3-year guarantee.

Available at leading jewellers nationwide.
For your nearest stockist, please call
(061) 472-722 during business hours.

www.solatrex.com

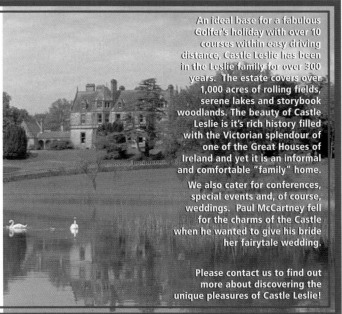

JUNIOR GOLFERS COMPETITION
Win a customised set of PING GOLF CLUBS

Yes that's right!

THE ESSENTIAL

GOLFERS GUIDE
IRELAND 2003

and

PING

have teamed up to give you the opportunity to win this fantastic prize.

The prize consists of a full set of
CUSTOMISED PING WOODS · CUSTOMISED PING IRONS
PING PUTTER & PING GOLF BAG

The winner and 11 runners up will also win a days golf at one of the 'Newcomers to Irish Golf Scene' Golf Courses (See Article pages 24-30). The winner will be announced on the day. All finalists will also receive hospitality and a goody bag.

To enter you must be a junior member of a GUI affiliated golf club. To be in with a chance to win, all you have to do is enter our free draw. Simply fill in the competition form and have it signed by a member of your golf clubs' committee or the junior officer at your club and return it to the address below along with an essay entitled:

'What a set of Pings would do for my game'...
The essay must contain between 300 and 500 words.
The winning essay will be published in next years ESSENTIAL GOLFERS GUIDE.

NAME:

ADDRESS:

TELEPHONE: EMAIL:

HANDICAP: HANDICAP ON 31-07-02:

SIGNATURE OF CLUB OFFICIAL:

The closing date for the competition is 31 July 2003.

Vista Marketing, Unit 1, Ballycummin Village, Raheen, Limerick
T: +353 61 306200   F: +353 61 306215   E: egl@eircom.net

Golf properties for sale

Costa Blanca, Spain

Project Santa Helena Houses:

House complete with swimming pool, terrace (upstairs option), large kitchen, livingroom, two bathrooms, one large and one small, four bedrooms, garden, and everything ready to live in.

Price: €205,789

Project Residence Beaulieu Houses:

Livingroom, kitchen, terrace, bathroom, two bedrooms. Upstairs planted terrace, one bedroom and one bathroom. House ready to live in. An additional 30,000 euro is added if you require a large garden.

Price: €205,700

Project Promo Noor Apartments:

Prices:		
First floor	€110,541
2 bedroom apartment	€121,573
3 bedroom apartment	€128,368
Rooftop apartment	€170,709

English speaking staff are waiting to talk to you about your dream home....

Contact: Lowyck Marina,
Tel: 0032 472 940 826,
Fax: 0032 538 089 70,
email: promo.sl.spain@skynet.be

Readers Competition

Answer the following three questions correctly and return your entry to the address below and you could be in with a chance of WINNING

Two Return Business Class Flights from Dublin to Johannesburg, South Africa via Zurich.

Courtesy of **THE ESSENTIAL GOLFERS GUIDE 2003** and
SWISS INTERNATIONAL AIRLINES
with
10 Runners-up receiving Free membership of the
EXECUTIVE GOLF & LEISURE PLATINUM CLUB
(See page 103 for details)

Questions:

1. **Name the 3 Irish members of the 2002 winning Ryder Cup Team? (See article pages 112-119).**
2. **What Greg Norman designed golf course opened in County Clare in 2002? (See page 29)**
3. **Name the Worlds No.1 lady golfer who will take part in a men's USPGA Tour Event 2003. (See page 122)**

Answers:

Question 1:	i	ii	iii
Question 2:			
Question 3:			

Name:
Address:

Contact Tel:	Email:
Home Club, if any:	

- Persons travelling must be over 18 years old. (winner of the competition and companion)
- Tickets must be utilised by 31 December 2003.
- The closing date for the competition is 31 July 2003.

All entries to:
Vista Marketing, Unit 1, Ballycummin Village, Raheen, Limerick
T: +353 61 306200   F: +353 61 306215   E: egl@eircom.net

THE UNOFFICIAL RULES OF
GOLF

1. The game of golf is 90% mental and 10% *mental*.

2. No matter how badly you are playing, it is always possible to play worse.

3. Never try to keep more than 300 thoughts in your head during your swing.

4. The less skilled the player, the more likely he is to share his ideas about the golf swing.

5. A golf match is a test of skill against your opponent's luck.

6. Nothing straightens out a nasty slice better than a sharp dogleg to the right.

7. It's often necessary to hit a second drive to really appreciate the first one.

8. You can hit a 2-acre fairway 10% of the time and a 2-inch branch 90% of the time.

9. A stroke does not occur unless it is observed by more than one golfer.

10. Every time a golfer makes a birdie, he must subsequently make a double bogey to restore the fundamental equilibrium of the universe.

11. Knowing the swing weight of your club is as indispensable to playing good golf as knowing the temperature of grass on the fairway.

12. There are two things you can learn by stopping your backswing at the top and checking the position of your hands: *how many hands you have and which one is wearing the glove.*

13. A two-foot putt counts the same as a two-foot drive.

14. It's a simple matter to keep your ball on the fairway if you're not too choosy which one it is.

15. For most golfers, the only difference between a one-dollar ball and a three-dollar ball is two dollars.

16. A ball you can see in the rough from 50 yards away is not yours.

17. If there is a ball in the fringe and a ball in the bunker, your ball is in the bunker.

18. If both balls are in the bunker, yours is in the footprint.

19. Since bad shots come in groups of three, a fourth bad shot is actually the beginning of the next group of three.

20 Don't buy a putter until you've had a chance to throw it.

IVAN MORRIS

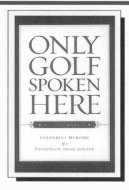

The Investment
Club Network

www.ticn.com

Empower yourself

Successful Stockmarket Investing.

- Clubs in Ireland, UK, Europe, Australia & USA.
- Over 5000 members in over 200 clubs & growing.
- Average Clubs Return - Dec. 2002*
  A Staggering 28%
- 100% Satisfaction Guarantee on all Courses.

We have strategic partnerships with:

TC2000 - Worden Bros Inc. - FREE Stockmarket CD-ROM.
Valueline.com - The Unique Site for Company Research.
TCBmarkets.com - with Doctor J the CBOE market trader.

TICN will teach you how to:

- Understand & Utilise Fundamental
  Company Research & Analysis.
- Understand & Utilise Technical Analysis
  (Graphs & Charts).
- Buy/ Sell Shares and Trade Covered
  Call & Put Options & Leaps.
- Generate a Monthly Income from your Shares.
- Trade ONLINE from home or office with skill & confidence.

* Subject to selection criteria to give average club performance.

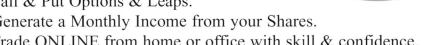

Tel: 1800 367 693 - Website: www.ticn.com

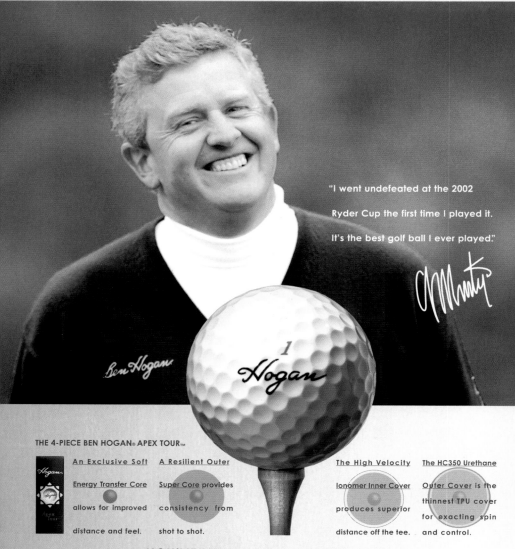